Research Trends in Artificial Intelligence: Internet of Things

Edited by

Sonali Mahendra Kothari

Department of Computer Science and Engineering
Symbiosis Institute of Technology
Symbiosis International (Deemed University)
Pune – 412115, India

Vijayshri Nitin Khedkar

Department of Computer Science and Engineering
Symbiosis Institute of Technology
Symbiosis International (Deemed University)
Pune – 412115, India

Ujwala Kshirsagar

Department of Electronics and Telecommunication
Engineering
Symbiosis Institute of Technology
Symbiosis International (Deemed University)
Pune – 412115
India

&

Gitanjali Rahul Shinde

Department of Computer Science & Engineering
(Artificial Intelligence & Machine Learning)
Vishwakarma Institute of Information Technology
Kondhwa (Budruk) Pune – 411048
Maharashtra, India

Research Trends in Artificial Intelligence: Internet of Things

Editors: Sonali Mahendra Kothari, Vijayshri Nitin Khedkar, Ujwala Kshirsagar and Gitanjali Rahul Shinde

ISBN (Online): 978-981-5136-44-9

ISBN (Print): 978-981-5136-45-9

ISBN (Paperback): 978-981-5136-46-3

First published in 2023.

need for a court order if at any point you breach any terms of this License Agreement. In no event will any delay or failure by Bentham Science Publishers in enforcing your compliance with this License Agreement constitute a waiver of any of its rights.

3. You acknowledge that you have read this License Agreement, and agree to be bound by its terms and conditions. To the extent that any other terms and conditions presented on any website of Bentham Science Publishers conflict with, or are inconsistent with, the terms and conditions set out in this License Agreement, you acknowledge that the terms and conditions set out in this License Agreement shall prevail.

Bentham Science Publishers Pte. Ltd.
80 Robinson Road #02-00
Singapore 068898
Singapore
Email: subscriptions@benthamscience.net

CONTENTS

FOREWORD

Artificial Intelligence (AI) in healthcare and biomedical applications is taking good shape nowadays. The convergence of AI, the Internet of Things, Blockchain and healthcare aims at delivering features such as scalability, security and privacy to high-level intellectual functions that are beneficial to the new era of digital information. In recent times, AI has touched major milestones by overcoming the challenges faced in realizing the full potential of projects in various fields such as smart homes, agriculture, smart cities, healthcare and medical, *etc.* Due to these transformations, the data is increasing at a faster rate in terms of size, complexity, variety, and heterogeneity, and in the sequel, computational intelligence, and machine learning the key contributors to improve business intelligence.

The book outline and contents show that the major coverage of the book includes a brief introduction to the domain, research challenges, literature review and state-of-the-art, different algorithms/techniques / deployment methods, data acquisition techniques including types of sensors used in IoT and communication, preprocessing and data cleaning, if required, application development and design issues, mathematical modeling of the engineering problems for ai based solution, different resources like datasets, APIs, software tools and packages evaluated or proposed, results, discussion and performance measures and future research directions. This will help readers to get detailed insights into the application of computational intelligence in the healthcare domain.

In addition to this, the communication and computing systems encompass every stage of professional and personal life, including education, healthcare, re- identification, transportation and social security. Data Science is used to analyze data from wearable trackers to ensure their patients' well-being, assist in hospital administration by reducing the waiting time and enhance public care. Cloud Security helps in the ease of scaling, increased reliability and availability, disaster recovery, and managing remote work. These key enablers for the healthcare and biomedical domain and more focus on IoT, big data and cloud will help readers to empower their research and learning in these areas.

Buyers, who belong to the category of researchers, will benefit from the state-of-art and future research directions provided in the book. Practicing engineers will benefit from the knowledge of the current challenges in technology, deployment methods and solutions. Post-graduate students will be introduced to new domains, and recent advancements in them. They will also be made aware of the rapid growth in technology and obsolesce.

Parikshit N. Mahalle
Department of Artificial Intelligence and Data Science
Bansilal Ramnath Agarwal Charitable Trust's
Vishwakarma Institute of Information Technology
Pune, India

PREFACE

Artificial intelligence (AI) has grown in popularity in today's world. It refers to the simulation of natural intelligence in machines that have been programmed to learn and emulate human actions. AI is being used by huge companies all over the world to make the lives of end-users easier. The smart sensors and actuators are two key components of the Internet of Things (IoT). The IoT enables seamless connection to devices irrespective of time and location and hence it is an important component of what is known as the Industrial Revolution 4.0. One of the most significant advantages of the IoT is the reduction of human errors and manual labor, as well as the increase in overall efficiency and cost-effectiveness, both in terms of time and cost. This book offers recent research work going on in different domains where AI and IoT can be used. This book is a one-stop-shop for real-time work to solve engineering problems in various domains. The first few chapters are focused on the importance and amalgamation of IoT and AI for smart farming. It gives details about the basics of AI and IoT, and different algorithms available in AI and IoT for solving problems in agriculture. Healthcare is an important domain where early prediction of disease can save valuable human lives. In view of this, the second section of the book includes chapters focusing on research in the health care domain.

In today's era where enormous data are generated every day, it is very important to analyze the data and find solutions to various problems, and predict future trends. The next section of the book is dedicated to such recent trends and research in different fields where IoT and AI can help in making better analyses, and predictions. In the real world, data comes for various use cases and there is a need for source-specific data science models. The book includes chapters highlighting research work done by various authors in multidisciplinary domains considering the needs of today and tomorrow.

Sonali Mahendra Kothari
Department of Computer Science and Engineering
Symbiosis Institute of Technology
Symbiosis International (Deemed University)
Pune – 412115, India

Vijayshri Nitin Khedkar
Department of Computer Science and Engineering
Symbiosis Institute of Technology
Symbiosis International (Deemed University)
Pune – 412115, India

Ujwala Kshirsagar
Department of Electronics and Telecommunication Engineering
Symbiosis Institute of Technology
Symbiosis International (Deemed University)
Pune – 412115
India

&

Gitanjali Rahul Shinde
Department of Computer Science & Engineering
(Artificial Intelligence & Machine Learning)
Vishwakarma Institute of Information Technology
Kondhwa (Budruk) Pune – 411048
Maharashtra, India

List of Contributors

A. Kannammal	Department of Computing (Decision and Computing Sciences), Coimbatore Institute of Technology, Coimbatore, Tamil Nadu-641014, India
Anjali B. Raut	Department of Computer Science & Engineering, H.V.P.M's, C.O. E.T., Amravati, Maharashtra, India
Gitanjali Rahul Shinde	Department of Computer Science & Engineering (Artificial Intelligence & Machine Learning), Vishwakarma Institute of Information Technology Kondhwa (Budruk), Pune – 411048, Maharashtra, India
Ishan Sarode	BTech-Information Technology, Vishwakarma Institute of Information Technology, Pune, India
Kiran Wani	Department of Mechanical Engineering, Symbiosis Institute of Technology, Symbiosis International [Deemed University], Maharashtra, India
Madhumita Bawiskar	Department of Computer Science and Engineering, Symbiosis Institute of Technology, Symbiosis International [Deemed University], Maharashtra, India
N. Pushyanth	Department of Computer Science, University of Oxford, Oxford, United Kingdom
Namrata Nishant Wasatkar	Vishwakarma Institute of information and Technology, Pune, (Maharashtra State), India
Prabhakar Laxmanrao Ramteke	H.V.P. M's College of Engineering and Technology, Amravati (Maharashtra State) Affiliated to Sant Gadge Baba Amravati University, Amravati, Maharashtra, India
Prashant Panse	Department of Information Technology, Medi-Caps University, Indore, India
Parul Bhanarkar	Department of Computer Science & Engineering, Jhulelal Institute of Technology, Nagpur, India
Pradnya Borkar	Department of Computer Science & Engineering, Symbiosis Institute of Technology, Nagpur, India
Pranali Gajanan Chavhan	Vishwakarma Institute of information and Technology, Pune, (Maharashtra State), India
Prajkta P. Chapke	Department of Computer Science & Engineering, H.V.P.M's, C.O. E.T., Amravati, India
Reena Thakur	Department of Computer Science & Engineering, Jhulelal Institute of Technology, Nagpur, India
Rupali R. Deshmukh	Department of Computer Science & Engineering, H.V.P. M's COET, Amravati, Maharashtra, India
Riddhi Mirajkar	Faculty, Vishwakarma Institute of Information Technology, Pune, India
Ruchi Doshi	University of Azteca, Chalco de Díaz Covarrubias, Mexico
Rahul Jadhav	Department of Computer Science and Engineering, Symbiosis Institute of Technology, Symbiosis International [Deemed University], Maharashtra, India

S. Chandia
Department of Computing (Decision and Computing Sciences), Coimbatore Institute of Technology, Coimbatore, Tamil Nadu-641014, India

Saurabh Sathe
San Jose State University, California, USA

Sonali Mahendra Kothari
Department of Computer Science and Engineering, Symbiosis Institute of Technology, Symbiosis International [Deemed University], Pune – 412115, India

Sina Patel
Department of Computer Science and Engineering, Symbiosis Institute of Technology, Symbiosis International [Deemed University], Maharashtra, India

Tanvi Raut
BTech-Information Technology, Vishwakarma Institute of Information Technology, Pune, India

Ujwala Kshirsagar
Department of Electronics and Telecommunication Engineering, Symbiosis Institute of Technology Symbiosis International (Deemed University), Pune – 412115, India

Vikas Kanifnath Kolekar
Vishwakarma Institute of information and Technology, Pune, Maharashtra State, India

Vijayshri Nitin Khedkar
Department of Computer Science and Engineering, Symbiosis Institute of Technology, Symbiosis International [Deemed University], Pune – 412115, India

Varad Vishwarupe
Department of Mechanical Engineering, Symbiosis Institute of Technology, Symbiosis International [Deemed University], Maharashtra, India

CHAPTER 1

IoT and AI-based Smart Farm: Optimizing Crop Yield and Sustainability

Namrata Nishant Wasatkar[1,*], Pranali Gajanan Chavhan[1] and Vikas Kanifnath Kolekar[1]

[1] *Vishwakarma Institute of information and Technology, Pune, Maharashtra State, India*

Abstract: The "Smart Farm" project is an IoT-based agriculture project aimed at optimizing crop yield and promoting sustainability in farming practices. By integrating various IoT devices and sensors, the project aims to improve the efficiency of farming operations, reduce waste, and enhance the quality and quantity of crop yields. The project focuses on using IoT technology to monitor and control various aspects of farming, including soil moisture, temperature, humidity, crop health, and livestock behaviour. By leveraging data from these sensors and devices, farmers can make more informed decisions about irrigation, pest control, and crop management, leading to increased productivity and sustainability. Overall, the Smart Farm project seeks to transform traditional farming practices into a more efficient, data-driven, and sustainable model that benefits both farmers and the environment.

Keywords: Agricultural robotics, Agricultural applications, Computer vision, Crop and soil management, Machine intelligence, Satellite drone.

INTRODUCTION

Agriculture is a critical industry that plays a significant role in global food security, economic development, and environmental sustainability. However, traditional farming practices often rely on manual labor, intuition, and guesswork, which can lead to inefficiencies, waste, and environmental degradation. In recent years, there has been a growing interest in using Internet of Things (IoT) technology to improve the efficiency and sustainability of farming operations. The "SmartFarm" project is an IoT-based agriculture project that aims to optimize crop yield and promote sustainability by integrating various sensors and devices into farming practices. By collecting and analyzing data from these devices, farm-

---
*** Corresponding author Namrata Nishant Wasatkar:** Vishwakarma Institute of information and Technology, Pune, Maharashtra State, India; E-mail: namrata.kharate@viit.ac.in

Sonali Mahendra Kothari, Vijayshri Nitin Khedkar, Ujwala Kshirsagar and Gitanjali Rahul Shinde (Eds.)

ers can make more informed decisions about irrigation, pest control, and crop management, leading to increased productivity and sustainability. This project represents a significant shift towards data-driven, efficient, and sustainable farming practices that benefit both farmers and the environment. In this paper, we will explore the various components of the SmartFarm project, including the sensors and devices used, the data analysis techniques employed, and the expected outcomes and benefits of the project.

Agriculture involves five steps are as follows:

- Preparing the soil.
- Planting.
- Spraying applications, fertilizer or chemicals.
- Harvesting.
- Managing: Determining what you did well and what you'll do next year by collecting data for all of these steps.

Smart farming, also known as precision agriculture or digital farming, is an advanced agricultural system that uses technology to optimize crop production and maximize yields while reducing waste, energy consumption, and environmental impact. It involves the use of various technologies, such as sensors, drones, machine learning, and data analytics, to monitor and control every aspect of the farming process [1].

The main goal of smart farming is to increase the efficiency and productivity of agriculture by making data-driven decisions based on real-time information [2]. For example, farmers can use sensors to measure soil moisture, temperature, and nutrient levels to determine the optimal time to plant, irrigate, or apply fertilizers. Drones equipped with cameras and sensors can help farmers monitor crop growth, detect pests and diseases, and identify areas that need attention.

Smart farming also involves the use of precision machinery and robotics, such as automated tractors and harvesters, to reduce labor costs and improve accuracy. In addition, data analytics and machine learning algorithms can help farmers analyze large amounts of data to identify patterns and optimize farming practices for better yields.

Overall, smart farming is a promising approach to modern agriculture, as it has the potential to increase yields, reduce costs, and minimize environmental impact.

CHALLENGES AND ISSUES

Farming faces several challenges and issues that can impact crop yield, profitability, and sustainability [2]. Here are some of the most significant issues in farming:

- Climate Change: Climate change is causing extreme weather events, such as droughts, floods, and heat waves, which can impact crop yields and soil health.
- Water Management: Access to water and efficient water management is critical for farming, especially in arid and semi-arid regions. Water scarcity and inefficient irrigation methods can lead to crop failure and reduced yields.
- Soil Health: Soil health is essential for crop growth, but soil degradation from erosion, overuse, and chemical use can lead to reduced yields and nutrient-poor crops.
- Pests and Diseases: Crop pests and diseases can devastate crops, reducing yield and quality, and increasing the need for pesticides and herbicides.
- Labor Shortage: Farm labor shortages can lead to increased costs and reduced efficiency, especially during peak seasons.
- Access to Markets: Farmers may face challenges in accessing markets to sell their products, especially small-scale and subsistence farmers.
- Food Security: Despite advancements in farming practices, many regions still face food insecurity due to poverty, conflict, and lack of access to resources.
- Sustainable Farming: Ensuring that farming practices are sustainable and do not harm the environment is becoming increasingly important to consumers and policymakers.

Addressing these issues will require a combination of technological advancements, policy changes, and changes in farming practices to ensure that farming remains a sustainable and profitable industry.

PROCESS OF SMART FARMING

The "SmartFarm" project involves several processes that are aimed at optimizing crop yield and sustainability through the use of IoT technology [3]. Agriculture, which provides a country with the necessary fuel, food, fibre, and feed, is its foundation. Due to the significant advancements in bioinformatics, which permeate many areas of our lives, the important industry has grown more adaptable and sophisticated. A significant chapter in the history of global agriculture is that of "smart agriculture," which began with the use of several cutting-edge technologies during various agricultural practises, including pre-cultivation, cultivation, seedling, fertilisation, weed detection, irrigation, pesticide spraying, till harvesting, and also pot-harvesting [4]. The following are the key processes involved in the project:

- Sensor deployment: The first step in the Smart Farm project is to deploy various sensors and devices in the farming area. This includes soil moisture sensors, temperature and humidity sensors, crop health monitoring sensors, and livestock monitoring sensors.
- Data collection: Once the sensors are deployed, they collect data on various aspects of the farming area, including soil moisture, temperature, humidity, crop health, and livestock behavior. This data is collected and transmitted to a central server for analysis.
- Data analysis: The data collected from the sensors is analyzed using various data analysis techniques, such as statistical analysis, machine learning algorithms, and predictive modeling. The analysis is used to identify trends, patterns, and anomalies in the data, which can be used to optimize farming operations.
- Decision-making: Based on the insights gained from the data analysis, farmers can make informed decisions about irrigation, pest control, crop management, and livestock health. These decisions are aimed at optimizing crop yield and promoting sustainability in farming practices.
- Feedback loop: The SmartFarm project also involves a feedback loop, where the decisions made by farmers are fed back into the system, and the sensors and devices are adjusted accordingly. This allows the system to continuously learn and improve over time.

Overall, the SmartFarm project involves a data-driven approach to farming, where IoT technology is used to optimize farming operations and promote sustainability. By collecting and analyzing data from various sensors and devices, farmers can make informed decisions that lead to increased productivity and reduced environmental impact.

There are several algorithms that can be used in smart farming to optimize crop yield and reduce resource waste [5]. Here are some examples:

Predictive Analytics

To evaluate vast volumes of gathered data, predictive analytics use machine learning algorithms from various sensors on the farm, such as soil moisture sensors, weather stations, and drone images, to forecast crop yields, plant diseases, and pest infestations.

Precision Farming

Precision farming involves using sensors and GPS technology to gather information on crop health and growth, soil conditions, and weather patterns. This information is then used to adjust the amount of fertilizers, water, and other inputs used in farming, reducing waste and maximizing yield.

Autonomous Equipment

Autonomous equipment, such as self-driving tractors and drones, can be programmed with machine learning algorithms to perform tasks such as planting, irrigation, and pesticide application, reducing labor costs and increasing efficiency.

Image Processing

Image processing algorithms can be used to analyze images captured by drones or other cameras to identify crop diseases, nutrient deficiencies, and other issues that may impact crop yield.

Blockchain Technology

Blockchain technology can be used to track the entire supply chain, from seed to final product, ensuring that all steps are transparent and traceable. This can help farmers to maintain high-quality standards and ensure food safety.

Decision Support Systems

Decision support systems use algorithms to analyze data and provide farmers with recommendations on the best course of action for planting, harvesting, and managing crops. This can help farmers to optimize crop yield and reduce waste.

Overall, these algorithms can help farmers to make data-driven decisions, improve crop yield, and reduce resource waste, resulting in more sustainable and profitable agriculture.

AUTONOMOUS EQUIPMENT FOR SMART FARMING

Autonomous equipment is becoming increasingly popular in smart farming as it allows farmers to increase efficiency, reduce labour costs, and optimize the use of resources [5, 6], shown in Fig. (**1**).

Here are some examples of autonomous equipment used in smart farming:

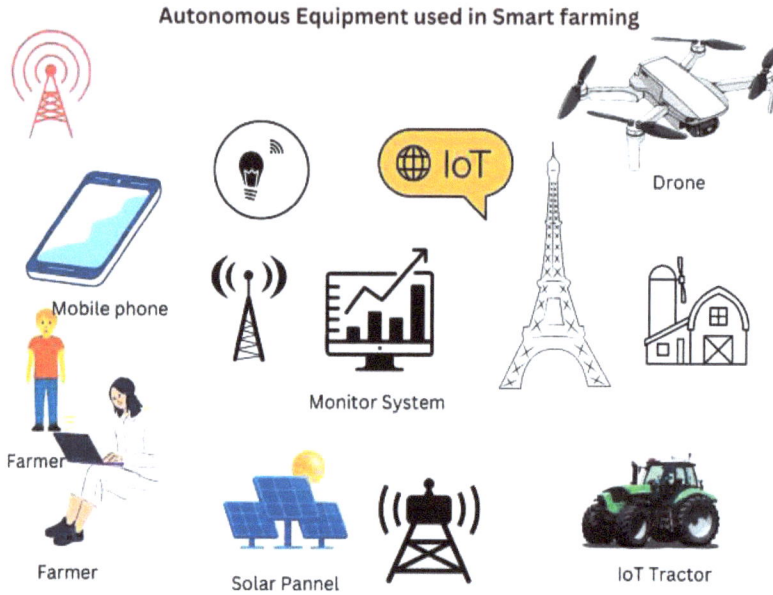

Fig. (1). Autonomous Equipment for smart farming.

Autonomous Tractors

Self-driving tractors can be programmed to perform tasks such as planting, tillage, and harvesting without the need for a human operator. They use sensors and GPS technology to navigate the field and perform tasks with precision.

Drones

Drones equipped with cameras and sensors can be used for a variety of tasks, such as crop mapping, plant counting, and monitoring crop health. They can also be used to apply pesticides and fertilizers with greater precision, reducing waste and environmental impact.

Robotic Harvesters

Robotic harvesters are designed to pick and sort fruits and vegetables without damaging them. They use computer vision and machine learning algorithms to identify ripe products and harvest them with precision.

Autonomous Seeders

Autonomous seeders can be used to plant crops with greater accuracy and efficiency. They can be programmed to plant seeds at precise depths and intervals, reducing the need for manual labor.

Autonomous Weeders

Autonomous weeders use machine learning algorithms to identify and remove weeds without harming the crops. They can be programmed to target specific types of weeds, reducing the use of herbicides.

Overall, autonomous equipment can help farmers to reduce labor costs, optimize resource use, and increase crop yield, resulting in more sustainable and profitable agriculture

In conclusion, smart farming has the potential to revolutionize agriculture by using IoT technology to optimize crop yield and sustainability. By collecting data from sensors and other devices, farmers can make data-driven decisions on when to plant, irrigate, and fertilize their crops. This can result in more efficient use of resources and higher crop yields. Additionally, smart farming can decrease waste and the use of pesticides and fertilisers to lessen the impact of agriculture on the environment. The IoT technology used in smart farming includes a variety of devices such as soil sensors, weather stations, drones, and autonomous equipment like tractors and harvesters. Machine learning algorithms can be applied to this data to provide insights and recommendations to farmers.

By adopting smart farming practices, farmers can improve their bottom line by reducing costs, increasing yields, and improving the quality of their products. Additionally, smart farming can help to ensure food security by producing more food with fewer resources, and improving the resilience of farming operations against climate change.

In general, smart farming might make agriculture a more efficient and sustainable enterprise and it is essential to invest in the development and adoption of these technologies to meet the growing demand for food while preserving our natural resources for future generations.

SENSORS IN SMART FARMS

There are several types of sensors that are commonly used in smart farms to collect data on various aspects of crop growth and environmental conditions. Some of the most common types of sensors used in smart farms include:

Soil Sensors

These sensors are used to measure soil moisture, temperature, and nutrient levels, which can help farmers determine when to irrigate, fertilize, or adjust other growing conditions.

In Fig. (**2**), soil moisture sensors are the usual name for sensors that monitor the volumetric water content. Volumetric Water Content (VWC), sometimes known as "soil moisture," is a measurement of how much water is retained in the soil and is stated as a percent of the entire mixture. The kind of soil affects both how much water a soil can hold and whether it is accessible to plants. For many applications, measuring soil moisture is a crucial quality (not limited to irrigation). Sensors can measure soil moisture using a number of different technologies and methodologies.

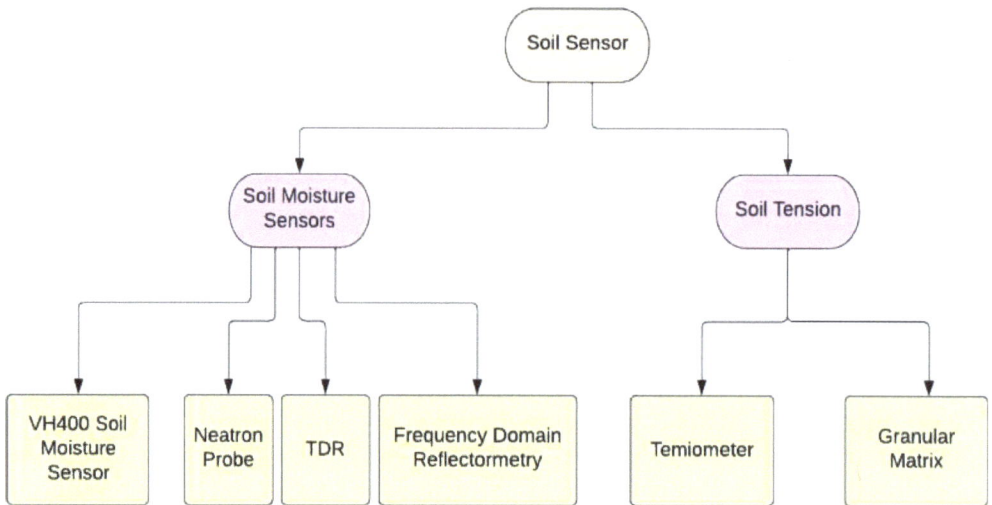

Fig. (2). Taxonomy of Soil Sensors.

Tensiometers (Soil Matric Potential Sensors) calculate the matric potential or soil water potential. The force needed to extract water from the soil, known as soil matric potential, is a sign of stress for plants and crops. It may be used to calculate the soil's water fluxes and the amount of water that is stored there. The neutron probe method is regarded to be the most accurate for measuring soil moisture.

Weather Sensors

These sensors are used to collect data on temperature, humidity, wind speed and direction, and precipitation, which can help farmers make informed decisions about when to plant, irrigate, or harvest crops.

Typically, the environmental variables that weather sensors measure are used to classify them. Types of weather sensors are as follows:

- Multi-weather sensors: Multi-weather sensors, as their name suggests, measure a number of variables using a single device. An illustration of a high-precision multi-weather sensor is the LAMBRECHT meteo WS7.
- Humidity and temperature sensors: Some of the most popular weather sensors are temperature and humidity sensors. They may be used to determine a plant's risk of harm from too much or too little moisture, compute a heat index, and more.
- Wind speed & quality sensors: Wind speed, direction, and quality sensors are used by people in a number of significant ways to analyse air-flow. Understanding winds is essential for choosing the best paths, conserving fuel, and ensuring the safety of the crew and cargo, for instance, in the marine industry.
- Water quality, level, & flow sensors: To keep communities safe, it is crucial to comprehend the volume, flow, and level of both natural and man-made bodies of water.
- Water quality sensors: These sensors measure the quality of water used for irrigation and animal husbandry, helping farmers identify potential issues and ensure the health of their crops and livestock.
- Sunlight & UV sensors: UV sensors measure the amount of sun radiation that enters a certain environment.
- Lightning sensors: Lightning sensors, as the name suggests, find lightning.
- Atmospheric pressure sensors: Understanding pressure is essential for many machine-driven industrial operations as well as comprehending the weather.
- Precipitation sensors: Rain, snow, sleet, and hail are all types of precipitation that are measured using precipitation sensors.
- Light sensors: These sensors are used to monitor the amount and quality of light that crops are receiving, which can help farmers optimize plant growth and yield.
- Air quality sensors: These sensors measure the quality of the air in the farming environment, including factors such as carbon dioxide and ammonia levels, which can impact crop growth and animal health.

Plant Sensors

These sensors can measure various aspects of plant growth, such as photosynthesis rates, leaf temperature, and chlorophyll content, which can help farmers detect early signs of stress, disease, or other issues.

- Plant disease sensors: Plant pathology uses digital photographs as crucial instruments for determining the health of plants. Red, Green, and Blue (RGB) digital pictures from digital cameras provide an easy source for illness detection, quantification, and diagnosis.

- Pest and disease sensors: These sensors can identify pests and illnesses in crops, enabling farmers to take preventative measures before they spread and do serious harm.
- Spectral sensors: Spectral sensors are often grouped according to their spectral resolution (*i.e.*, the quantity and width of wavebands that can be monitored), spatial scale, and detector type (*i.e.*, imaging or non-imaging sensor systems).
- Thermal sensors: Infrared thermography (IRT) measures plant temperature and has relationships with plant water status [7], crop stand microclimate [8], and variations in transpiration brought on by early plant pathogen infections [9].
- Fluorescence imaging Several chlorophyll fluorescence metrics are employed to calculate variations in plant photosynthetic activity.

Nutrient Sensors

These sensors are used to monitor nutrient levels in the soil and water, which can help farmers optimize fertilization practices and avoid over-fertilization. For detecting soil nutrients, two popular types of potentiometric electrochemical sensors are ion-selective electrodes (ISE) and ion-selective field effect transistors (ISFET).

GPS Sensors

These sensors can be used to track the location of farming equipment, such as tractors and harvesters, and optimize routes and schedules for maximum efficiency.

Overall, the use of IoT sensors in smart farming can provide farmers with real-time data and insights that can help them make better decisions about their farming practices, leading to increased efficiency, productivity, and sustainability.

BENEFITS OF SMART FARMING

Smart farming, also known as precision agriculture, is an innovative approach to farming that involves using advanced technology to optimize crop yields, reduce waste, and increase efficiency [4]. Here are some of the key benefits of smart farming:

Improved Efficiency.

Smart farming technologies such as sensors, drones, and GPS systems can help farmers monitor their crops in real-time and make data-driven decisions about when to water, fertilize, or harvest. This can help farmers optimize their use of resources and reduce waste, leading to increased efficiency and cost savings.

Increased Yields

By using precision agriculture techniques, farmers can gain a better understanding of their crops and their environment, which can help them optimize their growing conditions to achieve higher yields. For example, farmers can use sensors to monitor soil moisture levels and adjust irrigation systems accordingly, which can help plants grow faster and healthier.

Reduced Environmental Impact

Smart farming can help farmers reduce their environmental footprint by using resources more efficiently and reducing waste. By optimizing irrigation and fertilizer use, farmers can reduce runoff and pollution, which can have a positive impact on the environment.

Improved Quality and Safety

By monitoring their crops closely, farmers can detect problems early on and take action to prevent crop damage or contamination. This can help improve the quality and safety of their crops, which can lead to higher prices and increased demand from consumers.

Increased Profitability

By using precision agriculture techniques, farmers can optimize their yields and reduce their costs, which can lead to increased profitability. Smart farming can also help farmers diversify their income streams by enabling them to produce more crops on the same amount of land.

Overall, smart farming has the potential to transform the agricultural industry by increasing efficiency, improving yields, and reducing the environmental impact of farming.

THE IMPACT OF CLIMATE ON SMART FARMING

Climate has a significant impact on smart farming, as it affects crop growth and environmental conditions that are critical for farming. Climate change, in particular, has become a major challenge for farmers worldwide, as it has led to unpredictable weather patterns, more frequent extreme weather events, and changes in temperature and rainfall that can impact crop growth and yields [10].

Smart farming technologies can help farmers adapt to these changes by providing real-time data on weather conditions and soil moisture levels, allowing them to make informed decisions about irrigation, fertilization, and other farming practices. For example, if a smart farm sensor detects low soil moisture levels, the farmer can use that information to adjust irrigation practices to ensure that crops receive enough water to thrive.

In addition, smart farming technologies can help farmers reduce their environmental impact and carbon footprint by optimizing farming practices to use fewer resources and produce less waste. For example, precision irrigation can reduce water use, while precision fertilization can reduce the use of synthetic fertilizers, which can be harmful to the environment if overused.

Overall, smart farming technologies can help farmers adapt to the impacts of climate change and mitigate their environmental impact, while also improving crop yields and profitability. However, it is important to continue developing and improving these technologies to ensure that farmers have the tools they need to succeed in an increasingly unpredictable climate.

CASE STUDY OF SMART FARMING USING IOT

One example of smart farming using IoT is the project conducted by John Deere, a leading manufacturer of agricultural machinery, in collaboration with Intel and Climate Corporation. The project aimed to improve the efficiency and sustainability of farming operations by collecting and analyzing data from sensors and other IoT devices.

The project involved the deployment of sensors and IoT devices to gather data on soil moisture levels, temperature, and other environmental factors, as well as data on crop growth and yield. The data was then transmitted to a central hub, where it was analyzed using advanced algorithms to provide insights and recommendations to farmers.

Through this project, farmers were able to make more informed decisions about when and how much to water their crops, how much fertilizer to use, and when to harvest. This resulted in improved crop yields, reduced waste, and increased efficiency.

The project also enabled farmers to monitor and manage their operations remotely, using mobile devices and other IoT-enabled technologies. This allowed farmers to stay connected and informed, even when they were not physically on the farm.

The IoT is transforming the agricultural industry by giving farmers a wide range of tools to handle various problems they encounter in the field. With IoT-enabled devices, farmers can access their farms at any time and from practically anywhere [9].

Overall, the use of IoT in smart farming has the potential to transform the agriculture industry by providing farmers with new tools and insights to optimize their farming practices, reduce waste, and increase sustainability.

HOW TO USE AI FOR OPTIMIZING AND PREDICTING YIELD

AI can be utilized for yield prediction and optimization in various ways. Here are a few possible approaches:

Data Collection and Analysis

The first step towards yield prediction and optimization is to collect and analyze relevant data. AI algorithms can be trained to analyze large amounts of data, including weather patterns, soil characteristics, crop types, and yield history, to identify patterns and make predictions [11].

Predictive Modeling

AI algorithms can be trained to create predictive models that can forecast crop yields based on various factors such as weather conditions, soil moisture, and nutrient levels. Farmers may find it easier to plan when to sow, irrigate, fertilise, and harvest their crops as a result.

Machine Learning

Algorithms that use machine learning may be taught to recognise data patterns that are not immediately apparent to humans. This can be used to optimize crop yields by identifying the best combination of inputs, planting strategies, and harvesting techniques.

Crop Monitoring

AI-powered cameras and drones can be used to monitor crop health and identify areas where crops may be struggling. This can help farmers to take corrective actions before yield is affected.

Precision Agriculture

Precision agriculture involves using data-driven approaches to optimize crop production. Farmers can use various technologies such as sensors, drones, and satellite imagery to monitor soil conditions, weather patterns, and plant growth. This data is then used to adjust irrigation, fertilization, and pest management practices to maximize crop yield and quality. Precision farming techniques involve using sensors, GPS, and other technologies to monitor and manage crops on a real-time basis. AI can be used to analyze the data collected from these sensors and make recommendations about the optimal amount of water, fertilizer, and other inputs needed to maximize yield.

Automated Irrigation Systems

Smart irrigation systems use sensors and weather data to automate watering schedules and ensure that crops receive the right amount of water at the right time. This can help farmers conserve water and reduce the risk of overwatering or underwatering their crops.

Crop Monitoring

Smart farming technologies such as drones and satellite imagery can be used to monitor crops for signs of disease or pest infestations. This allows farmers to take action early and prevent further damage to their crops.

Livestock Monitoring

Sensors can be placed on livestock to monitor their health and behavior. This information can be used to optimize feeding and breeding practices and ensure that animals are healthy and productive.

Automated Machinery

Automated machinery such as robotic harvesters and autonomous tractors can help farmers reduce labor costs and increase efficiency. These machines can be programmed to perform tasks such as planting, harvesting, and tilling fields without human intervention. Governments at small farms and the business sector need to encourage smart agriculture more in emerging nations [7].

Overall, smart farming technologies are becoming increasingly important as farmers seek to optimize their operations and increase productivity while also reducing waste and environmental impact. By giving farmers real-time information and recommendations for maximising production, AI has the potential to completely transform the way farmers manage their crops.

CASE STUDY -AUTOMATED IRRIGATION SYSTEMS

Automated irrigation systems are a key component of smart farming technology, it is shown in Fig. (**3**). These systems use sensors and weather data to automate watering schedules and ensure that crops receive the proper quantity of water at the proper moment. Automatic irrigation systems save time, eliminate human error when regulating soil moisture levels, and increase net profits in line with factors like sales, product growth, and quality [12]. The major goal of an autonomous irrigation system is to help farmers save time, money, and electricity [8].

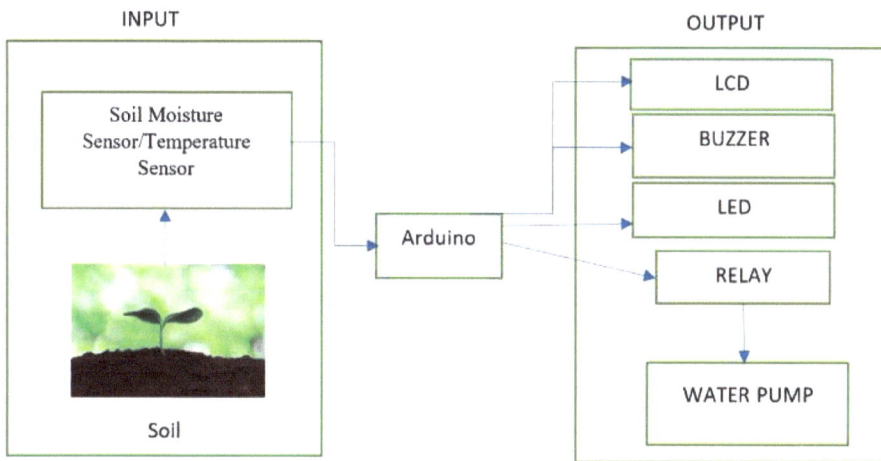

Fig. (3). Automated Irrigation Systems.

Here are some of the benefits of using automated irrigation systems in agriculture:

Water Conservation

Automated irrigation systems use sensors to measure soil moisture levels and adjust watering schedules accordingly. This helps to conserve water by reducing the amount of water used for irrigation.

Increased Crop Yield

By providing crops with the proper quantity of water at the proper moment, automated irrigation systems can help to increase crop yield, quality and making it cost efficient for farmers and reducing crop wastage [12].

Reduced Labor Costs

Automated irrigation systems can be programmed to run on a schedule, reducing the need for manual labor. This can save farmers time and money.

Improved Accuracy

Automated irrigation systems use sensors to measure soil moisture levels and adjust watering schedules accordingly. This improves the accuracy of irrigation and reduces the risk of overwatering or underwatering crops.

Flexibility

Automated irrigation systems can be programmed to adjust watering schedules based on weather patterns and other environmental factors. This allows farmers to adapt to changing conditions and ensure that crops receive the right amount of water.

Overall, automated irrigation systems are a cost-effective and efficient way to manage water usage in agriculture. By using sensors and weather data to optimize watering schedules, these systems can help farmers conserve water, increase crop yield, and reduce labor costs.

CONCLUSION

In conclusion, smart farming with the help of AI and IoT technologies is transforming the agriculture industry by optimizing farming operations and improving sustainability. Through real-time monitoring and analysis of crop data, farmers can make more informed decisions about planting, watering, fertilizing, and controlling pests. This results in better crop yields, reduced waste, and decreased environmental impact. By implementing precision agriculture techniques, farmers can efficiently use inputs such as water, fertilizer, and pesticides, thus protecting the environment and ensuring long-term sustainability. Smart farming with AI and IoT technologies is a promising solution to feed the growing global population while minimizing the negative impact of agriculture on the planet.

REFERENCES

[1]   J.H. Lenthe, E.C. Oerke, and H.W. Dehne, "Digital infrared thermography for monitoring canopy health of wheat", *Precis. Agric.,* vol. 8, no. 1-2, pp. 15-26, 2007.
[http://dx.doi.org/10.1007/s11119-006-9025-6]

[2]   E-C. Oerke, U. Steiner, H-W. Dehne, and M. Lindenthal, "Thermal imaging of cucumber leaves affected by downy mildew and environmental conditions", *J. Exp. Bot.,* vol. 57, no. 9, pp. 2121-2132,

2006.
[http://dx.doi.org/10.1093/jxb/erj170] [PMID: 16714311]

[3]   L. Raja, and S. Vyas, "The study of technological development in the field of smart farming", In: *Smart farm. technol. sustain. agricul. develop.* IGI Global, 2019, pp. 1-24.
[http://dx.doi.org/10.4018/978-1-5225-5909-2.ch001]

[4]   Zakaria Fouad Abdalla, and Hassan El-Ramady, "Applications and challenges of smart farming for developing sustainable agriculture",
[http://dx.doi.org/10.21608/jenvbs.2022.135889.1175]

[5]   E.M. Ouafiq, R. Saadane, A. Chehri, and S. Jeon, "AI-based modeling and data-driven evaluation for smart farming-oriented big data architecture using IoT with energy harvesting capabilities", *Sustain. Energy Technol. Assess.,* vol. 52, p. 102093, 2022. [http://dx.doi.org/10.1016/j.seta.2022.102093].

[6]   T. Sutjarittham, H. Habibi Gharakheili, S.S. Kanhere, and V. Sivaraman, "Kanhere, and Vijay Sivaraman. Experiences with iot and ai in a smart campus for optimizing classroom usage", *IEEE Internet Things J.,* vol. 6, no. 5, pp. 7595-7607, 2019.
[http://dx.doi.org/10.1109/JIOT.2019.2902410]

[7]   E. S. Mohamed, AA. Belal, S. K. Abd-Elmabod, M. A. A El-Shirbeny, A. Gad, and M. B. Zahran, "Smart farming for improving agricultural management", *The Egyp. J. Remote. Sens. Spac. Sci.,* vol. 24, no. 3, pp. 971-981, 2021.
[http://dx.doi.org/10.1016/j.ejrs.2021.08.007] [PMID: 1110-9823]

[8]   K. Kansara, V. Zaveri, S. Shah, S. Delwadkar, and K. Jani, "Sensor based automated irrigation system with iot: A technical review", *Int. J. Comput. Sci. Inf. Technol.,* vol. 6, no. 6, pp. 5331-5333, 2015.

[9]   K. Krishnaveni, E. Radhamani, and K. Preethi, *7 internet of things platform for smart farming. Internet of Things and Machine Learning in Agriculture.* De Gruyter, 2021, pp. 131-158.

[10]   A. L. Virk, M. A. Noor, and S. Fiaz, "Saddam Hussain, Hafiz Athar Hussain, Muzammal Rehman, Muhammad Ahsan, and WeiMa. Smart farming: an overview", *Smart village technology: concepts and developments,* pp. 191-201, 2020.

[11]   C.Z. Yang, S. Ramiah, and D. Padmakumar, "Web based agricultural monitoring and sales management system", In: *2022 IEEE 2nd Mysore Sub Section International Conference (MysuruCon),* 2022, pp. 1-5.

[12]   J. Doshi, T. Patel, and S. Bharti, "Smart Farming using IoT, a solution for optimally monitoring farming conditions", *Procedia Comput. Sci.,* vol. 160, pp. 746-751, 2019.
[http://dx.doi.org/10.1016/j.procs.2019.11.016]

CHAPTER 2

Impact of Automation, Artificial Intelligence and Deep Learning on Agriculture Crop Yield

Prabhakar Laxmanrao Ramteke[1,*]

[1] *H.V.P. M's College of Engineering and Technology, Amravati (Maharashtra State) Affiliated to Sant Gadge Baba Amravati, University, Amravati, Maharashtra, India*

Abstract: Every nation is concerned about the growing problem of agriculture automation. It is challenging to supply the food needs of the existing population due to rising numbers, frequent climate change, and scarce resources. Farmers are forced to wreak havoc on the land by applying dangerous pesticides more often since their old techniques cannot keep up with the growing demand. As a result, agricultural practices are significantly impacted, and the land gradually loses its fertility and becomes unproductive. The agriculture sector can benefit from technology like Artificial Intelligence (AI), deep learning, the Internet of Things (IoT), embedded systems, and automation. Artificial neural networks, the Internet of Things, fuzzy logic, machine learning, and other technologies may all be used to automate agricultural systems. Artificial intelligence technology is advancing quickly, and as a result, its employment is in a wide range of fields. Utilizing clever technologies, the agricultural industry has become able to regulate the field environment that is essential to the care of every plant. A suitable atmosphere and appropriate irrigation are provided by the plant's identification and suitable circumstances. In order to increase agriculture yields, it has become important to manage crops in controlled settings like greenhouses that can enhance the output. This chapter focuses on the use of artificial intelligence and IoT technology to improve the productivity of agricultural enterprises. AI technologies might help farmers overcome problems like weeds, pests, and climatic variability that lower output. Numerous uses of AI are now being deployed, such as automatic machine changes for weather forecasting and pest detection. The goal of implementing AI and IoT is to increase the possibility of producing healthy crops by recognizing damaged crops and crop yield growth.

Keywords: Agriculture crop yield, Artificial intelligence, Artificial neural networks, Automation, Drone, Deep learning, Fuzzy logic, Internet of things.

---

* **Corresponding author Prabhakar Laxmanrao Ramteke:** H.V.P. M's College of Engineering and Technology, Amravati (Maharashtra State) Affiliated to Sant Gadge Baba Amravati University, Amravati, Maharashtra, India; E-mail: pl_ramteke@rediffmail.com

INTRODUCTION

In this digital age, as technology advances, people are attempting to combine the functions of their natural and artificial brains. A whole new branch of artificial intelligence has emerged as a result of this continuous study. This is the method that allows people to build intelligent devices. The field of computer science, which includes AI, has the ability to be aware of its surroundings and should thrive to increase success rates. Based on prior experience, AI ought to be able to work. Machine learning, deep learning, CNN, ANN, IoT, and machine learning are some of the specialized fields that advance machine work and support the creation of more cutting-edge technology. The world's population has increased gradually and has already surpassed 7.7 billion people. By the year 2030, India's population is projected to exceed 1.5 billion, while the globe's population will increase from 7.7 billion in 2019 to over 8.5 billion. In the coming years, there will be a 70% rise in global food consumption and a major decrease in agricultural supply due to growing urbanization. By 2050, India will be the most populous nation on earth, and its domestic food production is already falling behind. The lack of planning, unexpected weather, incorrect harvest, irrigation technologies, and animals are the main causes of the decreased food output. Because of current global warming, nature has undergone a significant transformation. Because of the increase in the earth's average temperature, climatic conditions are unclear. The largest problem for farmers is persistent drought, not significant rain. Poor weather conditions cause farmers to earn 20–25 percent less money, according to India's yearly economic report.

One thought that comes to me is: What are all of these people going to eat? This inquiry is primarily directed at the agricultural sector. The population is not the only issue that modern farmers must deal with. What about the lack of workers and the need for eco-friendly food among consumers? Smart farming provides the solution to all of these issues. Software designed specifically for a certain site can save greenhouse gas emissions while also lowering the quantity of herbicides and fertilizers utilized (Impact of automation). Every nation's primary issue and the developing topic is agriculture automation. Given how quickly the world's population is expanding, there is an urgent demand for food. Farmers must apply toxic pesticides more often since their traditional methods are insufficient to meet the growing demand. This damages the soil and has a significant impact on agricultural operations, as the soil ultimately stays unfertilized. This chapter discusses several automation approaches and best practices, including the Internet of Things, wireless technology, artificial intelligence, machine learning, and deep learning. Crop diseases, improper storage management, misuse of pesticides, weed control, inadequate irrigation, and improper water management are a few issues affecting the agriculture sector. Machines were used to augment or replace human work throughout the industrial revolution. However, with the development of information technology in the twenty-first century, the idea of artificially intelligent machines was unavoidably born with the invention of the computer. The sustainability of any economy rests on the implementation of this technology in agriculture [1]. "Thing-to-thing" communication is what the word "IoT" refers to. System communication, automation, and cost-cutting are the three key objectives. AI is widely used in a variety of fields, including security, agriculture, economics, education, and many more. The machine learning process plays a role in the application of AI [2]. Agriculture used to be only concerned with growing crops and food [3]. But during the past 20 years, much has changed in terms of how crops and animal products are processed, produced, marketed, and distributed. Currently, agricultural operations provide the primary means of subsistence while increasing GDP [4, 5], contributing to national commerce, lowering unemployment, supplying raw materials for other sectors to produce goods from, and generally developing the economy [6 - 8]. It is essential that agricultural methods be examined with the goal of expanding creative techniques to sustain and enhance agricultural operations as the world's population grows geometrically. The use of technology in agriculture will be made possible by other developments like big data analysis, Internet of Things technologies, and artificial intelligence [9, 10]. Understanding concerns like the use of toxic pesticides, regulated irrigation, pollution management, and environmental repercussions in agricultural operations is urgently needed. It has been demonstrated that automating farming procedures increases soil productivity and improves soil fertility. Farm automation techniques can increase agriculture's profitability while simultaneously minimizing its environmental impact [11 - 13].

The use of computers in agriculture was first mentioned in a paper in 1983 [14]. The current issues in agriculture have been addressed using a variety of strategies, from databases to decision support systems [15, 16]. Agriculture is a dynamic industry, making it impossible to generalize problems and offer a universal fix. It can now accurately capture the intricate intricacies of each circumstance and offer the most appropriate answer using AI approaches. With the advancement of various AI approaches, extremely complicated issues are being handled gradually [17].

AI TECHNIQUES FOR PROBLEM SOLVING IN AGRICULTURE SECTOR

Following are some important AI approaches that may be utilized as targeted areas for issue-solving in the agricultural field:

Fuzzy Logic

Fuzzy logic is a promising technique that might swiftly gather the necessary information from the agricultural sector and produce reliable diagnosis choices. Based on the risk factors and symptoms, it will assess and forecast the likelihood of likely illnesses in agricultural plants. Applications of fuzzy logic in agriculture include locating appropriate land and forecasting weather. Fuzzy logic has been very useful in solving many real-world problems that are inherent to their uncertainty, complexity, impreciseness, and a high degree of randomness. Soft computing aims to mimic human thinking and thus solve problems as a human does. The systems embedded with one or more soft computing technologies tend to make decisions quicker (reducing the processing timeframe) and more accurately in the light of uncertain and indefinite data.

Artificial Neural Networks

They are often employed in order to complete different categorization and prediction tasks. They have also been used in farming, as it is widely understood. They might be included in decision assistance and precision agricultural systems.

Neuro- Fuzzy Logic

By replicating human vision to grasp language qualities, fuzzy logic offers a logical framework for coping with ambiguous circumstances, whereas neural networks imitate how humans learn, reason, and adapt. Systems that combine these two methods are known as "neuro-fuzzy systems." Soil quality may be monitored, managed, and improved through the use of an adaptive neuro-fuzzy inference system in agriculture [18].

Expert System

Expert systems in agriculture are able to combine the viewpoints of several fields, like plant pathology, entomology (the study of insects), horticulture, and agricultural meteorology, into a framework that best handles the kind of ad-hoc decision-making needed by contemporary farmers. It is a helpful decision-support tool for the growth of plants and crops [19].

OBSTACLES IN THE FIELD OF AGRICULTURE AND IN AI ADAPTATION

Farm automation is one approach to numerous problems. Why would hundreds of entrepreneurs finance mechanized farming? The industry of agriculture is currently facing issues that must be urgently addressed. These issues are nothing new for those who operate in the agricultural sector [20].

Consumer Inclinations

Demand for healthier food items has increased as a result of the glut of fast food and other unhealthy meals on the market. Due to the negative effects that eating poorly has had on our bodies, customers worldwide are yearning for healthy, plant-based cuisine. Farmers ought to produce it in substantial quantities to satisfy the growing consumer demand.

Lack of Labour

Nowadays, it is uncommon to meet an adolescent who wants to become a farmer. The reality is that as more people choose to live urban lifestyles, the farming industry must contend with a manpower deficit. Additionally, during the past ten years, contemporary farming methods have changed, making it more difficult to educate new personnel.

Environmental Accountability

The general public and local government anticipate environmentally conscious and responsible behavior from agricultural businesses. Farmers should choose to use fewer chemical substances, particularly insecticides. Farm automation can provide business owners in the agriculture industry with the answer they're seeking to this social and ecological requirement.

Tiny and Dispersed Landholdings

One of the key reasons for low agricultural output and a condition of backward agriculture is the sub-division and fragmentation of holdings. Moving animals, tools, manure, seeds, and other agricultural supplies from one plot of land to another wastes a lot of time and labour.

Seeds

To increase crop yields and maintain steady development in agricultural output, seeds are an essential and fundamental ingredient. The distribution of seeds of guaranteed quality is just as important as its manufacture. Unfortunately, the majority of farmers, especially small and marginal farmers, cannot afford high-quality seeds due to their high cost.

Land Mechanization

Very little to no machinery is used for the cultivation and processing phases of farming, such as excavating, planting, watering, gathering, cutting, and shipping farm products. It is particularly true for little and distant lands. As a result, a lot of human labour is wasted, and worker productivity becomes low.

Farm Automation or Smart Farming

Traditional farming has used a number of technological advancements to optimise the food production process and raise quality. As of right now, cutting-edge agricultural technology may be a vital component of a farmer's everyday tasks shown in Fig. (**1**).

Fig. (1). Farming in advance Source: Alexey Chalimov / 12th September 2019 / Digital Transformation eastern peak- by Ukraine.

Although AI has a lot of promise for applications in agriculture, farmers all over the world now lack knowledge of cutting-edge high-tech machine learning solutions. Agriculture is heavily dependent on environmental factors, including soil, weather, and insect attack susceptibility. Considering that it is impacted by unforeseen events, a yield production aim made at the beginning of the season might not appear wonderful once harvesting has begun. In order to develop their algorithms and produce precise forecasts and predictions, intelligent based system requires huge data. In conclusion, implementing cognitive solutions will be crucial for farming's future. Even though there is a lot of research being done right now and a lot of applications are now available, the farming industry still needs more help and is underserved. Farming with AI is still in its infancy, but it is harnessing AI decision-making systems and prediction solutions to solve the real-world demands and difficulties faced by farmers. The great potential of AI in agriculture has to be fully utilized.

Therefore, applications need to be more durable. When that happens, it will be capable of handling frequent shifts and changes in the environment on its own. This would facilitate the employment of the appropriate model or programme in the right sequence to efficiently gather contextual data. The high cost of many cognitive farming choices that are readily accessible on the market is the second important factor. In order to ensure technology reaches the farming industry, AI solutions must become more commercially feasible.

REQUIREMENT OF ARTIFICIAL INTELLIGENCE IN THE AGRICULTURE SECTOR

Different farming strategies have quickly adapted to the agricultural sector. Cognitive computing is the idea of using a computer model of human mental processes. As a result, agriculture was propelled by turbulent AI technology that assisted in comprehending, learning about, and responding to varied events based on the knowledge acquired to maximize efficiency. Microsoft Corporation is working with them to assist Indian farmers in the state of Andhra Pradesh with soil preparation, planting, fertilizing, and crop nutrition enhancements. A typical 30% increase in agricultural output per acre in comparison to previous harvests.

Numerous Applications of AI & other Technologies that can Boost Agriculture Yield

The list below includes the numerous fields in which solutions for advancing agriculture that include cognitive expertise are available.

Development Driven by the IoT

Each day, enormous amounts of data, both organized and unstructured, are produced. These facts include information on the weather, soil reports, fresh research, rainfall, insect attack susceptibility, and drone and camera images. Cognitive IoT technologies would perceive, recognize, and produce smart solutions to increase agricultural yields. The two basic methods for intelligent data fusion are near and far sensing. Testing the soil is a significant application of this high-resolution data. For proximity sensing, as opposed to distant sensing, just sensors that are closely associated with the soil are needed. Sensor integration with aerial or satellite systems is not necessary. This makes it easier to characterize the soil in a specific area based on the dirt below the surface. Robot hardware has already started combining data-collection software with robots to provide the optimal fertilizer for corn growing in order to maximize crop production. As a result, IoT, linked devices, and automation will almost certainly be applied in agriculture, enhancing nearly every aspect of it.

Ingenious Agriculture

It is mostly related to the use and applications of IoT-specific technology. Farmers may employ IoT-based sensors technology to better manage farming operations from livestock husbandry to agricultural cultivation. They may use a smart agriculture monitoring system remotely that helps to observe the crop status and decide how much pesticides and/or fertilizers they need to be used to achieve optimal efficiency. The definition of "smart farming" holds true as well. Despite not being as common as consumer-linked devices, smart agricultural IoT and industrial IoT in general are nonetheless quite popular. Agriculture IoT solutions are getting increasingly popular. According to current forecasts, the market for smart framing is expected to reach $6.2 billion by 2021. The worldwide smart agricultural business is expected to triple in size by 2025, from little more than $5 billion in 2016 to $15.3 billion. Businesses still have lots of options because the market is constantly expanding.

The technologies have already enabled agriculture fields like robots to have computational intelligence. It can pick up new knowledge, grasp it, and respond appropriately, as shown in Fig. (**2**) and Fig. (**3**) below:

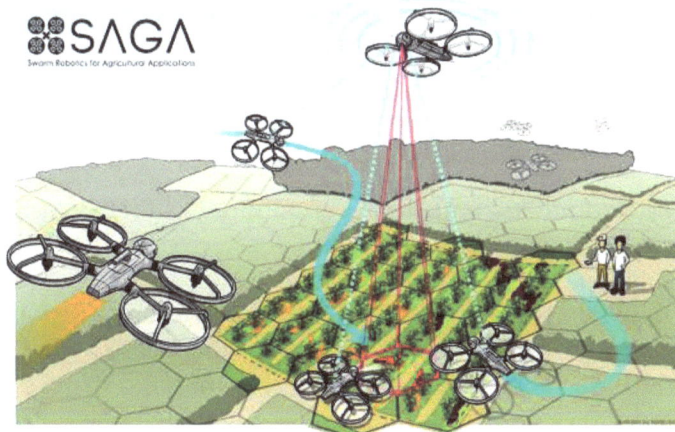

Fig. (2). Autonomous precision seeding by robotics with geomapping.

Fig. (3). IoT in Farming Source: Modern agriculture drones (Unpaprom *et al.,* 2018).

Machine Learning systems have entered and covered multiple applications in several sectors such as healthcare, agriculture, the automation industry, *etc.* Major electronic manufacturers such as Samsung, Apple, and others have stated that these technologies will be integrated into all of their products. IoT-enabled intelligent sensor devices will become mainstream in the near future. These intelligent sensors collect data from a range of sources, such as solar panels, agricultural fields for resource-efficient farming, disaster-prone areas, the processing industry, and so on.

Advantages of Intelligent Farming

- **Internet of Things and Agriculture:** Agriculture has the potential to change in many ways because of technology and IoT. There are specifically five ways that the IoT might enhance agriculture:
- **Countless data are gathered by smart agriculture sensors:** For instance, the state of the soil, the growing stage of the crop, or the health of cattle.
- **Reduced production risks as a result of better internal process control:** The ability to estimate manufacturing production allows for more effective product distribution planning. Knowing the exact number of crops that will be harvested assists you to ensure that the product does not go unclaimed.
- **Enhanced operational effectiveness thanks to process automation:** Many production cycle operations are automated with smart devices, such as pest control, fertilization, and irrigation.
- **Increased production quantities and quality:** By automating the production process, it is possible to maintain higher standards for crop quality and growth potential.

AGRICULTURE APPLICATIONS AND USE CASES

IoT sensors for agriculture and IoT applications in agriculture often come in a wide variety:

Climate Conditions Monitoring

Weather stations with many detectors for precision agriculture are undoubtedly popular for savvy farming technology. Climate and weather are the top influencing factors in the production of crops. Sensors are getting ubiquitous and playing an important role in sensing the environment as shown in Fig. (**4**). These include sensors for monitoring water, air, weather and soil.

Fig. (4). System for monitoring the climate Source: Alexey Chalimov / 12th September, 2019 / Digital Transformation eastern peak- by Ukraine.

Greenhouse Automation

Managing the greenhouse environment usually necessitates manual intervention. GreenIQ is an exciting idea that makes use of smart farm sensors. It is a smart sprinkler controller that allows for remote control of irrigation and lighting systems.

Cattle Management and Monitoring

There are IoT agricultural sensors available that can be installed on farm animals to measure performance and check health, similar to crop monitoring. Cattle tracking and monitoring are used to collect data on the condition, location, and well-being of livestock. Farmers may be able to save money on labour by employing drones to track livestock in real-time. This works in the same way as pet care IoT devices.

Precision Agriculture

Precision agriculture is concerned with exact decision-making. It is one of the most common and effective IoT applications in the agriculture system. Farmers may use soil information to more accurately estimate their crops' water, fertiliser, and pesticide needs.

Smart Farming Predictive Analytics

Farmers may use smart farming to estimate when to harvest crops, the probability of illnesses and pests, and so forth. Agriculture is critically dependent on the controlled and predictable use of data analytics techniques.

A SMART FARMING SOLUTION

There are countless applications for IoT in agriculture. The performance and income of farms may be improved in a variety of ways with the aid of smart technologies. However, creating IoT applications for agriculture is not a simple operation. If one is considering making an investment in smart farming, there are some issues that one needs to be aware of:

IoT Hardware

Before designing an IoT solution for agriculture, the device's sensors must be chosen. The selection will be made based on its function, and its success will be assessed by quality sensors. IoT hardware requirements vary as per the needs of agriculture applications. Let's see the IoT hardware requirements for crop protection from animals. Farm crops are frequently destroyed by neighborhood wildlife, including buffalo, cows, goats, birds, *etc.* For the farmers, this results in enormous losses. Farmers are unable to enclose entire fields in barricades or patrol them around-the-clock. So, here we provide a strategy for automatically protecting crops from animals. This system is based on a microcontroller from the PIC family. A motion sensor is used by this system to identify approaching wild animals in the field. The sensor instructs the microcontroller to operate in this situation. The microcontroller now emits an alarm to entice the animals out of the field and sends an SMS to the farmer so that he is aware of the problem and may respond if necessary, as shown below in Fig. (**5**).

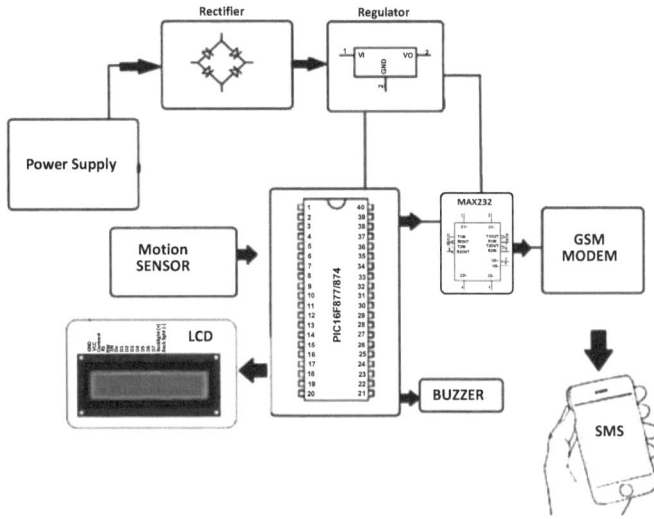

Fig. (5). Block Diagram for Automatic Crop protection from Animals Source: Nevon Solutions Pvt. Ltd, Vihan Commercial Complex, Walbhatt Road Goregaon East, Mumbai.

Connectivity

The necessity for data transfer across several agricultural units continues to hinder the development of smart farming. To allow operation, the connection must be robust.

Data Gathering Intervals

The necessity for data transfer across several agricultural units continues to hinder the development of smart farming. To allow operation, the connection must be robust.

The Farming Sector's Data Integrity

Large data quantities are required by a technology, which increases the risk of security gaps that criminals may exploit for data theft and hacker attempts; hence, data integrity is required.

Disease Detection

Image sensing and analysis are used to split pictures of plant leaves into surface sections such as the background and sick region of a plant leaf.

Before appropriate control measures can be recommended, a quick and precise diagnosis of the disease is required. It is the first phase of any disease study. The majority of the time, a diagnosis is made based on the diseased plant's distinctive characteristics. The diagnosis also depends on the pathogen's identification. The diagnosis process entails three steps: meticulous observation and categorization of the facts; appraisal of the facts; and a reasoned determination of the cause.

The typical appearance of an affected plant species, its local air and soil environment, the cultural conditions in which it is growing, the infections known to infect the area, and the pathogen's capacity to cause illness are all things that a trained diagnostician must be familiar with. The growing plant should be present for the diagnosis to be made. When a plant starts to die in part or in its entirety, for instance, disease is suspected. Blossoms, leaves, stems, roots, or other plant components that are deformed, curled, discoloured, overdeveloped, or underdeveloped are additional symptoms of disease shown in Fig. (**6**). Additionally, it is common for diseased plants to exhibit abnormal responses to other advised techniques like pruning, insect and mite management, fertilisation, and watering.

Fig. (6). Image based Plant Disease detection Source: Deshana Shah *et al.,* Conference Paper First Online: 01 February, 2022 (Springer).

AUTOMATION TECHNIQUES FOR IRRIGATION AND RE-ASSISTING FARMER ABILITY

AI-trained devices that are knowledgeable about past weather patterns, the condition of the soil, and the kind of crops that should be produced may automate irrigation and boost total productivity. Irrigation uses over 70% of the world's freshwater supply; automation can help farmers manage their water issues while also saving water.

Using Drones and Robots to Automate Agriculture

Since smart farming is such a large field, a company's specific demands will determine how they are used. Will robots or drones be more suitable for the industry? Let's see what functions they are good for in various situations.

Robots and Autonomous Machines

Agriculture is a suitable industry for robotics breakthroughs since farmers typically have to deal with repeated operations in the field that require a lot of effort. Agricultural robots, also known as "agrobots," can perform a variety of tasks such as harvesting, watering, and sowing. Let's examine their work more closely.

Robotic Weeding and Seeding

Planting robots are highly accurate and concentrate on a specific area of the field. The use of artificial intelligence and computer vision in this sort of agricultural robot allows for a reduction in pesticide use in the field as it is entirely autonomous and runs on solar energy. This is the most ecologically friendly method: a little four-wheel equipment goes over the field spraying herbicides with the least amount of environmental and crop damage.

Automatic Irrigation

Subsurface Drip Irrigation (SDI) systems and specialised sensors make up the bulk of robot-assisted irrigation systems. In the agricultural sector, SDI is well-known because it offers a precise way to manage how much water is used and when it is delivered to the plants. Even though these systems are undoubtedly more sophisticated than manually watering each plant individually, they still need some human input [25]. More advanced IoT sensors are able to independently check the moisture levels and communicate real-time information to a smart device. Such sensors and SDI work together to develop automated agricultural machinery that streamlines work and conserves water.

Automation of Harvest

Machines must be delicate enough to avoid damaging fruits and vegetables because harvesting is not an easy task for them. However, there are already harvest robots that are capable of handling their jobs. For instance, Abundant is the original for-profit business that specialises in apple picking as shown in Fig.

7). Use a vacuum instead of graspers or other comparable tools to pull off the feat. A machine typically involves a camera or multiple cameras feeding information to the robot that allows it to locate and access the crops around it. Machine vision makes it possible for robots to perform tasks like weed picking, growth monitoring, harvesting, sorting, and packing. In contrast, Agrobot is situated closer to the ground since it creates robots specifically for strawberry harvesting. This invention uses AI to assess the fruit's level of ripeness.

Fig. (7). Harvesting Automation Source: Alexey Chalimov / 12th September, 2019 / Digital Transformation eastern peak- by Ukraine.

AGRICULTURE AUTOMATION BENEFITS

The future can be altered by only one agrobot. Technology for intelligent agricultural automation has the potential to have a huge impact. This area of technology has the key to developing eco-friendly solutions to many global issues.

The Agricultural Sector Satisfies Consumer Demand

It has been noted that shifting customer wants and tastes are present. We all want our food to be delivered quickly to markets and stores while still being fresh. Farmers may save time and money by using agrobots.

The Industry's Labour Deficit is Becoming Better

In some farming specialties, labour expenses might account for up to 50% of total expenses. This issue is made much more serious by the manpower scarcity.

Robotic sowing, harvesting, watering, and monitoring reduce the requirement for hiring workers for a variety of repetitive operations.

Agriculture is Becoming More Environmental-friendly

Many people are terrified by the use of pesticides, which is why agriculture is developing a repulsive reputation. Robots are changing the game's rules to be more ecologically friendly since they can inject pesticides with extreme accuracy, which is nearly impossible for a human to accomplish as shown in Fig. (8). Sustainable agriculture consists of environment-friendly methods of farming that allow the production of crops or livestock without damage to humans or natural systems.

Fig. (8). Eco-friendly Agriculture Source: Alexey Chalimov / 12th September, 2019 / Digital Transformation eastern peak- by Ukraine.

Look at where we are today compared to a few years ago, when seeding drones were merely the imagination of a few courageous innovators. Drones and robots collaborate to create interconnected smart farms. They communicate with one another, share knowledge, and enable agriculture to stay one step ahead and feed billions of people. No matter how complicated the farm is, all IoT solutions need software tools that support and stand behind them. To properly assess the plants in the field, every drone or autonomous tractor requires a brain.

MODERN AI-BASED PREDICTION MODEL APPLICATIONS IN AGRICULTURE RELATING TO SOIL, CROP, DISEASES, AND PEST MANAGEMENT

Soil Administration

It is the use of procedures, methods, and treatments to enhance the functionality of soil. A conventional soil survey technique can be used to assess if urban soils contain contaminants [21]. Compost and manure applications increase soil aggregation and porosity. Better aggregation shows the presence of organic components, which are crucial in avoiding the development of soil crusts. To stop the physical deterioration of soil, alternate tillage techniques can be used. To enhance the quality of the soil, organic materials must be used. Several soil-borne diseases that need to be controlled by soil management frequently have a substantial impact on the production of vegetables and other consumable crops.

Crop and Yield Management

Crop management approaches to deal with water scarcity caused by the soil, weather, or insufficient irrigation. It is desirable to utilise crop management systems that are flexible and decision-based. Drought timing, intensity, and predictability are all important considerations when picking between cropping alternatives.

Plant Disease Control

Disease management is essential for agricultural harvests to provide their best yield. Diseases in plants and animals are a significant barrier to increased output. These diseases, which affect both plants and animals, are caused by a variety of variables, including genetics, soil type, rain, dry weather, wind, temperature, and others. These technologies save the excess use of water, pesticides, and herbicides, maintain the fertility of the soil, also help in the efficient use of manpower, elevate productivity and improve quality of crops [22].

Weed Management

The use of herbicides directly affects both the environment and human health. Modern AI techniques are being used to manage weeds effectively and precisely, reducing the need for pesticide use. The farmers' anticipated production and profit are continuously reduced by weeds. According to a survey, uncontrolled weed infestations will result in a 50% decrease in the output of dried bean and maize harvests. Due to weed competition, wheat output is reduced by roughly 48%. These losses might occasionally reach 60%. According to research on the effects of weeds on soybean production, the output was reduced by between 8% and 55%.

Pest Management

One of the most concerning issues in agriculture that causes significant economic losses is insect pest infestation. Researchers have been working on computerised systems that can recognise pests that are active and offer treatment options for decades in an effort to reduce this threat.

Monitoring and Storage Control Management for Agricultural Products

Aside from keeping an eye out for pests and illnesses, farmers must also carefully grade, store, and dry gathered products. We must deal with a variety of artificial intelligence-based food monitoring and quality control systems.

Manage Yield Prediction

The crop yield projection greatly benefits marketing plans. Additionally, prediction models may be used to analyse pertinent aspects that have a direct impact on the yield.

The farmers were used to of traditional methods of farming and today artificial intelligence is making a revolution in agriculture by replacing traditional methods with more efficient methods.

In order to improve a wide range of agriculture-related tasks throughout the entire food supply chain, the industry is turning to artificial intelligence technologies. These technologies can help produce healthier crops, control pests, monitor soil and growing conditions, organise data for farmers, ease workloads, and help with a variety of other tasks.

SOLUTIONS FOR MONITORING SMART FARMING

Farmers may now overcome their everyday obstacles thanks to a wide variety of smart farming technologies as a result of the expanding aggrotech sector. Agriculture field monitoring gathers a variety of metrics for planting, watering, crop collection, and pest management that farmers may use to manage these chores efficiently, see Fig. (**9**) a below [23].

Fig. (9). Smart monitoring of Agriculture Source: Alexey Chalimov / 12th September, 2019 / Digital Transformation eastern peak- by Ukraine.

Monitoring the State of Soil

Farmers utilize soil conditions to determine the best crop. Soil moisture and salinity are alerted instantly by IoT devices monitoring soil parameters. One such system is CropX, an agro-tech platform for remote monitoring of agricultural operations. It collects data using sophisticated agricultural sensors and converts it into intelligible information for processing and storage in the cloud. Soil moisture is a critical parameter in agriculture. If there is a shortage or overabundance of water, plants may die. At the same time, this data depends on many external factors, primarily weather conditions and climate changes. That is why it is so vital to understand the most effective methods for analyzing soil moisture content. Modern farmers have a wide range of options: in addition to traditional sensors, there is modern satellite technology. Soil condition monitoring is shown below in Fig. (**10**).

Fig. (10).   Soil condition Monitoring Source: Alexey Chalimov / 12th September, 2019 / Digital Transformation eastern peak- by Ukraine.

Agriculture Weather Monitoring

It is a prominent IoT application area. Crop cultivation is greatly unstable. Farmers are kept aware of changing weather parameters such as temperature, precipitation, humidity, solar radiation, and wind speed through devices employed [24] see Fig. (**11**) below.

Fig. (11). Weather monitoring System.

Source: Alexey Chalimov / 12th September, 2019 / Digital Transformation eastern peak- by Ukraine

Systems for Automating Greenhouses

A delicate and sensitive greenhouse environment needs constant upkeep and management. The use of remote sensing in agriculture is demonstrated by smart agriculture technologies like Growlink, Farmapp, and GreenIQ for greenhouse automation. They control temperature, lighting, humidity, CO_2, and other environmental factors to assist in maintaining the ideal microclimate. The effectiveness of greenhouse farming is maximized by immediate notifications and improved management skills as shown in Fig. (**12**).

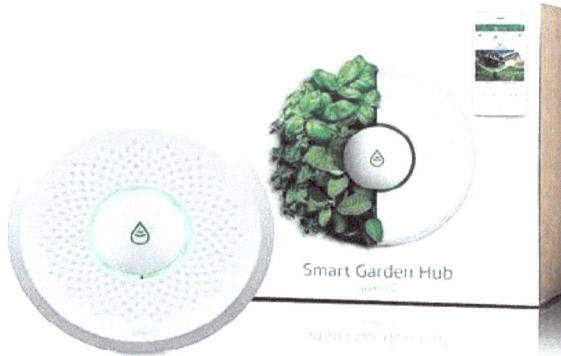

Fig. (12). Automation for green houses.

Source: Alexey Chalimov / 12th September, 2019 / Digital Transformation eastern peak- by Ukraine.

System for Monitoring Crops

Many things might go wrong while crops develop and ripen: illnesses, pest infestations, or unfavorable weather circumstances could possibly result in permanent damage before farmers even realize it, see Fig. (**13**). Smart sensing technology is used in crop monitoring to collect data on crop status (temperature, humidity, health indicators, and so on) and allow farmers to respond immediately if something goes wrong.

Fig. (13). System for Monitoring Crops.

Source: Alexey Chalimov / 12th September, 2019 / Digital Transformation eastern peak- by Ukraine.

CONCLUDING REMARKS

This chapter focuses on several aspects of intelligent agricultural growth for human use. There are many unfinished masterpieces, and we must display them all. We present major elements of the technology's influence on agriculture in this chapter, along with numerous difficulties and accessible support systems to increase agricultural productivity. These also include the current key agricultural sectors where AI is effective and has a lot of potential. To preserve the confidence and needs of the next generation, it is crucial to develop and apply such AI-based systems to today's agricultural areas.

ACKNOWLEDGEMENTS

I want to express my gratitude to my faculty friends and colleagues, Ms. Trupti Kantale, Mr. Bharat Dhak, and Ms. Sneha Khupse, who deserve a particular word of appreciation for their collaboration. I give sincere thanks to Principal Dr. Anant B. Marathe for his advice.

REFERENCES

[1]   M.A. Kekane, "Indian agriculture-status, importance and role in Indian economy", *Int. J. Agricul. Food. Sci. Technol.,* vol. 4, no. 4, pp. 343-346, 2013.

[2]   K. Jha, and A. Doshi, "A comprehensive review on automation in agriculture using artificial intelligence", *Int. J. Adv. Res.,* p. 30, 2018.

[3]   M. Fan, J. Shen, L. Yuan, R. Jiang, X. Chen, W.J. Davies, and F. Zhang, "Improving crop productivity and resource use efficiency to ensure food security and environmental quality in China", *J. Exp. Bot.,* vol. 63, no. 1, pp. 13-24, 2012.
[http://dx.doi.org/10.1093/jxb/err248] [PMID: 21963614]

[4]   Sneha Deshmukh, *Dr. Prabhakar L. Ramteke, "A Review on Use of IOT in Precision Agriculture using ML Algorithm", IJIRSET,,* vol. 10, no. 8, August 2021.

[5]   O. Oyakhilomen, and R.G. Zibah, "Agricultural production and economic growth in Nigeria: Implication for rural poverty alleviation", *Z. Ausl. Landwirtsch.,* vol. 53, no. 3, pp. 207-223, 2014.

[6]   T.O. Awokuse, *Does agriculture really matter for economic growth in developing countries?* The American Agricultural Economics Association Annual Meeting: Milwaukee, Newark, USA, 2009.

[7]   O. Badiene, *Sustaining and Accelerating Africa's Agricultural Growth Recovery in the Context of Changing Global Food Prices IFPRI Policy Brief 9,* 2008.

[8]   S. Block, and C. Timmer, *Agriculture and Economic Growth: Conceptual Issues and the Kenyan Experience.* Harvard Institute for International Development, 1994.

[9]   C.R. De Kimpe, and J.L. Morel, "Urban soil management: A growing concern", *Soil Sci.,* vol. 165, no. 1, pp. 31-40, 2000.
[http://dx.doi.org/10.1097/00010694-200001000-00005]

[10]   M. Li, and R.S. Yost, "Management-oriented modeling: optimizing nitrogen management with artificial intelligence", *Agric. Syst.,* vol. 65, no. 1, pp. 1-27, 2000.
[http://dx.doi.org/10.1016/S0308-521X(00)00023-8]

[11]   E.M. López, M. García, M. Schuhmacher, and J.L. Domingo, "A fuzzy expert system for soil characterization", *Environ. Int.,* vol. 34, no. 7, pp. 950-958, 2008.
[http://dx.doi.org/10.1016/j.envint.2008.02.005] [PMID: 18378310]

[12]   H.H. Kadar, and S.S. Sameon, "Sustainable water resource management using IOT solution for agriculture", *2019 9th IEEE International Conference on Control System, Computing and Engineering,* 29 Nov.–1 Dec. 2019, Penang, Malaysia, ISBN: 978-1-7281-3501-4.
[http://dx.doi.org/10.1109/ICCSCE47578.2019.9068592]

[13]   V. Palazzi, and F. Gelati, "Leaf-compatible autonomous RFID-based wireless temperature sensors for precision agriculture", *IEEE Topical Conference on Wireless Sensors and Sensor Networks,* 2019.
[http://dx.doi.org/10.1109/WISNET.2019.8711808]

[14]   S. Tajik, S. Ayoubi, and F. Nourbakhsh, "Prediction of soil enzymes activity by digital terrain analysis: Comparing artificial Neural n/w and multiple linear regression models", *Environ. Eng. Sci.,* vol. 29, no. 8, pp. 798-806, 2012.
[http://dx.doi.org/10.1089/ees.2011.0313]

[15]   E. Rich, and Knight. Kevin, *Artificial intelligence* McGraw-Hill: New Delhi, 1991.

[16]   D.N. Baker, J.R. Lambert, and J.M. McKinion, *"GOSSYM: A simulator of cotton crop growth and yield", Technical bulletin.* Agricultural Experiment Station: South Carolina, USA, 1983.

[17]   V. Dharmaraj, and C. Vijayanand, "Artificial Intelligence in Agriculture International Journal of Current Microbiology and Applied Sciences", 7(12): 2122-2128, ISSN: 2319-7706, Volume: 7, Number: 12, 2018.

[18]   H.S. Saini, R. Kamal, and A.N. Sharma, "Web based fuzzy expert system for integrated pest management in soybean", *Int. J. Inform. Technol.,* vol. 8, no. 1, pp. 55-74, 2002.

[19]   P. Martiniello, "Development of a database computer management system for retrieval on varietal field evaluation and plant breeding information in agriculture", *Comput. Electron. Agric.,* vol. 2, no. 3, pp. 183-192, 1988.
[http://dx.doi.org/10.1016/0168-1699(88)90023-3]

[20]   K.W. Thorpe, R.L. Ridgway, and R.E. Webb, "A computerized data management and decision support system for gypsy moth management in suburban parks", *Comput. Electron. Agric.,* vol. 6, no. 4, pp. 333-345, 1992.
[http://dx.doi.org/10.1016/0168-1699(92)90004-7]

[21]   K. Neil Harker, "Survey of yield losses due to weeds in central Alberta", *Can. J. Plant Sci.,* vol. 81, no. 2, pp. 339-342, 2001.
[http://dx.doi.org/10.4141/P00-102]

[22]   T. Talaviya, D. Shah, N. Patel, H. Yagnik, and M. Shah, "Implementation of artificial intelligence in agriculture for optimisation of irrigation and application of pesticides and herbicides", *Artificial Intelligence in Agriculture,* vol. 4, pp. 58-73, 2020.
[http://dx.doi.org/10.1016/j.aiia.2020.04.002]

[23]   A.C. Hinnell, N. Lazarovitch, A. Furman, M. Poulton, and A.W. Warrick, "Neuro-Drip: estimation of subsurface wetting patterns for drip irrigation using neural networks", *Irrig. Sci.,* vol. 28, no. 6, pp. 535-544, 2010.
[http://dx.doi.org/10.1007/s00271-010-0214-8]

[24]   W. Yong, L. Shuaishuai, L. Li, L. Minzan, L. Ming, K.G. Arvanitis, C. Georgieva, and N. Sigrimis, "Smart sensors from ground to cloud and web intelligence", *IFAC-PapersOnLine,* vol. 51, no. 17, pp. 31-38, 2018.
[http://dx.doi.org/10.1016/j.ifacol.2018.08.057]

[25]   Available   from: https://easternpeak.com/blog/smart-agriculture-monitoring-solutions-to-opt-mize-farming-productivity/

CHAPTER 3

AIoT: Role of AI in IoT, Applications and Future Trends

Reena Thakur[1,*], **Prashant Panse**[2], **Parul Bhanarkar**[1] and **Pradnya Borkar**[3]

[1] *Department of Computer Science & Engineering, Jhulelal Institute of Technology, Nagpur, India*

[2] *Department of Information Technology, Medi-Caps University, Indore, India*

[3] *Department of Computer Science & Engineering, Symbiosis Institute of Technology, Nagpur, India*

Abstract: Technology such as the Internet of Things (IoT), big data, cloud computing, fog computing, edge computing, and blockchain can be a perilous factor when it comes to encouraging the integration of new technologies. Artificial Intelligence (AI) is an integral part of agricultural and industrial development. This chapter describes the extensive evolution of AI and IoT. Researchers and practitioners will find this chapter essential for understanding AI and IoT, along with models, current status, future trends, and industrial development. There are a number of issues with AI, but overall, it is considered to be an advanced and revolutionary assistant in a wide range of fields. The purpose of this chapter is to present a comprehensive study on AIoT that explains the convergence of AI and IoT. Herein, we summarize some innovative AIoT applications that are likely too intense for our world.

Keywords: Artificial intelligence, Agriculture, Green development, Internet of Things.

INTRODUCTION

Researchers spent more than 50 years creating the autonomous learning capabilities of computers, starting with the development of computers that needed human manipulation in the 1950s. This development is a turning point for computer science, business, and society. In a way, computers have developed to the point where they are capable of finishing new tasks on their own. Future AI will communicate with humans using their native language, gestures, and emotions to adapt to them and learn from them. People will live in real physical space and remain in the digitally virtualized network as a result of the widespread

* **Corresponding author Reena Thakur:** Department of Computer Science & Engineering, Jhulelal Institute of Technology, Nagpur, India; E-mail: en19cs601002@medicaps.ac.in,

Sonali Mahendra Kothari, Vijayshri Nitin Khedkar, Ujwala Kshirsagar and Gitanjali Rahul Shinde (Eds.)

use and interconnection of various intelligent terminals. The distinctions between humans and machines will already be blurred in this cyberspace [1 - 3].

- **Artificial Intelligence (AI)** is an intelligent machine that can simulate the intellect of a human by using this branch of computer science. AI seeks to replicate human qualities like perception, reasoning, comprehension, *etc.* in machines. In order to improve productivity and create new goods and services, intelligent systems in many different industries are built on extremely disruptive AI capabilities as shown in Table **1**.

Table 1. Key definitions.

Artificial Intelligence	Machines, devices, or systems that learn and perform new tasks.
The Internet of Things	It involves collecting, sending, and processing data from devices connected to the internet.
Artificial Intelligence of Things	Collects data and intelligence. After analyzing the information, AIoT will perform tasks without any human intervention.

- **The Internet of Things (IoT),** on the other hand, is a network of interconnected things or gadgets that, through software or sensors built into them, can gather and transmit data in real time. The use of IoT enables significant levels of automation across a variety of functions and sectors. IoT devices produce a ton of data from sensors and human input.

ROLE OF AI IN IOT

The IoT is transforming how we connect devices in our surroundings and throughout the cities, including long-distance communications. This type of network generates vast information about online activities happening every moment. The daily data generated by these networks are 5 quintillion bytes/1 Billion Gigabytes/ 5 Exabytes. The technologies, including Artificial Intelligence, 5G networks, and Bigdata, are the key to creating and managing these networks. IoT and AI are combined to form AIoT that a smart network of connected devices with AI, unleashing data's power better and faster than ever.

Artificial Intelligence and Machine Learning models set over connected devices like edge domains, cloud centers, *etc.*, allow AIOT to collect real-time information through various sensors. This data can then be utilized for positioning, comparison, prediction, scheduling, and many more tasks. IoT provides AI with the data to feed the training algorithms, whereas AI provides IoT with perception and recognition capabilities. The two combined provide a platform for upgrading the economy sector, improving the industry, and optimizing the experience. In urban areas, AIoT businesses were implemented in mass around 2019. Several research articles and references present AI and Machine learning models being utilized in the domain of IoT [1].

In an IoT-enabled device, the environment is sensed, the data is captured, processed, and actions are taken. The action performed determines the intelligence of the device [1]. The goal of IoT devices powered by AI technology involves automation and adaptation. A few of the developments in current AIOT applications are described in this section.

VOICE ASSISTANTS

A voice service agent works as a personal assistant for users using cloud-based services. Smart devices within their proximity are controlled by them. They can also perform query replying like calling cabs, making restaurant reservations, *etc.* A few well-known assistants include Alexa from Amazon and Siri from Apple Inc [4].

ROBOTS

The development of robots that mimic humans and can communicate with them through the understanding, reciprocation, and expression of specific human emotions is one of the results of recent advances in this field of robotics [5]. An example is SoftBank's Pepper, which can understand human emotions such as anger, sadness, and joy. Hanson Robotics' Sophia can express emotions with over 50 facial expressions.

SMART DEVICES

Robots and voice assistants aren't the only IoT SO/devices that can help people with their tasks. Deep neural networks, transfer learning, computer vision, object identification, face and speech recognition, speech and expression recognition, and speech are all used by AI-enabled SOs. Using Honeywell's HD Wi-Fi doorbell, SkyBell, consumers may use their smartphone or voice assistant to open the door. The video camera on the doorbell alerts the homeowner when someone is at the door and streams a live view to their phone.

INDUSTRIAL IOT

In addition to being used in smart homes, IoT has a wide range of applications in various industrial sectors. In addition to identifying potential problems early, it can assist operators in making any necessary changes, from a small sensor to an entire facility. IoT-based industrial solutions such as Plutoshift are also available.

It enables businesses to continuously track asset performance, measure financial impact, and make informed decisions. Therefore, the possibilities and capabilities of AI and IoT can be expanded by combining them. ML and BDA are capable of finding highly valuable insights within the data generated by IoT. AI can benefit from data generated by the IoT [6].

➤ **How does AIoT work?**

Understanding the technology's driving force becomes crucial once the technologies are combined. Here is the entire workflow of AIoT as follows:

- **Data Collection:** Data collection and creation are the initial steps. A variety of data sets are collected with the help of sensors in the devices.
- **Data Transference:** Once collected, the data is usually stored in cloud storage services. A cloud storage system is more cost-effective than installing hardware and can store large amounts of data.
- **Data Processing:** Cloud servers process data stored on them. An extraction and cleansing process based on key data is carried out step by step.
- **Data Projection:** Various networks are used to communicate the processed data. In order to turn them into actionable information, they are aggregated and analyzed.
- **Execution of Information:** A practical application is then made of the actionable information collected.

IoT is impossible without AI, these two work together to create a potent technology. IoT merely collects information through online-connected devices. But AI creates the methodology, separating the machines, gadgets, or apps. IoT and AI are technologies that affect many different businesses. They can lead the Industry 4.0 revolution and is the industrial automation of the future. By giving people access to handle the gadgets in their hands, AI in IoT makes life easier for people. In IoT, AI is primarily responsible for boosting enterprises and improving their competence in optimizing revenue and improving efficiency. AI integrates the M2M (machine-to-machine) learning component with IoT. Connecting such sophisticated gadgets brings us one step closer to full automation. IoT provides chances for AI as well. IoT links AI to many devices so it can learn from them and advance for the following generation.

➤ **Benefits of AI in IoT**

- **Increase in Efficiency:** AI has helped automate sectors with its machine learning abilities. In accordance with the information gathered it may also foresee and carry out tasks. To accomplish the objective, AI can teach IoT devices to be more intuitive. IoT AI facilitates routine operations and improves efficiency by redirecting energy to more important goals.

- **Effective Risk Management:** AI analyzes data that IoT devices generate to forecast risk. After determining the threat, it makes an effort to reduce the potential risks. Companies are more equipped to deal with fraud, financial losses, and cyber threats.
- **Real-Time Monitoring:** IoT devices benefit from AI while it monitors actions and activity. It aids organizations in monitoring the data inflow and actions made on it.
- **Innovation:** Collaborations between AI and IoT open up novel economic options, which increase the potential for creating novel AI and IoT-based products, services, and solutions that improve the quality of life.
- **Improving Cyber security:** In the world, we live in today, data is essential. So, it is crucial to protect that data. The solutions that AIoT provides are advantageous for businesses of all sizes, in all industries, and with all kinds of goals. IoT environments are made more dependable and safer for enterprises with the use of AI-enabled security solutions.

More data than ever before is being produced by IoT devices. According to a report by IDC, there will be 55.7 billion linked devices worldwide by 2025, and connected IoT devices would generate 73.1 billion ZB of data. Comparatively, 18.3 billion ZB were used in 2019. Regrettably, most IoT data is never retained or examined, whether we like to admit it or not. In other words, when we talk about "data-driven" decisions today, we are probably talking about just 1% of the data being examined or used. This restriction on human involvement necessitates the use of AI and Machine Learning (ML) techniques to create AIoT applications.

Practical AIoT applications, on the other hand, necessitate a high level of response from highly decentralized IoT devices. In addition to its burden on network bandwidth and communication latency, it also creates a significant burden on the traditional cloud computing paradigm. It is also impractical and costly to send raw data to a central cloud daily. Edge-Cloud Collaborative Computing was born out of this need. Among other things, edge computing provides faster response times and reduces bandwidth consumption by moving computation tasks and data storage closer to network edges.

APPLICATIONS

• Healthcare

Healthcare is a service that everyone requires. AIoT can assist in delivering personalized health insurance policies, as shown in Fig. (**1**) Healthcare is a vast ecosystem with virtually limitless AIoT applications. The insurance sector is incorporating IoT technology into a variety of product lines in order to predict and prevent risky situations. Smart sensors allow for real-time gathering and monitoring of vital human signs. These numbers indicate our current physical and mental health. Such a vast amount of data is impossible for humans to understand and would need to be processed and analyzed by AI algorithms to give us the information, so we need to follow proper steps to improve our health [7]. There is an increasing integration of AIoT technology in medical services, including hospitals, clinics, diagnostic centers, health insurance, pharmaceuticals, real-time health systems (RTHS), robotics, and smart pills. AIoT technologies will be used in digital health, affecting therapeutics, diagnostics, and infrastructure.

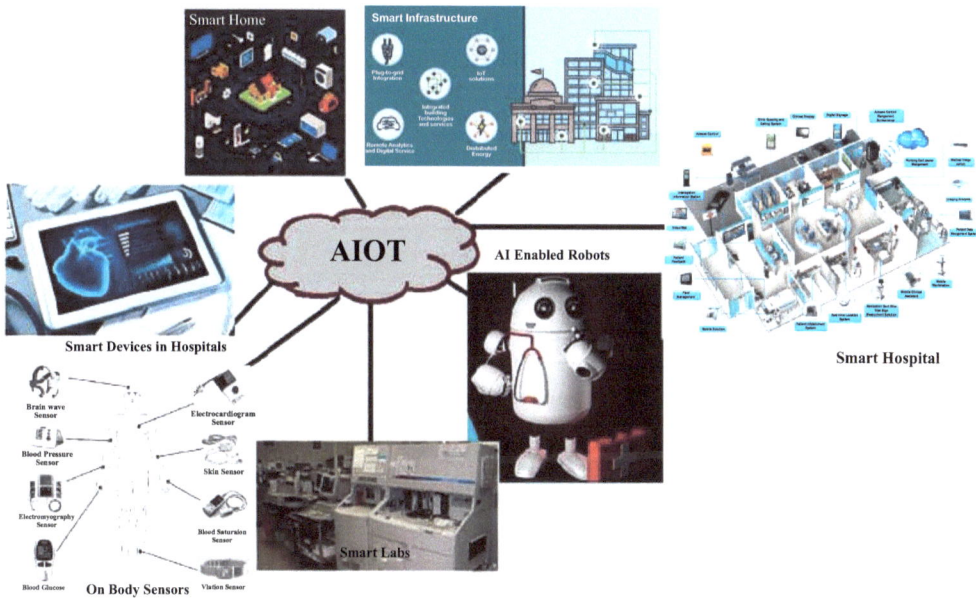

Fig. (1). AIOT in Smart Healthcare.

● Automated Vehicles

Autonomous vehicles can safely go from one location to another without human involvement. IoT is the most important modern technology that makes this possible. Tesla's cars are an excellent example of how AI and IoT can radically alter the vehicle business. People use such a smart technology to make sure that automated driving is safe. Sensors, gadgets, cameras, and many other things ensure that. Autonomous vehicles' computers may collect and evaluate data from multiple sources in real-time to make the most accurate driving decisions [8]. Autonomous cars are a great example of Edge AI, where scattered computers are connected *via* the cloud and analyze pictures without dumping data locally (on-device).

● Video Surveillance

Video surveillance becomes smarter with the addition of AI and IoT. Multiple video feeds must be checked by human operators using video management systems (VMS). There is much room for error, limited attention, and different reaction times when security cameras are manually operated. Machine learning algorithms are combined with camera video feeds to evaluate real-time data, detect objects, recognize people, and automatically identify events. Retail stores frequently use smart video surveillance [9]. For example, Walmart, the world's largest grocery chain, employs image recognition cameras at checkouts to prevent theft. Weapon detection and intrusion event detection are two other popular deep-learning security applications.

● Monitoring Traffic

IoT-based sensors and devices are extensively utilized in intelligent cities for real-time traffic analysis. An AI system that can assess crowd density and do traffic volume analysis is a smart drone. AIoT systems with computer vision capabilities can identify traffic jams or accidents in the transportation sector [10]. Fig. (**2**) illustrates how AIoT systems are utilized in traffic analysis to identify potentially harmful circumstances, such as stopped vehicles.

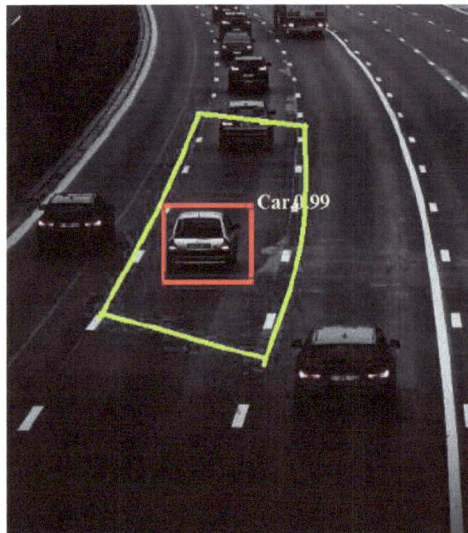

Fig. (2). Traffic Analysis.

• Manufacturing and Production

IIoT, or the Industrial Internet of Things, frequently uses AIoT technologies. These sophisticated systems are employed in manufacturing to monitor machinery in real-time and find problematic components. For quality control, contemporary deep learning technologies are progressively replacing traditional machine vision systems [11].

• Smart Buildings

Smart building applications frequently use IoT sensors and cameras to detect room occupancy in real-time, for example. These systems are utilized to ensure the safety and security of employees. Why not construct a structure to go with these smart homes and create new workspaces to go with them? More innovative residential and commercial buildings are more efficient, cost-effective, and ecologically friendly. The safety of people working or living in these smart buildings is improved. It can also detect the presence of humans and change the temperature accordingly [12].

• Retail Analytics

AIoT has also aided retail shops and businesses, as shown in Fig. (**3**). The use of sensors and other AI techniques has made inventories, staff, and other activities easier to manage. IoT devices, such as digital devices like webcams, work as sensors to track the movements of customers and employees. The information gathered can assist employees in preparing for busy hours and possible customers. This data is beneficial for managing and developing plans and predicting a customer's behavior until they make a final purchase. Even if the customer does not complete the transaction, knowing where they stopped in the process and being able to adjust that aspect is still important [13].

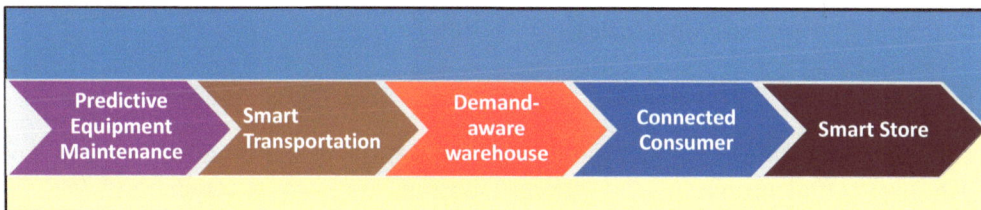

Fig. (3). AIOT in Retail Analysis.

● **Traffic Management**

Google Maps is an excellent example of the Internet of Things in traffic management. Artificial intelligence is used to assess traffic and data is obtained from a range of devices. Similarly, there are sensors and drones operated by the government that monitors traffic [14]. It promotes road etiquette and reduces traffic violations. Traffic management also allows for the tracking and monitoring of cars regularly. Government officials, criminals, or anyone in great danger are transported in these cars.

● **Wearable Devices**

IoT in entertainment includes wearable technology such as VR headsets and smart watches. It provides augmented reality, healthcare technology, and other services. The information collected by these devices is gathered *via* the Internet. The devices then utilize artificial intelligence to learn from the user's actions and adapt to their preferences. Wearable devices are an excellent approach to begin learning about bionics. They were created to improve people's lives, but they can now also be used to replace body parts [15].

● Smart Agriculture

Almost half of the food consumed on the earth is produced by crops, which are vital to human nutrition. Grains, sugarcane, fruits, vegetables, and oil crops all fall under the category of plant-based foods. Ammonia evaporation caused a significant amount of garbage to leak into the soil and be lost to the environment, and oxidized nitrogen-fixing set off an unsteady vicious cycle. The development of environmental preservation has been hampered by it. By establishing green crop production, we will be able to meet the concerns of sustaining food security while also safeguarding the environment. Machine learning is used for weather forecasting, disease detection, crop identification, and soil nutrient management during production [16]. ML evaluates the demand and plants production throughout the processing phases.

● **Cyber-security Applications**

New cyber threats emerge every day. Cybersecurity must be able to learn from these threats and protect against them. Cyber security must advance in lockstep with the expectations and, on occasion, be ahead of the threats. With the help of IoT, this becomes possible. AI learns and acts based on data collected from various internet-connected devices [17].

● **Edge Computing:** Today, IoT is greatly helping build Smart Homes and Smart Cities. Edge computing technology can potentially build home robotic devices and other autonomous devices.

● **Voice AI:** There are a number of AI-enabled assistants available these days, such as Google Home, Alexa, Siri, *etc*. It is possible to make payments on-demand and with voice authentication using IoT using NLP.

Impact of A IoT on Society

1. AI, like all other technologies, has been advancing through time. Any computer, gadget, or application that makes decisions based on calculated and intelligent insights is considered AI.

2. Using NLP and IoT, payments can be made on-demand and with voice authentication. However, there are still limitations to what it can accomplish.

3. Today's machines are different from those we see in movies. There is still a long way to go before they become self-aware.

4. Healthcare, industry, entertainment, online commerce, and various other fields have benefited greatly from AI.

5. It has aided healthcare practitioners in automating daily duties such as medical record management using artificial intelligence. This allows experts to focus on their patients and offer them the needed help.

6. AI has also had an impact on the industrial business. It has improved worker safety by automating several operations. Globally, AI services, software, and hardware will reach $327.5 billion in 2021, according to the International Data Corporation. With a CAGR of 17.5%, it is expected to reach $554.3 billion by 2024.

CONCLUSION

This chapter concludes an all-inclusive study on AIoT. It explores how AI can authorize the IoT to make it quicker, greener, smarter, and harmless. Further, this briefly presents the AIoT architecture in the framework of new technologies. Following, we summarize some innovative applications of AIoT that are likely too intense for our world. Finally, we highlighted the challenges and issues facing AIoT and some possible research opportunities.

REFERENCES

[1]   F. Doshi-Velez, and B Kim, "Towards a rigorous science of interpretable machine learning", *arXiv:1702.08608,* 2017.

[2]   S.J. Russell, and P. Norvig, *Artificial intelligence: A modern approach.* Pearson Education: Malaysia, 2016.

[3]   B. Goertzel, *Artificial general intelligence.,* C. Pennachin, Ed., vol. 2. Springer: New York, 2007. [http://dx.doi.org/10.1007/978-3-540-68677-4]

[4]   A. Poushneh, "Humanizing voice assistant: The impact of voice assistant personality on consumers' attitudes and behaviors", *J. Retailing Consum. Serv.,* vol. 58, p. 102283, 2021. [http://dx.doi.org/10.1016/j.jretconser.2020.102283]

[5]   M. Dohler, T. Mahmoodi, M.A. Lema, M. Condoluci, F. Sardis, K. Antonakoglou, and H. Aghvami, "Internet of skills, where robotics meets AI, 5G and the Tactile Internet", *2017 European Conference on Networks and Communications (EuCNC),* pp.1-5, 2017. [http://dx.doi.org/10.1109/EuCNC.2017.7980645].

[6]   Z. Bi, Y. Jin, P. Maropoulos, W.J. Zhang, and L. Wang, "Internet of things (IoT) and big data analytics (BDA) for digital manufacturing (DM)", *Int. J. Prod. Res.,* pp. 1-18, 2021. [http://dx.doi.org/10.1080/00207543.2021.1953181]

[7]   K.H. Yu, A.L. Beam, and I.S. Kohane, "Artificial intelligence in healthcare", *Nat. Biomed. Eng.,* vol. 2, no. 10, pp. 719-731, 2018. [http://dx.doi.org/10.1038/s41551-018-0305-z] [PMID: 31015651]

[8]   D.A. Abbink, P. Hao, J. Laval, S. Shalev-Shwartz, C. Wu, T. Yang, S. Hamdar, D. Chen, Y. Xie, X. Li, and M. Haque, "Artificial intelligence for automated vehicle control and traffic operations: challenges and opportunities", *Lecture Notes in Mobility,* vol. 8, pp. 60-72, 2022. [http://dx.doi.org/10.1007/978-3-030-80063-5_6]

[9]   A. Rego, A. Canovas, J.M. Jiménez, and J. Lloret, "An intelligent system for video surveillance in IoT environments", *IEEE Access,* vol. 6, pp. 31580-31598, 2018. [http://dx.doi.org/10.1109/ACCESS.2018.2842034]

[10]   V. Mandal, A.R. Mussah, P. Jin, and Y. Adu-Gyamfi, "Artificial intelligence-enabled traffic monitoring system", *Sustainability,* vol. 12, no. 21, p. 9177, 2020. [http://dx.doi.org/10.3390/su12219177]

[11]   R. Rai, M.K. Tiwari, D. Ivanov, and A. Dolgui, "Machine learning in manufacturing and industry 4.0 applications", *Int. J. Prod. Res.,* vol. 59, no. 16, pp. 4773-4778, 2021. [http://dx.doi.org/10.1080/00207543.2021.1956675]

[12]   K. Alanne, and S. Sierla, "An overview of machine learning applications for smart buildings", *Sustain Cities Soc.,* vol. 76, p. 103445, 2022. [http://dx.doi.org/10.1016/j.scs.2021.103445].

[13]   K. Oosthuizen, E. Botha, J. Robertson, and M. Montecchi, "Artificial intelligence in retail: The AI-enabled value chain", *Australas. Mark. J.,* vol. 29, no. 3, pp. 264-273, 2021. [http://dx.doi.org/10.1016/j.ausmj.2020.07.007]

[14]   A. Farahdel, S.S. Vedaei, and K. Wahid, "An IoT based traffic management system using drone and AI", 2022 14th International Conference on Computational Intelligence and Communication Networks (CICN) (pp. 297-301). IEEE. 2022. [http://dx.doi.org/10.1109/CICN56167.2022.10008357]

[15]   C.Y. Jin, "A review of AI technologies for wearable devices", *IOP Conf. Series Mater. Sci. Eng.,* vol. 688, no. 4, p. 044072, 2019. [IOP Publishing.]. [http://dx.doi.org/10.1088/1757-899X/688/4/044072]

[16]   J. Li, "Cyber security meets artificial intelligence: A survey", *Front. Inform. Technol. Electron. Eng.,* vol. 19, no. 12, pp. 1462-1474, 2018.

[http://dx.doi.org/10.1631/FITEE.1800573]

[17]   A. Mitra, S.L. Vangipuram, A.K. Bapatla, V.K. Bathalapalli, S.P. Mohanty, E. Kougianos, and C Ray, "Everything you wanted to know about smart agriculture", *arXiv:2201.04754,* 2022.

CHAPTER 4

The Role of Machine Intelligence in Agriculture: A Case Study

Prabhakar Laxmanrao Ramteke[1,*] and **Ujwala Kshirsagar[2,*]**

[1] *H.V.P.M's College of Engineering & Technology, Amravati (Maharashtra State) Affiliated to Sant Gadge Baba Amravati University, Amravati, Maharashtra, India*

[2] *Department of Electronics and Telecommunication Engineering, Symbiosis Institute of Technology Symbiosis International (Deemed University), Pune – 412115, India*

Abstract: India's GDP is heavily reliant on agricultural products and business management. Therefore, it is crucial for the agriculture industry to comprehend the most common uses of artificial intelligence (AI) through case studies. To increase its production, this industry must overcome a number of obstacles, such as soil treatment, plant disease and pest effects, crop management, farmers' innovative methods, and the use of technology. The major ideas behind AI in agriculture are its adaptability, excellence, accuracy, and economy. It is critical to examine AI applications for managing soil, crops, and the environment, and plant or leaf diseases. Food security continues to be seriously threatened by deforestation and poor soil conditions, both of which harm the economy. The application's advantages, constraints, and methods for employing expert systems to increase productivity are all given particular attention. Businesses are utilizing robots and automation to assist farmers in developing more effective weed control strategies for their crops. See & Spray, a robot created by Blue River Technology, is said to use computer vision to monitor and accurately spray weeds on cotton plants. Crop and Soil Monitoring - Businesses are using deep learning and computer vision algorithms to interpret data taken by drones and/or software-based technologies to monitor the health of crops and soil. Crop sustainability and weather forecasting are accomplished *via* satellite systems. A Colorado-based startup employs satellites and machine learning algorithms to examine agricultural sustainability, forecast weather, and assess farms for the presence of diseases and pests. Utilizing predictive analytics, machine learning models are being created to monitor and forecast various environmental factors, such as weather variations. Drones and computer vision are used for crop analysis, while machine learning is used for identifying soil flaws.

Keywords: Agricultural robotics, Agricultural applications, Computer vision, Crop and soil management, Machine intelligence, Satellite drone.

---

[*] **Corresponding authors Prabhakar Laxmanrao Ramteke and Ujwala Kshirsagar:** H.V.P.M's College of Engineering & Technology, Amravati (Maharashtra State) Affiliated to Sant Gadge Baba Amravati University, Amravati, Maharashtra, India; & Department of Electronics and Telecommunication Engineering, Symbiosis Institute of Technology Symbiosis International (Deemed University), Pune – 412115, India; E-mails: kshirsagarujwala9@gmail.com; pl_ramteke@rediffmail.com

INTRODUCTION

The foundation of India's economy is agriculture. For more than 58 percent of rural households, it serves as their primary living area. The development and application of machine learning have improved agricultural benefits. Because artificial intelligence (AI) can be applied broadly to a variety of issues, particularly those that humans find difficult to handle effectively, it is gaining relevance extremely quickly. Therefore, farming solutions driven by AI help farmers produce more with less while improving quality and offering speedy go-to-market strategies for their crops.

In order to increase efficiency, agriculture is powered by AI, which examined its services in acquiring, comprehending, and responding to various situations. In order to increase production and efficiency, artificial intelligence technology is helping several agricultural industries.

The management of irrigation systems and soils is extremely important in agriculture. Crop loss and poor crop quality are caused by improper irrigation and soil management. To increase production, a smart management system is therefore required. The Internet of Things based smart irrigation system may automate the watering process by assessing the soil moisture and weather conditions. Because artificial intelligence is aware of previous weather conditions and patterns, soil, and its contents' quality, and the varieties of crops or yields to be cultivated, it may skip irrigation, one of the labor-intensive farming operations. The goal of automated irrigation systems is to boost average yields by utilizing real-time machines that can continuously maintain the correct soil conditions, considerably lessen the farmers' laborious tasks, and also has the ability to lower production costs. The awareness of AI would have a significant influence on reducing water loss for agriculture, which uses around 70% of the nation's freshwater.

Understanding Essential Agriculture Stages

Lack of information at each level of agriculture can cause new issues to appear or exacerbate existing ones, raising the cost of farming. The demand for the agricultural industry is exacerbated by the daily population expansion. From crop selection to harvest and product sale, agribusiness suffers from extremely high overall losses. Since knowledge is power, farmers may be able to make better decisions and lessen issues linked to agriculture by following the information regarding crops, the changing environment, and the targeted market. Information may be collected and processed using technologies including blockchain, IoT, edge computing, machine learning, deep machine learning, and cloud computing.

Applications of machine learning, computer vision, and IoT will assist to enhance the quality, raise production, and eventually increase the productivity and economy of farmers and related industries. The various stages required in Agriculture production are shown in Fig. (1).

Agriculture's Stages

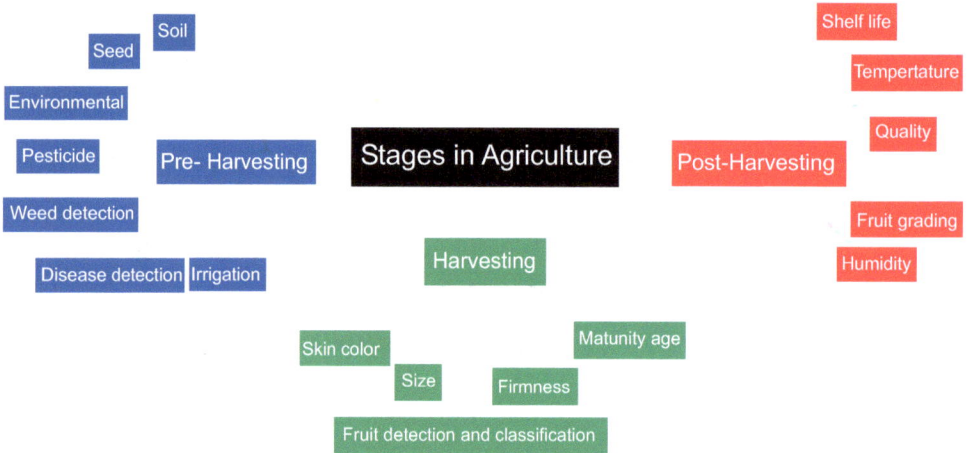

Fig. (1). Stages in Agriculture. Source: V. Meshram, K. Patil *et al*. Artificial Intelligence in the Life Sciences 1 (2021), Elsevier.

CASE STUDIES

An IOT-based System for Crop Irrigation

In smart irrigation systems using IoT, Gursimran Singh suggested machine learning technologies to improve irrigation water use by forecasting the future soil moisture of a field. To anticipate futuristic soil moisture, field real-time data from different sensors such as temperature, humidity, moisture of soil, and UV radiation are combined with weather forecasts through the internet. The analysis of several machine learning methods for forecasting future soil moisture shows the outcomes of several machine learning techniques. The system architecture of an IOT-based crop irrigation system is shown in Fig. (2).

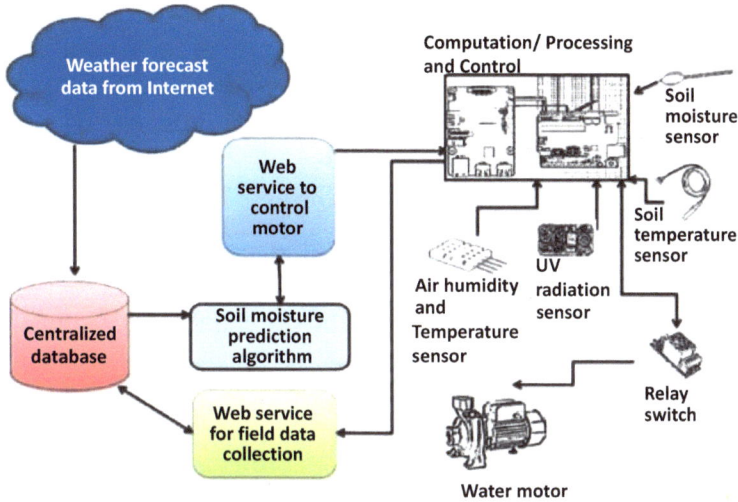

Fig. (2). IoT-based Crop Irrigation System Architecture. Source: Gursimran Singh *et. al.*, 'Machine Learning based Soil Moisture Prediction for IoT based.

Smart Irrigation System', IEEE explore-10 Feb, 2020.

The sensor node is built with Raspberry Pi and Arduino Uno based computing, processing, and control platform with sensors for taking into account temperature, soil moisture, humidity, and radiation, as well as a relay for managing irrigation through the water pump or dc motor. The centralized database from the sensors deployed in the field transceiving data through web services. Additionally, information about weather prediction is retrieved from the internet and used to forecast soil moisture for the future days [1].

Applications of Machine Learning Algorithms in High Precision Agriculture

In a comprehensive study of machine learning applications in agriculture, Abinav Sharma, Arpit Jain, *et al.* focused on forecasting agricultural yield, weed and disease identification in crops/yields, and various species recognition. Soil factors like carbon and content in soil moisture are also predicted. To measure crop quality and yield, Machine Learning with computer vision is examined for the categorization of a variety of crops and their photos. This strategy may be applied to improve livestock output by forecasting reproductive patterns, detecting eating problems, and predicting the behavior of cattle based on machine learning models employing sensor data.

Smart farming, sometimes referred to as precision agriculture, has become a cutting-edge instrument for addressing the present issues with agricultural sustainability. Precision agriculture refers to a system where the farmer or caretaker is only directly involved when absolutely necessary, such as in the event of an emergency or system breakdown. The set standards of parameters required for agricultural day-to-day operations are maintained with the aid of IoT. In order to reduce the direct involvement of farmers, the parameters may be monitored using the necessary sensors and sent through an IoT for remote monitoring. The IoT cloud may also be used for control, for instance, to detect and prevent animal infiltration in agricultural fields. Without sensors, monitoring and controlling become nearly difficult tasks in the IoT for precision agriculture [2].

Key components of the agricultural revolution are machine learning (ML) and an Internet of Things (IoT)-based enabled farm. To measure crop quality and yield, ML with computer vision is examined for the categorization of a variety of crop photos. This strategy may be applied to improve livestock output by identifying trends in fertility, detecting eating problems, and forecasting the behavior of cattle using machine learning models and sensor data, among other applications. Intelligent irrigation uses drip irrigation. The graphical abstract of machine learning applications for precision agriculture is shown in Fig. (3) below.

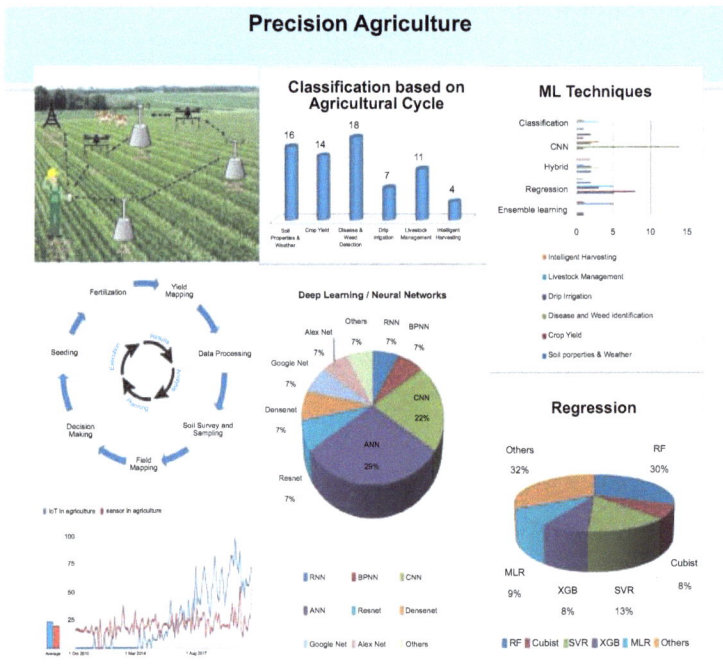

Fig. (3). A graphical abstract for Machine Learning Applications for Precision Agriculture. Source: Abhinav Sharma *et al.*, 'Machine learning applications precision Agriculture: A comprehensive review', 2021 IEEE.

Soil Characteristics and Weather Forecasting

The soil characteristics are an essential issue to consider since they are closely tied to the topography and climate of the area being used. Predicting soil qualities mostly entail foreseeing soil nutrients, soil surface humidity, and meteorological conditions during the crop's lifespan. The characteristics of soil and by extension, the capacity to produce crops have been greatly impacted by human activities. There are 17 key components overall. The nutrients present in a certain soil determine how well crops develop. Sensors that use electricity and electromagnetic fields primarily measure soil nutrients. Farmers can decide which species of the crop is best for the available agricultural land based on its nutrients in the soil. The use of AI algorithms to anticipate weather and soil characteristics depends on a number of variables. The prediction method that is most accurate and resistant to noise, nonlinearity, outliers, *etc.* Extreme Learning Machine, Random Forest, Support Vector Regression, and Cubist are the algorithms that are used the most frequently. The essential plant nutrient elements are listed in the Table **1**.

Table 1. Essential Plant Nutrients.

Essential Plant Element		Symbol	Primary Form
Non- Mineral Elements	Carbon	C	CO_2 (g)
	Hydrogen	H	H_2O (1), H^+
	Oxygen	O	H_2O (1), O_2 (g)
Mineral Elements			
Primary Micronutrients	Nitrogen	N	NH_4^+, NO_3^-
	Phosphorus	P	$H2PO4^-$, $HPO4^{2-}$
	Potassium	K	K^+
Secondary Micronutrients	Calcium	Ca	Ca^{2-}
	Magnesium	Mg	Mg^{2-}
	Sulfur	S	SO_4^{2-}

(Table 1) cont.....

Micronutrients	Iron	Fe	Fe^{3+}, Fe^{2+}
	Manganese	Mn	Mn^{2+}
	Zinc	Zn	Zn^{2+}
	Copper	Cu	Cu^{2+}
	Boron	B	$B(OH)3$
	Molybdenum	Mo	$4MoO^{2-}$
	Chlorine	Cl	Cl
	Nickel	Ni	Ni^{2+}

Source: https://www.the-compost-gardner.com/soil-texture.html

Crop Yield Forecast- The difficulty of applying AI approaches to agricultural production prediction is enormous, and the lack of a general model makes developing the algorithm difficult. Regression algorithms and neural networks are the most promising crop yield prediction methods.

Weed and disease detection- The advancements in image processing are principally responsible for the implementation of AI approaches in disease and weed identification. The most popular option for creating a system for diagnosing diseases is CNN's.

Drip Irrigation- In addition to being crop-friendly, intelligent irrigation systems are also environmentally benign. AI and IoT working together minimize manual involvement while making the most use of the resources at hand to prevent environmental damage.

Production and Management of Livestock- The primary goal of livestock management is the welfare of farm animals, and it makes use of modern image recognition algorithms (CNN) and regression approaches to identify and forecast illness occurrence.

Intelligent Harvesting- AI harvesting applications serve largely as a support system for autonomous harvesting systems. The development of image processing is crucial for harvesting prediction systems; CNNs are the most useful model for creating such systems.

MODELLING SOIL WATER BALANCE

To estimate crop irrigation needs, modeling water balance is used. According to the FAO56 technique, L.S. Pereira *et al.* advocated using the soil water balance (SWB) model to estimate the irrigation of crops, their needs and the schedule of irrigation. Measurements of temperature, relative humidity, wind speed, and sun radiation are necessary for the Food and Agriculture Organization approach (FAO 56). Standard vs. real Kc ideas, single and dual Kc methods, and baseline notions such as standard vs. actual Kc concepts are all taken into account while discussing the Kc-ETo methodology. The calculation of crop evapotranspiration (ET_c) is performed under standard conditions. No limitations are placed on crop growth or evapotranspiration from soil water and salinity stress, crop density, pests and diseases, weed infestation or low fertility. ET_c is determined by the crop coefficient approach whereby the effect of the various weather conditions are incorporated into ET_o and the crop characteristics into the K_c coefficient: $ET_c = K_c ET_o$. This provides the requirements for accurate soil water balance and suitable parameterization, and calibration. Before reviewing the FAO56 technique to compute and partition crop evapotranspiration and associated soil water balance, the one-step vs. two-step computing methodologies are compared [3].

DESIGN AND IMPLEMENTATION OF A SENSOR NETWORK-BASED SMART NODE

Sensor network-based smart node is designed for a precision agricultural system. Juan M. *et al.* proposed the design and implementation of a precision agriculture system's Smart Node for farmers of white cabbage in Panama/China utilizing sensor networks as the foundation. The key goals are the transfer of knowledge and justifying the impacts of soil and change in climate on white cabbage [4]. Agroclimatic parameters such as temperature, soil moisture, relative humidity, and luminosity that are beyond our control can cause production losses. It has now discovered the ideal ranges to minimize these losses and maximize productivity. The Smart node system is shown in Fig. (**4**) below.

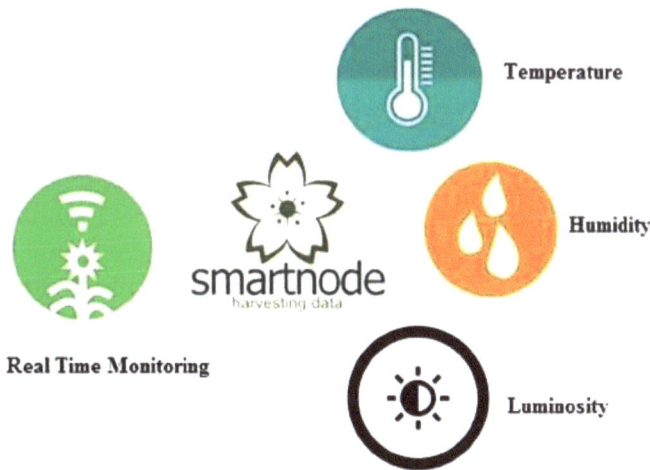

Fig. (4). Smart node. Source: Juan M. *et. al.* 'Design and implementation of Wireless Sensor Network for precision agriculture in white cabbage crops', 2017 IEEE.

Smart-node Hardware

Smart-node uses batteries and renewable energy. The ATmega328p microcontroller is used in the system, being the main component responsible for data acquisition, data sending, and receiving. The system consists of a soil moisture sensor to measure soil moisture, and a Temperature sensor to measure soil temperature and atmospheric temperature. If the network coordinator failed, the entire network would stop working.

Acquisition Programme, Connectivity Architecture and Software

There are two types of network designs created for the proposed system. First, the database and local server are used in networks that enable continuous crop monitoring. Secondly, real-time monitoring of climate factors and soil may be done using an IoT and a mobile application called Time Distance in the case of connectivity in the field, such as a cellular network [4].

IN IRRIGATION MANAGEMENT DECISION SUPPORT SYSTEM: ANALYSIS AND APPLICATION

In order to ascertain the quality and mistakes in relation to expert judgment, Roque Torres-Sanchez *et al.* investigated a variety of learning strategies. The agriculture industry places a high value on automatic irrigation scheduling systems because of their capacity to handle deficit irrigation methods and conserve water. Due to the numerous aspects that the technician must take into account while controlling irrigation in the best possible way, developing an effective and functioning autonomous irrigation system is a highly challenging undertaking. By automatically developing forecasts based on an agronomist's knowledge, autonomous training and learning systems provide an alternative to traditional irrigation. The purpose of this research is to examine various learning methodologies in order to assess the accuracy and precision of expert judgment. The suggested irrigation decision support system was evaluated on nine orchards in 2018 utilizing the methodologies like linear regression, random forest regression, and support vector regression. In three of these orchards, the learning methods' outcomes and the agronomist's judgments over the course of a full year were compared [5]. The most accurate regression model was chosen based on the mistakes in the prediction model. The findings support the notion that these techniques may be used to create systems for autonomous irrigation scheduling.

- Users can quickly compare several possibilities with the use of decision-support tools.

- Prior DSS development was driven more by technology than end-user demand.
- Few DSS support the ability to make strategic (long-term) decisions or incorporate uncertainty into their results.
- DSS heuristics may have been successfully applied if there has been a decline in DSS use or acceptance.
- Greater uptake of DSS knowledge results from demand-driven participatory methods.

MACHINE LEARNING RECOMMENDED IRRIGATION METHODS

Lior Fink, Anat Goldstein, and others proposed a study that intends to use the gathered data for irrigation advice prediction in addition to crop monitoring and control. Leading jojoba product manufacturer Jojoba Israel has orchards with sensors that gather information about moisture level for real time plant requirements monitoring. The company's agronomist prepares a weekly watering plan based on these facts. Additionally, information about the weather, irrigation, and production is gathered from additional sources. A dataset was specifically created by combining data acquainted for two years from 22 soil sensors which were distributed across four primary plots (which were further subdivided into 28 sub-plots and 8 irrigation system groups), from a meteorological platform, and from the collected irrigation records. On this dataset, several regression and classification techniques were used to create models that could forecast the weekly irrigation plan suggested by the agronomic. To identify the factors that consistently increased prediction accuracy, eight distinct subsets of variables were used in the model development process. Data from 22 soil sensors distributed across four key areas, from a weather station, and from real irrigation records were combined to create a dataset over the course of approximately two years.

On this dataset, several regression and classification techniques were used to create models that could forecast the weekly irrigation plan advised by the agronomic [6].

The study used a standard data mining methodology, which included the steps of dataset design, extraction transformation loading (ETL), ML algorithms to train the dataset with recommended models, evaluation of the trained models, and selection of the best-recommended model.

The Decision Tree Regression, Random Forest Regression, and GBRT models were taken into account for regression trees. The logistic classifier, random forest classifier, decision tree classifier and BTC classification methods were contrasted for classification. In terms of classification precision, BTC was the most accurate classifier of them. Therefore, the three Machine learning models of BTC, linear regression and GBRT were created. To determine which model was the most effective, each of these models was created using eight distinct feature-set subsets. The findings demonstrated that GBRT and BTC models, which are non-parametric models, were most effective in predicting decisions about irrigation.

Cotton Centre Pivot Irrigation is Efficiently Scheduled and Controlled by a Mechanism based on Canopy Temperature

In an automated center, pivot irrigation system, S.A. O'Shaughnessy and S.R. Evett scheduled irrigations for alternate blocks beneath a 3-span center pivot using the time-temperature threshold (TTT) algorithm. The yields of treatments that were automatically watered and those that had irrigations scheduled were compared [7].

Intelligent Irrigation Monitoring with Thermal Imaging in Smart Agriculture with the Internet of Things

Kim-Kwang, Paul Rad and Mehdi Roopaei Presenting Raymond Choo many facets of intelligent irrigation management that might benefit from thermal imaging. Before exploring alternative solutions, this article explores the main needs, technological challenges, and legal concerns that enable the usage of the Cloud of Things to manage data connected to water sources. Intelligent Irrigation Monitoring Smart System with Thermal Imaging in the Cloud of Things is useful for agriculture [8 - 10].

IRRIGATION SENSOR COUPLED TO AUTOMATIC WATERING SYSTEM

Automated Irrigation System is depicted in Fig. (**5**). A grayscale image formed by various water contents in the soil serves as the foundation for the irrigation sensor's pixel distinction. Using Matlab R2014a, a series of photos between those taken when the soil is fully dry and those taken when it is saturated with 300 ml of water were compared using their histograms in the grayscale range of 0 to 255 to estimate this differential. These two photos serve as a representation of the system's dynamic range limitations, which are determined by the percentages of sand, loam, and clay in the soil [11 - 16].

For two-year dataset for maize crop under dripping irrigation with a film of mulch, Zhijun Chen *et al.* suggested a method where a temporal convolution network (TCN) with two engineering algorithms, Maximal Information Coefficient (MIC) and Principal Component Analysis (PCA) was established to predict environmental terms and conditions. The study is still evaluating the TCN models' predictions of Kc values as compared to those found in the literature.

According to the findings, the seven most crucial factors influencing maize evapotranspiration are the temperature of the soil, mean value temperature, maximum range of temperature, humidity, the height of plants, radiation, and leaf area index [17 - 21].

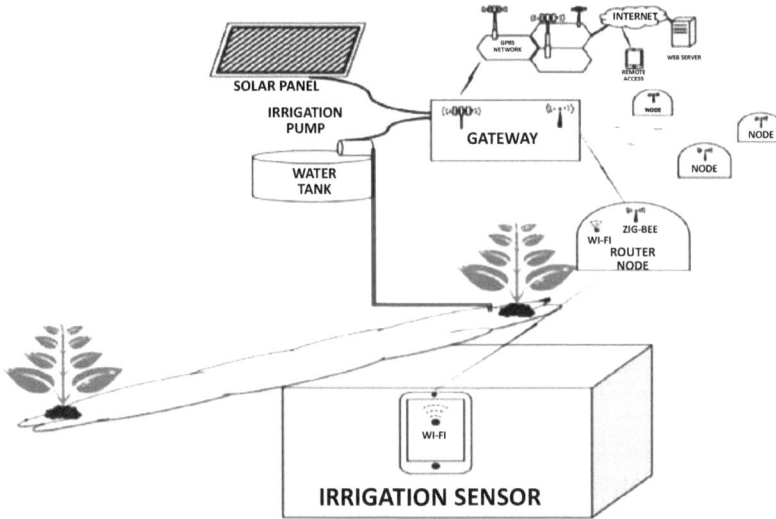

Fig. (5). Irrigation sensor linked to the Automated Irrigation System. Source: Joaquin Gutierrez *et.al.*, 'Smartphone Irrigation Sensor', 20 May, 2015 IEEE Sensors Journal.

PREDICTION FOR CROP YIELD AND FERTILISER

S. Bhanumathi, M. Vineeth and N. Rohit, proposed a crop yield prediction system using an ML algorithm and proposed how much quantity of fertilizers or nutrients should be used to get a high-quality yield for the crop. The proposed architecture diagram for crop yield and the amount of fertilizer is given in Fig. (**6**).

Considering data from different environments and agriculturally based parameters, crop yield was predicted. Based on the data related to the state, city, temperature, humidity, moisture, and fertilizers required, they have built a machine learning (ML) model, trained it, and forecast production. After that, the appropriate fertilizer dosage was calculated to get the desired yield. The amount of nitrogen and phosphorus are the input parameters; the amount of the appropriate fertilizer to use is the output. Back propagation algorithm is used to build a model from the fertilizers' dataset. The output value or characteristic of the back propagation technique is fixed to the dataset. Campo Verde *et al.* proposed a system to manage agricultural operations in terms of a model for irrigation using IoT, sensors and smart boards such as Raspberry Pi and Arduino. The idea was compared to a traditional irrigation system, which normally operates on a threshold for soil moisture, and humidity and makes choices in accordance with that setting. However, this paradigm becomes useless for judgments that are made repeatedly throughout time [22].

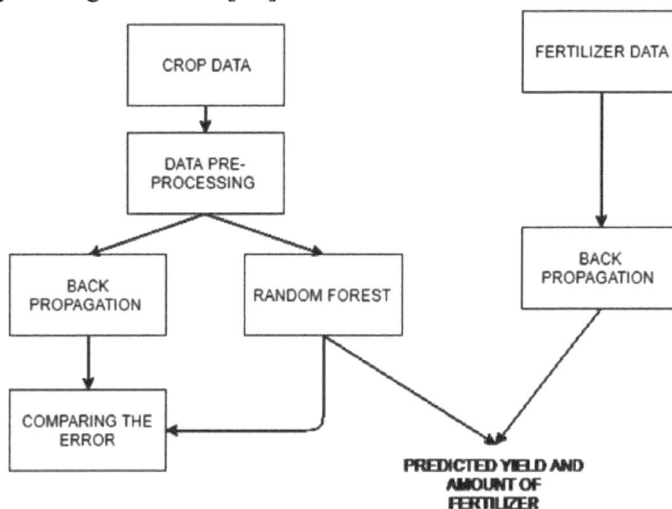

Fig. (6). Architecture for crop yield and the amount of fertilizer. **Source:** S. Bhanumathi *et al*. Crop Yield prediction and efficient use of fertilizers, 1 April 2019.

CLASSIFICATION MODEL FOR RICE PLANT DISEASE DETECTION THAT IS OPTIMAL

In the context of smart farming, R. Sowmyalakshmi *et al*. created a novel CNN inception with ResNset v2 model and Optimal Weighted Extreme Learning Machine (CNNIR-OWELM) for identifying and categorizing rice plant illnesses.

The suggested approach for rice plant disease detection is depicted. IoT devices primarily collect photos of rice plants from agricultural regions and send them to a cloud server for analysis. Pre-processing, segmentation, feature extraction, and ultimately classification are some of the steps that are used in the proposed method's server-side execution.

To increase the image's degree of contrast, the input photos are pre-processed. In order to identify the unhealthy areas in a picture of a rice crop, a histogram-based segmentation method is also provided. The segmented image's feature vectors are then retrieved by Inception using the ResNet v2 model. The generated feature vectors are then used to classify the plant disease using the FPA-WELM model.

Multi-Rotor Drone

The most basic type of drone is multi-rotor models, depicted in Fig. (**7**), which come with capabilities like camera framing from above. Multirotor drones are able to regulate the angles from which they capture pictures, producing images with more accuracy. Less endurance and speed are the multirotor drawbacks. Due to this, only a few agricultural tasks are performed with these sorts of drones.

Fig. (7). Several-Rotor Drone. **Source:** Suhas M.V *et. al*. AgrOne: An Agricultural Drone using IoT, Data analytics, and cloud computing features, 2018.

Fixed-Wing Drone

Fixed-wing Rotor drones operate using structures resembling wings, shown in Fig. (**8**). In contrast to other drones, fixed-wing rotor drones take off using wings like those of an airplane. To start moving, inertia must first be supplied by an outside force. Due to this characteristic, these drones are once again restricted to certain agricultural operations.

Fig. (8). Static Wing Drone. **Source:** Suhas M.V *et. al*. AgrOne: An Agricultural Drone using IoT, Data analytics, and cloud computing features, 2018.

Single-Rotor Helicopter Drone

As compared to other variety of drones, single rotor helicopter drones have greater advantages, shown in Fig. (**9**). They are fixed with a gas controlled mechanism for long lasting durability. Aerodynamic principles emphasize that a system's efficiency will increase and spin decrease if its rotor blades are bigger. Single rotor helicopters are more beneficial in agricultural settings since they have lengthy rotor blades.

Fig. (9). Drone Helicopter with Just One Rotor. **Source:** Suhas M.V *et. al.* AgrOne: An Agricultural Drone using IoT, Data analytics, and cloud computing features, 2018.

FARMING USING ARTIFICIAL INTELLIGENCE

A revolution in agriculture has resulted from it. The agricultural output has been shielded by this technique from a number of circumstances, including population expansion, job challenges, and food security concerns. The primary goal of this study is to evaluate the numerous ways artificial intelligence is being used in agriculture to optimize irrigation, spraying and weeding with the use of sensors and embedded systems built into drones and robots. Such technologies reduce the overuse of water, pesticides, and herbicides, preserve soil fertility, assist in making effective use of labor, boost output, and enhance the quality [21].

THE USE OF THE INTERNET OF THINGS AND CLOUD COMPUTING TO CREATE A CUSTOM AGRICULTURAL DRONE

Suhas M. V. *et al.* have suggested the Internet of Things and cloud computing technologies to create one's own agricultural drone as shown in Fig. (**10**) below.

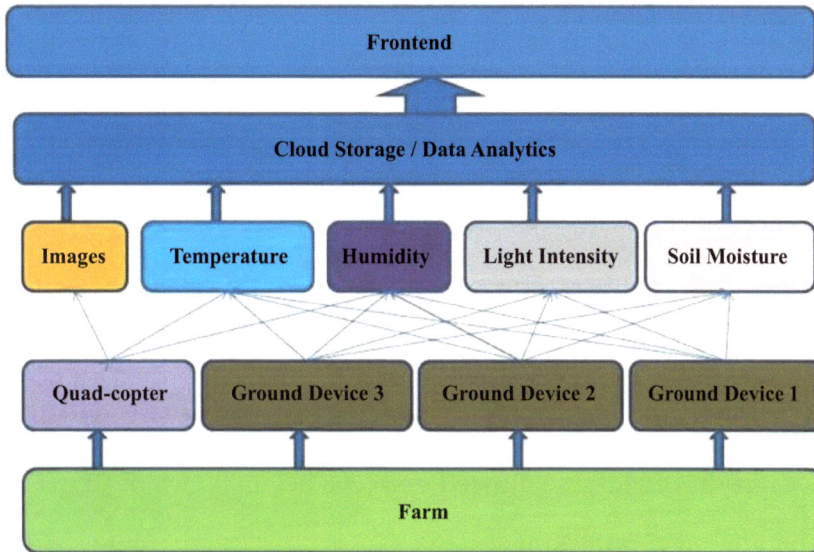

Fig. (10). Framework for Agrone. **Source:** Suhas M.V *et al.* AgrOne: An Agricultural Drone using IoT, Data Analytics, and cloud computing features, 2018.

The quadcopter flies autonomously and takes pictures of the field, which are then analysed to determine how well the crops are doing. This photograph and its associated result are both kept in the cloud. For greater yields, the sensors on the quadcopter and on the ground assist to keep an eye on the temperature and humidity [22]. Users are having stable access to farm data remotely monitored by utilising the cloud. Results gained demonstrate how drone and on-ground sensor devices for agricultural help may be created using current trends in technology. Additionally, the project's prospective extensions by conducting sophisticated image processing, as well as its future path.

Autonomous Quadcopter

A payload of about one kilogram should be transportable by the quadcopter. The Raspberry Pi is being used for onboard image processing. This will increase overall efficiency and decrease the burden on the Storage Cloud. Due to the fact that the quadcopter needs accurate GPS coordinates, external telemetry assists in making the device autonomous [23].

Telemetry will assist you in moving the quadcopter while also preserving its acceleration, pitch, yaw, and altitude.

On-Ground Sensor Nodes

It suggests a battery-operated wireless sensor network for humidity, soil moisture, temperature, and light intensity. Such Sensor Nodes would be spread out over the area. Each sensor node will have a preset Unique ID that corresponds to its deployment location. This will make it easier to keep an eye on and manage various farm regions [24].

Image Processing

An onboard camera will be put to the quadrocopters. Once the quad-copter passes over a certain area of the field, it will take a picture of it based on data from the telemetry system. The Raspberry Pi attached to the camera will process this picture. The data that has been analysed will reveal details about a green portion of the photograph, which have utilized as a crop health indicator [25].

Cloud Analytics and Data Storage

It is suggested to use cloud services because the Raspberry Pi's processing and storage capabilities are constrained particularly Data Analytics as a Service and Storage as a Service. The photographs taken by the quadcopter will first be compressed and transferred to the Cloud for Historical Processing on the Raspberry Pi.

Frontend

Users may see data and comprehend the relevant inferences using the frontend interface. Data is extracted from both cloud services and then populated.

INTERACTIVE CULTIVATION SENSING SYSTEM POWERED BY IOT

A technique for generating composite growth data in diverse habitats and crops intended for backyard gardens and paddy fields is proposed by Kesevan Veloo *et al*. To guarantee the daily continuous development of crops under ideal circumstances, an interactive cultivation sensor system made of IoT-based technologies is created and implemented. With this, progress will be made in figuring out the best circumstances for machine-learning farming and in solving any future agricultural difficulties. Multiple sensors attached to the suggested cultivation kit are utilized to retrieve data that impact crop development.

This information includes soil moisture, pH level, carbon dioxide level, water level. Using a camera, pictures of the crops are also captured. The degree of growth would then be assessed using both the data and the photos.

The culture kit has network capabilities, and the server gathers sensor data. Machine learning may be carried out as big data, together with picture data, based on sensor data gathered from diverse backyard gardens and other outside areas. Consequently, it is feasible to link sensor data to the crop growth status [26]. The interactive cultivation sensing system is shown in Fig. (**11**).

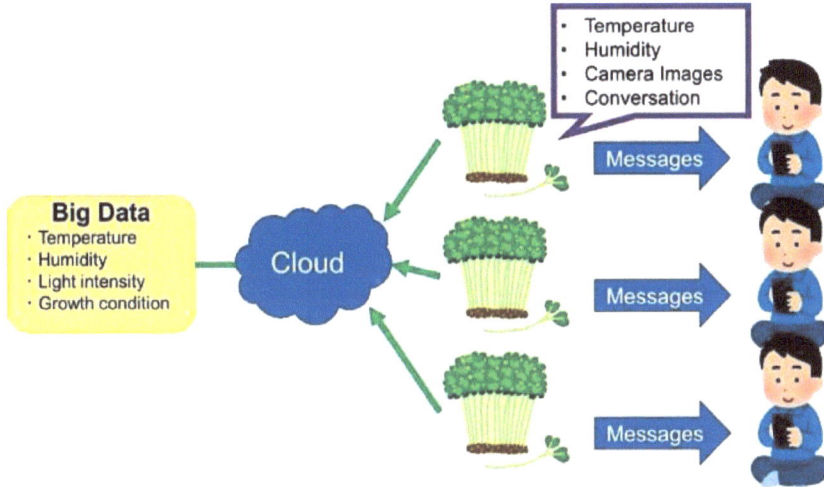

Fig. (11). System for Interactive Cultivation Sensing. **Source: Kesevan Veloo *et. al.*,** 'Interactive Cultivation System for the Future IoT-Based Agriculture', 2019.

Use of Weather Forecasting

Farmers find it challenging to decide the best time to plant seeds due to climate change and rising pollution. With the use of artificial intelligence, farmers may analyze weather patterns using weather forecasting to assist them plan the type of crop that can be cultivated and when seeds should be sown. System for assessing the health of crops and soil:

The kind of soil and nutrition of the soil has a significant impact on the crops that are grown and their quality. The quality of the soil is deteriorating as a result of growing deforestation, making it difficult to assess. A German technology startup named PEAT has created an AI-based program called Plantix that can detect nutritional deficits in the soil, as well as plant pests and diseases. Using smartphones, the farmer may take pictures of his or her plants. Through brief movies on this program, it can also view soil restoration methods with advice and other alternatives. In a similar vein, Trace Genomics is another machine learning-based business that aids farmers in conducting a soil study. Such an app assists farmers in keeping track of the health of their crops and soil, which results in healthier crops that are more productive.

Using Drones to Assess Crop Health

Crop health monitoring systems based on drone-based Ariel imagery have been introduced by SkySqurrel Technologies. This method uses a drone to collect data from fields, which are subsequently sent by a USB drive to a computer for expert analysis. This analyzes the photographs it has collected using algorithms and then provides a thorough report on the state of the farm. It aids in the identification of pests and germs, enabling farmers to utilise pest control measures and other approaches when necessary to take the necessary action [27].

Predictive Analytics and Precision Agriculture

The use of AI in agriculture has produced tools and applications that assist farmers in conducting accurate and controlled farming by giving them the necessary instructions regarding water management, crop rotation, timely harvesting, and the type of crop to be grown, the best time to plant, pest attacks, and nutrition management. With equipment as basic as an SMS-enabled phone and the Sowing App, farmers without connectivity may profit from AI right away. Farmers with Wi-Fi connectivity may utilise AI apps to acquire a constantly AI-tailored plan for their farms, in the meanwhile. Farmers can fulfill the world's rising food demand with these IoT- and AI-driven solutions, expanding output and earnings sustainably without depleting priceless natural resources [28].

A System Using AI that can Identify Pests

One of the deadliest enemies of farmers because of agricultural damage are pests. AI systems employ satellite photos and historical data to determine if any insects have landed and, if so, which species—such as locusts, grasshoppers, and others—have done so. AI aids farmers in their battle against pests by sending notifications to their smartphones so that farmers may take the necessary measures and employ the necessary pest management [29].

IMPACT OF ARTIFICIAL INTELLIGENCE ON AGRICULTURAL CROP YIELD

• The Need for AI in the Agriculture Sector.

AI's different farming strategies have quickly adapted to the agricultural sector. Cognitive computing is the idea that uses a computer model of human mental processes. This leads to tumultuous AI-powered agriculture technology that provides assistance in interpreting, learning about, and responding to various circumstances (depending on the learning collected) to increase efficiency. Farmers may be provided with solutions *via* platforms like Chatterbot in order to profit from current developments in the farming sector and reap benefits in the field.

- Different Applications of AI and Other Technologies that Can Boost Agriculture Yield.

The various areas where the solutions for benefitting agriculture involving cognition possess knowledge are furnished below:

The Internet of Things (IoT) Driven Development

Development is driven by the Internet of Things. Each day, enormous amounts of data, both organized and unstructured, are produced. These facts include information on the weather, soil reports, fresh research, rainfall, insect attack susceptibility, and drone and camera images. Cognitive IoT technologies would perceive, recognize, and produce smart solutions to increase agricultural yields. Proximity and distant sensing are the two main technologies used for intelligent data fusion. Testing the soil is a significant application of this high-resolution data. Contrary to remote sensing, proximity sensing only needs sensors that are physically attached to the object being sensed.

The Development of Understanding *via* Images

Precision farming is one of the most debated aspects of agriculture in the modern world. Drone imaging can help with in-depth field analysis, crop monitoring, and field scanning. In order to ensure that the farmers act quickly, a mix of computer vision technologies, drone data, and IoT will be used. Precision farming would be accelerated if data from drone images were used to generate real-time alerts. Commercial drone manufacturers like Aerialtronics have mandated Visual Recognition APIs and IBM Watson IoT Platform for in-the-moment picture processing.

Identifying Diseases

Images of plant leaves are divided into surface areas like the background, the sick area, and the non-diseased part of the leaf using image sensing and analysis to make sure this happens. After being cropped, the unhealthy or infected region is submitted to the lab for further diagnosis. Additionally, this helps in identifying pests and detecting vitamin deficiencies.

Determine the Crop's Readiness

To determine how ripe the green fruits are, white and UVA light images of various crops were taken. The farmers might develop several levels of preparedness of fruits or crops using the results of this investigation. After that, they are stacked in different ways before delivering them to the market.

Field Administration

By creating a field map and identifying the places where crops need water, fertilizers, and pesticides, real-time calculations may be made throughout the period of cultivation using high-definition photos from drone and copter systems. This really helps with resource optimization.

Determining the Best Combination of Agronomic Goods

With reference to factors like soil quality, weather predictions, seed types, and pest infestation in a particular region, cognitive solutions advise farmers on the best hybrid crops to grow. A customized suggestion is given based on the needs of the farm, the local environment, and information on previous instances of successful farming. To help farmers make informed decisions, various external considerations such as market trends, crop prices, customer demands, requirements, and aesthetics may also be taken into account.

Crop Health Surveillance

The construction of agricultural metrics over thousands of acres of arable land requires the use of remote sensing methods, hyperspectral photography, and 3D laser scanning. From a time and effort standpoint, it has the potential to bring about a revolutionary change in how farmers monitor their farmlands. Crops will be monitored using this technology throughout their whole life cycle.

Irrigation Automation Methods that Help Farmers

The most labor-intensive farming practices are irrigation. AI-trained devices that are knowledgeable about past weather patterns, the condition of the soil, and the kind of crops that should be produced may automate irrigation and boost total productivity. Irrigation uses around 70% of the world's freshwater supply; automation can help farmers manage their water problems while also saving water.

Precision Farming

Precision farming is a more precise and regulated kind of farming that, in addition to offering advice on crop rotation, replaces the tedious and labor-intensive aspects of farming. High-precision positioning systems, geological mapping, remote sensing, integrated electronic communication, variable rate technology, optimal planting and harvesting time estimators, water resource management, plant and soil nutrient management, and rodent and pest attacks are among the notable key technologies that enable precision farming.

APPLICATIONS OF AI TO AGRICULTURE

The majority of the procedures and steps involved in agriculture are manual. AI can simplify the most difficult and common activities by enhancing already-adopted technology. When used in conjunction with other technologies, it can collect and analyze large amounts of data on a digital platform, determine the best course of action, and even start that action. The function of AI in the cycle of agricultural information management is shown in Fig. (**12**).

Fig. (12). Smart Agriculture farming.
Source: *MDPI – From Smart Farming towards Agriculture 5.0.*

PRODUCT RECOMMENDATIONS USING AI: CASE STUDY

A mobile application utilizes machine learning and image analytics to identify crop illness and give precise treatment suggestions in real time. Background information is pertinent: Farmers spend billions of dollars annually managing crop diseases, yet until recently, they lacked access to reliable diagnostic tools. Numerous crop diseases may be eliminated using targeted therapies, but it's crucial to choose the right one. Farmers may turn to treatments that are at best ineffective and at worst just as detrimental as the diseases they are trying to treat if they are armed with erroneous diagnoses. The environmental effects of these unintentional mistakes can be catastrophic, ranging from pollution to a decline in vital pollinator species like bees and butterflies [30, 31].

Crop diseases are extremely difficult to identify without extensive subject matter. Manufacturers of crop disease treatments realized that their goods could not be utilized productively as long as consumers lacked the necessary information to make wise purchase selections. Only after the condition being treated has been appropriately identified can the treatment advice be useful. Customer-specific treatment advice could not be given without physically inspecting each specimen. Plant pathologists are unable to visit all farms that want assistance.

The Solution: Give the pathologists access to the information.

Solution Overview

Machine learning-powered enhanced picture analytics are used during the diagnosis procedure.

Fig. (13). Analytics of Images through Machine Learning.

Source: Machine Learning (ML): Google's ML Engine's sophisticated deep learning capabilities were used to build disease categorization capabilities. To train the neural network, it utilized Google's high-performance infrastructure and more than 50,000 photos. The neural network's training time is significantly shortened using Google's Tensor flow Processing Units (TPUs), enabling quick and affordable model updates when new photos are gathered and filtered, as shown in Fig. (**13**).

Artificial Intelligence in Agriculture Sector: Case Study of Blue River Technology

Nowadays, agriculture is adopting advanced innovative technology for agriculture-based activities. In authors' research work, they have discussed how artificial intelligence changed the whole agricultural sector in the context of business model, SWOT, and PESTEL analysis of blue river technology company. The study results found the main role of artificial intelligence in agriculture like precision farming, machine learning, and demand forecasting and it will play a key role in sustainable Indian Agriculture [32].

CONCLUDING REMARKS

The most significant vocations in the world are farming and agriculture. It is important to India's economic sectors. Land, water, and other resources are running out due to the growing world population, making it difficult to maintain the demand and supply chain. Therefore, it is necessary to adopt a wiser strategy and increase the farm's efficiency in order to maximize productivity. Through case studies, it is clear that artificial intelligence has shown to be valuable for real-time data monitoring in the agricultural industry. This has been put in place to control yield, weeds, pests, and crops. It will take some time before artificial intelligence is used in agriculture. A thorough analysis of AI, ML, and IOT applications in agriculture is provided in this chapter. Humans continue to profit from artificial intelligence, which is the automation of intelligent behavior, in many facets of daily life. Water waste will be reduced and existing water will be used as effectively as possible by using IOT and ML algorithms for agricultural irrigation.

Utilizing artificial intelligence to estimate agricultural production and identify diseases enables farmers to decide which crops to cultivate by predicting crop output based on soil characteristics, environmental factors, and historical data. Recent studies predict that the worldwide drone market for agriculture would expand at a CAGR of 35.9 percent and reach $5.7 billion by 2025. For farmers and agronomists to evaluate the health of their crops, drones are a great instrument. Drones may be used to get a general perspective.

ACKNOWLEDGEMENTS

I want to express my gratitude to my colleague and friends Mr. Bharat Dhak and Ms. Sneha Khupse who deserve a particular word of appreciation for their help and collaboration. I want to thank Principal Dr. A. B. Marathe from the bottom of my heart for his advice.

REFERENCES

[1]   G. Singh, D. Sharma, and A. Goap, "Machine learning based soil moisture prediction for internet of things based smart irrigation system", *5 th IEEE International Conference on Signal Processing, Computing and Control (ISPCC 2k19).*, 2019 JUIT, Solan, India [http://dx.doi.org/10.1109/ISPCC48220.2019.8988313]

[2]   A. Sharma, A. Jain, P. Gupta, and V. Chowdary, "Machine learning applications for precision agriculture: A comprehensive review", *IEEE Access,* vol. 31, no. December, pp. 4843-4873, 2020.

[3]   L.S. Pereiraa, and P Paredesa, "Soil water balance models for determining crop water and irrigation requirements and irrigation scheduling focusing on the FAO56 method and the dual Kc approach",

Agricultural Water Management, vol. 241, p. 106357, 2020.

[4] M. Juan, "Design and implementation of WSN for precision agriculture in white cabbage crops", *IEEE XXIV International Conference on Electronics, Electrical Engineering and Computing (INTERCON),* Cusco, Peru, pp.1-4, 2017.

[5] R. Torres-Sanchez, H. Navarro-Hellin, A. Guillamon-Frutos, R. San-Segundo, M.C. Ruiz-Abellón, and R. Domingo-Miguel, "A decision support system for irrigation management: Analysis and implementation of different learning techniques", *Water,* vol. 12, no. 2, p. 548, 2020.
[http://dx.doi.org/10.3390/w12020548]

[6] Anat Goldstein, *Applying machine learning on sensor data for irrigation recommendations: Revealing the agronomist's tacit knowledge", Precision Agric.* vol. 19. Springer: New York, 2018, pp. 421-444.

[7] S.A. O'Shaughnessy, and S.R. Evett, "Canopy temperature based system effectively schedules and controls center pivot irrigation of cotton", *Agric. Water Manage.,* vol. 97, no. 9, pp. 1310-1316, 2010.
[http://dx.doi.org/10.1016/j.agwat.2010.03.012]

[8] M. Roopaei, P. Rad, and Kim-Kwang Ray. Choo, "Cloud of things in smart agriculture: Intelligent irrigation monitoring by thermal imaging", *IEEE Cloud Computing,* vol. 4, no. 1, pp. 10-15, 2017.
[http://dx.doi.org/10.1109/MCC.2017.5]

[9] P. Sneha, and L. Sharma, "A review on use of iot in precision agriculture using ml algorithm", *IJIRSET,* vol. 10, no. 8, 2021.

[10] A. Goap, D. Sharma, A.K. Shukla, and C. Rama Krishna, "An IoT based smart irrigation management system using machine learning and open source technologies", *Comput. Electron. Agric.,* vol. 155, pp. 41-49, 2018.
[http://dx.doi.org/10.1016/j.compag.2018.09.040]

[11] Sharma. Deepak, "A technical assessment of iot for indian agriculture", *IJCA Proceedings on National Symposium on Modern Information and Communication Technologies for Digital India MICTDI,* pp.1-5, 2016.

[12] H.H. Kadar, and S.S. Sameon, "Sustainable water resource management using iot solution for agriculture", *9th IEEE International Conference on Control System, Computing and Engineering,* Penang, Malaysia, 2019.
[http://dx.doi.org/10.1109/ICCSCE47578.2019.9068592]

[13] V. Palazzi, and F. Gelati, "Leaf-compatible autonomous rfid-based wireless temperature sensors for precision agriculture", *IEEE Topical Conference on Wireless Sensors and Sensor Networks.,* 2019 Orlando, FL, USA
[http://dx.doi.org/10.1109/WISNET.2019.8711808]

[14] G. Gyarmati, and T. Mizik, "The present and future of the precision agriculture", *IEEE 15th International Conference of System of Systems Engineering (SoSE).,* 2020 Budapest, Hungary
[http://dx.doi.org/10.1109/SoSE50414.2020.9130481]

[15] C. Kamienski, J.P. Soininen, M. Taumberger, R. Dantas, A. Toscano, T. Salmon Cinotti, R. Filev Maia, and A. Torre Neto, "Smart water management platform: IoT-based precision irrigation for agriculture", *Sensors,* vol. 19, no. 2, p. 276, 2019.
[http://dx.doi.org/10.3390/s19020276] [PMID: 30641960]

[16] J. Gutierrez Jaguey, J.F. Villa-Medina, A. Lopez-Guzman, and M.A. Porta-Gandara, "Smartphone irrigation sensor", *IEEE Sens. J.,* vol. 15, no. 9, pp. 5122-5127, 2015.
[http://dx.doi.org/10.1109/JSEN.2015.2435516]

[17] Zhijun Chen, and Shijun Sun, "Temporal convolution-network-based models for modeling maize evapotranspiration under mulched drip irrigation", *Computers and Electronics in Agriculture,* vol. 169, p. 105206, 2020.
[http://dx.doi.org/10.1016/j.compag.2019.105206]

[18] S.S. Ramaprasad, "Intelligent crop monitoring and protection system in agricultural fields using IoT",

4th International Conference on Recent Trends on Electronics, Information, Communication & Technology (RTEICT), 2019 Bangalore, India [http://dx.doi.org/10.1109/RTEICT46194.2019.9016770]

[19]   A. Gupta, "Smart crop prediction using IoT and machine learning", *Int. J. Eng. Res. Technol.,* vol. 2021, 2021.

[20]   M. Lavanaya, "Soil nutrients monitoring for greenhouse yield enhancement using ph value with iot and wireless sensor network", *Second International Conference on Green Computing and Internet of Things,* pp. 547-552, 2018.

[21]   T. Talaviya, D. Shah, N. Patel, H. Yagnikc, and M. Shahd, "Implementation of artificial intelligence in agriculture for optimization of irrigation and application of pesticides and herbicides", *Artificial Intelligence in Agriculture,* vol. 4, pp. 58-73, 2020.

[22]   L.M.S. Campoverde, M. Tropea, and F. De Rango, "An IoT based smart irrigation management system using reinforcement learning modeled through a Markov decision process", *IEEE/ACM 25th International Symposium on Distributed Simulation and Real Time Applications (DS-RT).,* 2021 Valencia, Spain [http://dx.doi.org/10.1109/DS-RT52167.2021.9576130]

[23]   X. Nie, L. Wang, H. Ding, and M. Xu, "Strawberry verticillium wilt detection network based on multi-task learning and attention", *IEEE Access,* vol. 7, pp. 170003-170011, 2019. [http://dx.doi.org/10.1109/ACCESS.2019.2954845]

[24]   A. Seyedzadeha, and S. Maroufpoor, "Artificial intelligence approach to estimate discharge of drip tape irrigationbased on temperature and pressure", *Agric. Water Manage.,* vol. 7, pp. 170003-170011, 2019.

[25]   R. Sowmyalakshmi, "An optimal classification model for rice plant disease detection", *Comput. Mater. Continua,* vol. 68, no. 2, pp. 1751-1767, 2021. [http://dx.doi.org/10.32604/cmc.2021.016825]

[26]   V. Kesevan, K. Hayate, and T. Shogo, "Interactive cultivation system for the future IoT-based agriculture", *Seventh International Symposium on Computing and Networking Workshops,* 2019 Nagasaki, Japan

[27]   M. Manoj Vihari, N. Usha Rani., and M. Purna Teja, "IoT based unmanned aerial vehicle system for agriculture applications", *International Conference on Smart Systems and Inventive Technology,* 2018 Tirunelveli, India

[28]   T. Tanha, S. Dhara, P. Nivedita, Y. Hiteshri, and S. Manan, "Implementation of artificial intelligence in agriculture for optimisation of irrigation and application of pesticides and herbicides", *Artificial Intelligence in Agriculture,* vol. 4, pp. 58-73, 2020.

[29]   Available   from:https://www.analyticsvidhya.com/blog/2020/11/artificial-intelligence-in-agricult-re-using-modern-day ai-to-solve-traditional-farming-problems/#h2_6

[30]   M. Vishal, P. Kailas, M. Vidula, H. Dinesh, and S. D. Ramteke, "Machine learning in agriculture domain: A state-of-art survey", *Artificial Intelligence in the Life Sciences,* vol. 1, p. 100010, 2021.

[31]   S. Bhanumathi, M. Vineeth, and N. Rohit, "Crop yield prediction and efficient use of fertilizers", *International Conference on Communication and Signal Processing,* pp. 0769-0773, 2019. Chennai, India [http://dx.doi.org/10.1109/ICCSP.2019.8698087]

[32]   S. Panpatte, and C. Ganeshkumar, "Artificial intelligence in agriculture sector: Case study of blue river technology", *Proc. Sec. Int. Conf. Inform. Manag. Mach. Intell,* pp.147-153, 2021. [http://dx.doi.org/10.1007/978-981-15-9689-6_17]

CHAPTER 5

Optimal Feature Selection and Prediction of Diabetes using Boruta- LASSO Techniques

Vijayshri Nitin Khedkar[1,*], Sonali Mahendra Kothari[1], Sina Patel[1] and Saurabh Sathe[2]

[1] *Department of Computer Science and Engineering, Symbiosis Institute of Technology, Symbiosis International [Deemed University], Maharashtra, India*

[2] *San Jose State University, California, USA*

Abstract: Diabetes prediction is an ongoing research problem. The sooner diabetes is detected in a human, the sooner lives and medical resources can be saved. Predicting diabetes as early as possible with easy to measures parameters with optimal accuracy is an ongoing problem. When dealing with large data, feature selection plays an important role. It not only reduces the computational cost but also increases the performance of a model. This study ensemble three different types of feature selection techniques: filter, wrapper and embedded. Ensembling Boruta and LASSO features give optimal results. Also, effectively handling class imbalance leads to better results.

Keywords: Diabetes Prediction, Ensembling features, Feature selection, SMOTE.

INTRODUCTION

Diabetes is a metabolic disease identified by the high insulin levels in the blood [1, 2]. Also known as diabetes mellitus, it often leads to complicated diseases like heart attack, kidney failure, stroke and nerves. Diabetes is grouped into mainly three types: diabetes type 1, diabetes type 2, and gestational diabetes. Type 1 Diabetes occurs when there is a lack of insulin in the body which permanently damages cells that produce the pancreas. The second type of diabetes is when the body cannot effectively use the insulin produced by it, and gestational diabetes is usually seen in pregnant women.

Identifying diabetes at an early stage is a strenuous task since most medical data are correlated, structured, nonlinear and intricate in nature. The use of machine le-

---

* **Corresponding author Vijayshri Nitin Khedkar:** Department of Computer Science and Engineering, Symbiosis Institute of Technology, Symbiosis International [Deemed University], Maharashtra, India; E-mail: vijayshri.khedkar@sitpune.edu.in

arning-based systems has emerged in the field of healthcare [3, 4], not only for diabetes but for other diseases like coronary arteries, heart disease, and cancer. Machine learning-based systems can be used for feature selection and classification. A very important pre-processing step while training any data is variable selection. The main aim of this step is to filter out non-contributing features from the training dataset. Performing feature selection comes with many benefits: it deals with the problems related to dimensionality, avoids overfitting problems and reduces the total time cost for training the model.

Majorly, methods for features selection are categorised into filter methods, wrapper methods, and embedded methods [5 - 8]. Previously, authors have aimed at comparing various feature selection methods for varied domains. However, many studies have been developed based on one type of feature selection technique. There are different advantages and disadvantages of using a particular type of technique, and using a single type of algorithm has its own drawbacks. To overcome this drawback, the ensemble feature selection method is being explored recently. Ensemble-based feature selection techniques generate different subsets and get a final output. However, these studies are mainly limited to a single algorithm; not all three categories are considered in an ensemble feature selection. Also, many methods are being used for predicting or diagnosing diabetes. Mainly, these methods use advanced lab test results for prediction, which is time and cost-consuming. It is necessary to predict diabetes as early as possible using easy to measure features that can save time, money and health for health professionals and patients.

In this study, we focus on inspecting how different machine learning models behave and perform with different feature selection techniques along with various combinations of filter, wrapper and embedded feature selection methods. Also, identifying easy to measure features that do not require advanced lab tests for predicting diabetes as early as possible. This paper demonstrates that aggregation of Boruta and LASSO for feature selection and combining it with random forest gives better results for the data.

RELATED WORKS

A study [9] used decision trees, Naive Bayesian, Random forest, Support Vector Machine, and K nearest neighbour for predicting diabetes in an early stage based on data collected from UCI called PIDD dataset. The main aim was to select the correct attribute by iteratively checking the correlation between attributes. Different metrics were used for evaluating the models. RF and DT outperformed in terms of specificity. However, NB gave better accuracy. Various machine learning algorithms such as Logistic regression, gradient boost, and random forest were compared [10]. The main finding of this study was that logistic regression gave the highest accuracy of 96% with the private dataset used, which has features like insulin, BMI, Blood pressure, age, job type, and glucose. In comparison, gradient boost and AdaBoost classifiers gave 77% accuracy with the PIMA dataset.

Another study [11] proposed its own dataset for predicting type 2 diabetes. The class imbalance was treated by SMOTE technique, and for feature selection, Chi-square, and logistic regression were used. By comparing various ML algorithms, out of which the decision tree outperformed the proposed dataset. It was found out that smoking, healthy diet, blood pressure, BMI, gender and region were significant factors contributing to prediction accuracy. A study [12] used the NHANES dataset for predicting diabetes by extracting features like age, ethnicity, body mass index, fitness, drinking habits, smoking habits, nutrition intake, cholesterol, and calorie consumption. Moreover, linear SVM and bagged trees were compared, giving 88.5% and 87% accuracy. However, after removing outliers and missing values, the dataset was very small, which cannot be validated in real-time situations.

DATASET USED

A publicly available dataset from National Health and Nutrition Examination Survey (NHANES), which is cross-sectional ongoing survey data, was utilised for experiments. The survey collects health, nutrition, and lab examinations which consist of different measurements such as cholesterol, blood pressure and other specimens for lab testing. Survey participants were recognized as positive diabetic patients if any one of the following conditions were met:

  i. Plasma fasting glucose >=126 mg/dL
 ii. Glycohemoglobin >=6.5%
iii. Serum glucose >= 2000 mg/dL
 iv. Responding 'Yes' when asked, "Did a doctor tell you that you have diabetes?"

Table 1. Detailed Description of Data set.

Feature Selection Techniques	AGE	RAC	EDU	GEN	WAI	MAR	HEI	LEG	WEI	BMI	CHO	HYP	DYS	SYS	HEA	EXE	ALC
ReliefF	✓	✓	✓	✓	-	✓	-	-	-	-	-	✓	-	-	✓	-	✓
Boruta	✓	-	-	-	✓	-	✓	✓	✓	✓	✓	-	-	✓	-	-	-
LASSO	✓	-	✓	✓	✓	✓	-	✓	✓	✓	✓	-	-	✓	✓	✓	-

(Table 1) cont.....

ReliefF ∪ Boruta	✓	✓	✓	✓	✓	✓	✓	✓	✓	✓	✓	✓	-	✓	✓	-	✓
ReliefF ∩ Boruta	✓	-	-	-	-	-	-	-	-	-	-	-	-	-	-	-	-
ReliefF ∪ LASSO	✓	✓	✓	✓	✓	✓	✓	✓	✓	✓	✓	✓	-	✓	✓	✓	✓
ReliefF ∩ LASSO	✓	-	✓	✓	-	✓	-	-	-	-	-	-	-	-	✓	-	-
Boruta ∪ LASSO	✓	-	✓	✓	✓	✓	✓	✓	-	-	-	-	-	✓	✓	✓	-
Boruta ∩ LASSO	✓	-	-	-	✓	-	-	✓	✓	✓	✓	-	-	✓	-	-	-

A total of 6039 respondents were observed after excluding unusual observations and missing values. Complete information about the dataset is given in Table **1**.

Handling Class Imbalance

The adverse effect of class imbalance was treated by a technique called Synthetic Minority Oversampling Technique (SMOTE). The variance between the two classes of the dataset is considerably high, which can lead to decreased accuracy in predicting classifiers. The problem of class imbalance arises when there is a huge dissimilarity between two binary classes, that is, the majority class and minority class [13]. This leads to inaccurate classification and over-fitting of the model due to underperformance of the model or bias is not elongated for the majority class [14]. A handful of studies have shown that with balanced data, good classification and model performance can be achieved. There are various methods which are called "Sampling Methods," to tackle this issue of class imbalance. The main aim of these techniques is to alter the target class values in the original dataset to equal the distribution. In this study, we proposed our approach to classification models based on the Synthetic Minority Oversampling Technique (SMOTE). Few studies have observed that SMOTE performed better with some datasets [15].

SMOTE method is an oversampling technique that is mostly used in imbalanced data with many features that are being used in healthcare [15]. To expand the count of instances in the original dataset, new random data points of minority class are generated. These instances are created from the nearest neighbours of the minority class in the original dataset. In this study, we applied SMOTE technique resulting in a new training set. SMOTE increased the positive sample from 6039 instances to 11546 instances.

The steps for creating new synthetic samples for continuous features are:

1. Distance between the feature characteristic minority class and its K-nearest neighbours is calculated.

2. The outcome in step 1 is multiplied by an arbitrary number in the range [0,1].

3. The value derived in step 2 is aggregated to the feature value of the initial feature vector.

We get a new feature vector as:

$$\gamma_{new} = \gamma_0 + (\gamma_{0i} - \gamma_0) \times \eth$$

γ_{new}: new produced sample.

γ_0: minority class data point's feature vector

γ_{0i}: i[th] selected neighbor of γ_0.

$\eth$: arbitrary number in [0,1].

The samples for numerical data is produced by the following steps:

1. The 'majority vote' of variables under consideration and their respective KNN for numerical data is derived; if there's a tie, then pick any random value.

2. Assign the result derived in step 1 to SMOTE data.

RESEARCH APPROACH

In this paper, data from NHANES (2009-2012) is extracted with a total of 18 features with 9 categorical and 9 numerical variables. In this study, we focus on analysing and recognizing which fusion of feature selection techniques performs best with classification algorithms. Filter, embedded, and wrapper are three varieties of attribute selection techniques. Two different types of variable selection techniques are combined.

Given any training dataset having N different variables, each feature selection technique produces different reduced sets whose dimensions are lower than N. In this study, union and intersection are applied for aggregating various reduced dataset that contains selected features only. For instance, all features selected in set F(filter) and W(wrapper) are used to do union of a reduced set of F∪ W. On the other hand, the intersection is only based on common or common variables that appear both in F and W, giving a new set F ∩ W. Fig. (**1**) and Fig. (**2**) show research approaches and feature selection strategies, respectively.

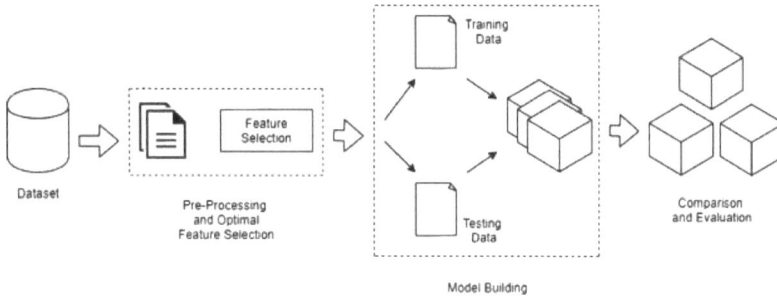

Fig. (1). Research Approach.

FEATURE SELECTION METHODS

Filter-based methods usually select features from the dataset irrespective of the use of any machine learning algorithm. This type of technique is inexpensive computationally and is very fast. It works well in removing correlated and redundant features; however, it does not remove multi-collinearity. The second type of technique is the wrapper method [16].

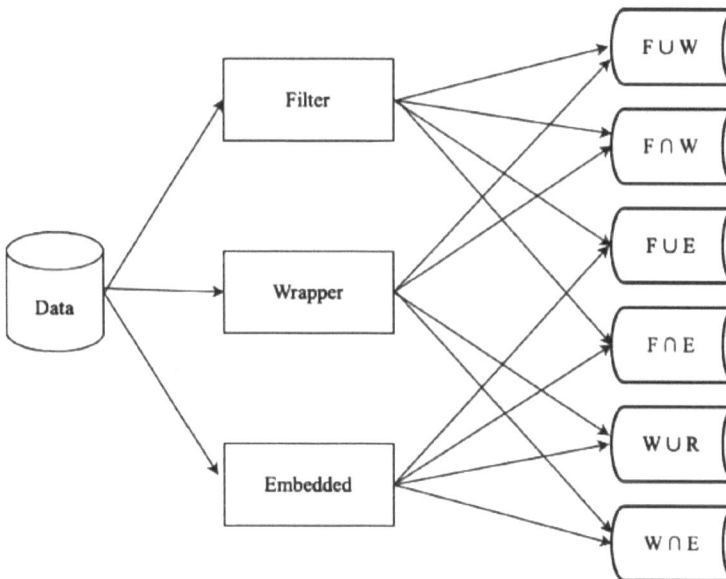

Fig. (2). Ensemble strategy for feature selection.

They are often referred to as greedy algorithms by selecting features in an iterative manner till a particular stopping criterion is not reached. This stopping criterion is pre-defined such as when a specific number of features has been achieved. The main advantage of these type of methods is that it provides an optimal set of features for the training model which results in better accuracy but high computational resources [17]. Moreover, the third type of variable selection technique is the embedded method which uses a learning algorithm itself to select features that is it selects features during model training. It solves drawbacks encountered in filters and wrappers by merging their advantages. It is faster than filter methods and also takes into consideration the interaction of features like wrapper techniques do.

ReliefF

ReliefF algorithm is a filter-based proposal for selecting attributes that are considerably reactive to variable interactions. It is based on identifying feature value differences between the nearest neighbour instance pairs. The variable score reduces if the attribute value difference is observed in a neighbouring instance pair with the same class [18]. On the other hand, it increases the feature score if there is a difference between a neighbouring data point pair with varied class values. ReliefF uses Manhattan (L1) norm to find near-hit or near-miss instances. The weight is updated by the following equation:

$$w_i = w_i - (x_i - nearHit_i)^2 + (x_i - nearMiss_i)^2$$

Boruta

Boruta is a feature selection algorithm that works as a wrapper around the random forest. It tries to select all relevant features in the dataset by taking multi-variable relationships into consideration. It first creates shadow columns by creating duplicate features and shuffling them, and then trains the classifier to calculate feature importance. Furthermore, it checks shadow features with real features by comparing Z-score. At every iteration, it compares Z-score and selects the better performer and marks the feature as important.

Lasso

The least absolute shrinkage and selection operator (LASSO) is an embedded feature selection algorithm. It is a forward-looking feature selection method by transforming each coefficient by a constant component λ and truncating a zero. If LASSO recognizes a high correlation in the feature set, then it only selects one among them and shrinks the others to zero. LASSO estimate can be defined as:

$$\beta = min\left\{\left\{\frac{1}{2}\left(\sum_{i=1}^{N} \quad y_i - \beta_0 - \sum_{j=1}^{p} \quad x_{ij}\beta_j\right)^2\right\} + \gamma \sum_{j=1}^{p} \quad |\beta_j|\right\}$$

The accuracy of a classification and interpretability of a model is enhanced by LASSO by integrating the high characteristics of subset selection and ridge regression.

Many previous studies show that random forest gives promising results when dealing with such data. In this study, feature selection techniques are analysed by merging them with two classification algorithms, namely the Random forest algorithm, Logistic Regression, and Naïve Bayes algorithm.

RESULT ANALYSIS

Feature Selection Results

Table **2** shows the result of different feature sets selected by different techniques experimented. Four variables, namely: age, waist, cholesterol and systolic blood pressure were included and marked important by all types of feature selection schemes. LASSO individually considered almost all features as important except BMI.

Evaluation *Metrics*

Various statistical parameters or metrics can be utilised to differentiate the performance of the model classifiers. Different types of evaluation metrics provide different information. Some of the metrics are classification accuracy, ROC, F1 measure score, mean square error, and confusion matrix. In this study, we have used classification accuracy (CA) and area under the curve (AUC) as our performance metrics.

The ratio of correct guesses to the total number of instances in the data is called CA. Evaluating the model with CA is effective when data is evenly balanced.

$$CA = \frac{True\ Positive\ +\ True\ Negative}{Total\ Number\ of\ Samples}$$

AUC is another metric that is widely used when dealing with binary classification problems. AUC is the likelihood that a model will mark a selected first group example greater than a randomly selected second group selected instance. The first group is for positive instances, and the second group is for negative instances. It takes a true positive rate (TPR) and False-positive rate (FPR) into consideration where TPR is the ratio of positive data points which are accurately identified to be included in the first group against all first group data points and FPR is the ratio of second group data points that are erroneously considered as positive against all second group data points. The plot between FPR and TPR is in the range [0,1] and is called AUC. It is AUC, and the performance of the model is directly proportional.

Table 2. Selected features by different feature selection techniques.

Feature Selection Techniques	Classification Techniques					
-	Random Forest		Naïve Bayes		Logistic Regression	
-	CA	AUC	CA	AUC	CA	AUC
ReliefF	97.4	0.893	59.9	0.827	96.4	0.889
Boruta	93.1	0.921	71.1	0.78	74.2	0.889
LASSO	97.6	0.901	63.6	0.87	93.5	0.989
ReliefF ∪ Boruta	97.5	0.894	70	0.84	91.2	0.989
ReliefF ∩ Boruta	82.6	0.778	71.3	0.792	72.8	0.789
ReliefF ∪ LASSO	95.1	0.874	66.6	0.87	92.8	0.889
ReliefF ∩ LASSO	97.3	0.912	64.9	0.846	96	0.889
Boruta ∪ LASSO	97.8	0.997	66.6	0.87	92.8	0.889
Boruta ∩ LASSO	93.9	0.955	72.3	0.798	73.9	0.889

Cross-Validation

Cross-validation (CV) is also known as data partitioning. CV is used for partitioning the dataset into a training set and testing set. There are various CV protocols employed for reducing the variability in the data, such as K2, K5, and K10. A poorly chosen CV protocol may result in mis-interpretative results such as scores with high variance or high bias. In this study, we have used the K10 protocol, which is commonly used in machine learning and statistics. In the K10 protocol, the dataset is split into 10 equal parts, where ninety percent is used for training the model and the remaining for testing or validating the model. Tenfold CV generally yields good results with low bias and acceptable variance through previous studies.

Classification Method Results

The comparison of three classifiers along with different feature selection schemes used is shown in the figure. Ten old stratified cross-validations were used for evaluating the results. It is recognized that Random forest (RF) yields good results for all types of feature selection schemes when matched to the other two classifiers. It is also discovered that RF, when employed with Boruta and lasso feature selection schemes gives the highest AUC as well as the accuracy of 0.995 and 97.8%, respectively. Moreover, for Naive Bayes, LASSO feature selection yields better results in terms of AUC, and that for accuracy is the intersection of Boruta and LASSO compared to other variable selection techniques. In comparison, logistic regression gave better results with the reliefF method of feature selection both for accuracy and AUC. Random forest classifiers performed exceptionally well with all types of feature selection schemes. For random forest, when comparing individual variable selection techniques, ReliefF yielded the best AUC of 0.993, and LASSO gave a 97.6% of accuracy. Table **3** shows a detailed comparison of all approaches. Fig. (**3**) and Fig. (**4**) represent a graphical comparison of classification accuracy and area under the curve of classifiers, respectively.

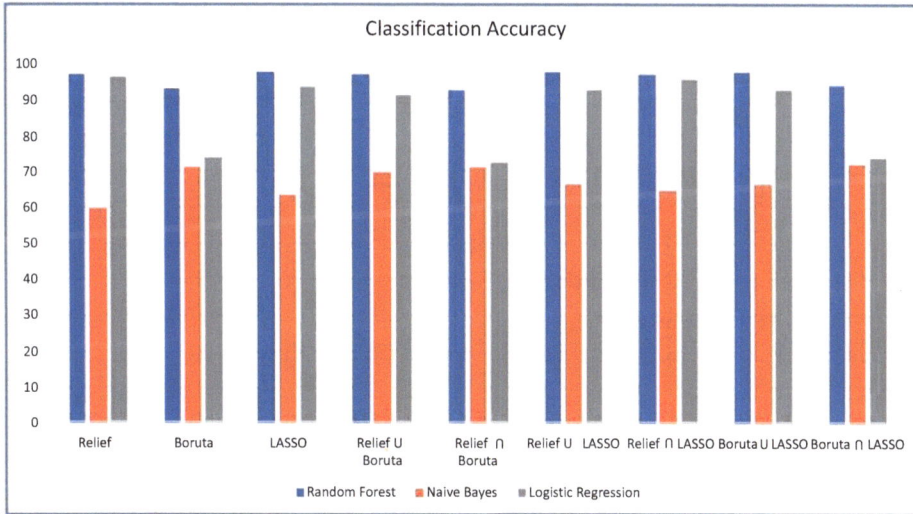

Fig. (3). Classification Accuracy Comparison.

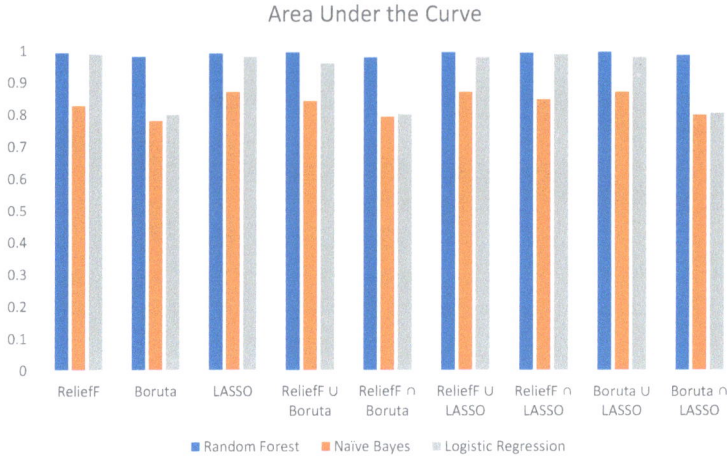

Fig. (4). AUC Comparison.

Evaluation of Receiver Operating Characteristics (ROC)

A graph plotted between sensitivity and 1-specificity is called a ROC graph. AUC is derived from this ROC graph which is a metric for evaluating the classifiers. Orange 3.26.0 software was used to compute these curves. After observing ROC curves of three different feature selection techniques (ReliefF, Boruta and LASSO) for random forest classifier, it is seen that LASSO with random forest is better, giving optimal AUC in comparison with other approaches in this study. It is observed that AUC for ReliefF is 0.993, 0.827 and 0.989 for RF, NB, LR algorithms, respectively and that of Boruta, it is 0.981, 0.827 and 0.989, respectively.

Table 3. Model Evaluation (CA: Classification Accuracy, AUC: Area under the curve).

Authors	Year	Dataset	FST	Classifier	PT	ACC	AUC
[16]	2017	PIMA	NO	GPC	K5,K10	81.96	NO
[17]	2018	NHANES	FEATURE IMPORTANCE	ENSEMBLE(LR,KNN,GB,RF)	K10	96	0.75
[3]	2020	NHANES	LOGISTIC REGRESSION	RANDOM FOREST	K2,K5,K10	94.25	0.95
[18]	2019	NHANES	XGBOOST FEATURE IMPORTANCE	RANDOM FOREST	K10	NO	0.841
[19]	2010	NHANES	NO	SVM,LR,KNN,RF,GB,SVM	K10	83.5	0.842
[20]	2017	NHANES	RF	DECISION TREE	K10	N0	0.84

(Table 3) cont.....

[21]	2020	CROSS SECTIONAL SURVEY DATA	FORWARD LOGISTIC REGRESSION	SVM	NO	82.1	0.822
[22]	2021	EHR SAUDI ARABIA	PERMUTATION IMPORTANCE & HIERARCHICAL CLUSTERING	LR,KNN,RF,GB,SVM	NO	82.1	NO
OUR APPROACH	2021	NHANES	BORUTA & LASSO	RANDOM FOREST	K10	97.8	0.995

DISCUSSION

In this study, we have presented and experimented with various feature selection and machine learning-based approaches to predict patients as diabetic or non-diabetic. The data we have used is easy to measure and can predict diabetes at an early stage without advanced lab reports. Electronic health records play a vital role in such cases. Moreover, data from smartwatches can also be utilised. Three feature selection techniques: ReliefF, Boruta, and LASSO, were experimented with three classifiers: Random forest, Naive Bayes and logistic regression. We hypothesised that random forest would perform better with Boruta and LASSO. The common high-risk factors identified by all different approaches were namely age, waist, cholesterol and systolic blood pressure. Since the data was highly imbalanced, SMOTE technique was applied. Further, various aggregations of sets derived from these variable selection techniques were given as input to various classifiers. Also, K10 cross-validation was applied for the generalisation of the prediction.

This study shows prediction and identifies risk status of patients with diabetes for 6301 nondiabetic and 306 diabetic patients. This data was balanced by the SMOTE technique giving a total of 11,546 instances. Our result demonstrates that the aggregation of Boruta and LASSO for feature selection and combining it with random forest gives better results for the data. It gives 0.995 AUC and an accuracy of 97.8%. Table **4** shows key differences from previous studies.

Table 4. Key differences from previous studies.

Feature Name	Description	Values	Code
Age	Age of the person.	Continuous	RIDAGEYR

(Table 4) cont.....

RACE	Race/Ethnicity	1-Mexican 2-Hispanic 3-White 4-Black 5-Other	RIDRETH1
EDUCATION	Education Level	1-Less than 9th 2- 9th-11th grade 3- high school grade 4-some college 5-college graduate 7-refused 9-don't know	DMDEDUC2
GENDER	Gender	1-Male 2-Female	RIAGENDR
MARITAL	Marital Status	1- Married 2-Widowed 3-Divorced 4-Seperated 5-Never Married 6-Live in Partner 77-Refused 99-Don't Know	DMDMARTL
WAIST	Waist Circumference(cm)	Continuous	BMXWAIST
HEIGHT	Standing Height(cm)	Continuous	BMXHT
LEG_LEN	Upper Leg Length(cm)	Continuous	BMXLEG
WEIGHT	Weight(kg)	Continuous	BMXWT
BMI	Body Mass Index(kg/m**2)	Continuous	BMXBMI
CHOLESTEROL	Total Cholesterol (mg/dL)	Continuous	LBXTC
HYPERTENSION	Ever told you have hypertension?	1-Yes 2-No 7-Refused 9-Don't Know	BPQ057
DYSBP	Diastolic : Blood Pressure mm Hg	Continuous	BPXDI1
SYSBP	Systolic : Blood Pressure mm Hg	Continuous	BPXSY1
HEALTH RISK	Ever told you have health risk of Diabetes?	1-Yes 2-No 7-Refused 9-Don't Know	DIQ170
EXERCISE	Vigorous work activity	1-Yes 2-No 7-Refused 9-Don't Know	PAQ605
ALCOHOL	Had alcohol in last 12 months?	0 - No 1 - Yes	ALQ120Q

(Table 4) cont.....

DIABETES	Diabetic or not?	0 - No 1 - Yes	-

CONCLUSION

Diabetes Mellitus is a life-threatening disease that is identified by high blood sugar. If it is identified at an early stage through features easy to measure without advanced lab tests, much time, resources and lives can be saved. In this study, it can be seen that ensemble variable selection methods that are based on different criteria can produce better results. Various feature selection techniques give distinctive results. The experiment, however, showed that the aggregation of LASSO and Boruta, when combined with random forest, gave better results in terms of AUC as well as accuracy. Nevertheless, many different feature selection techniques or ensembling these methods through different criteria are yet to be explored when dealing with medical data.

FUTURE SCOPE

In the proposed work, an existing dataset is used. Some studies [9-12]. have also used the existing dataset for working with machine learning models. To improve the prediction and better monitoring of user health, dataset preparation is an important task. Considering this, the proposed work will continue its training with the dataset captured using IoT devices. The real-time data collected from wearable devices will help in better health monitoring of the diabetic patient. The model trained in the proposed work will be used with IoT devices to early predict chronic diseases like diabetes. The use of IoT technologies in monitoring diabetic patients' health, such as continuous glucose monitoring (CGM) and Insulin infusion pumps, can improve the life quality of diabetic patients.

One concern of using IoT devices is security and privacy of the user health parameters monitored through various IoT sensors. In the future scope, the proposed work will focus on securing any breach of IoT data while it is being used or monitored for user health and avoid any consequences to the user.

REFERENCES

[1]　A. D. Association, *Diagnosis and classification of diabetes mellitus Diabetes Care, vol. 33, no. SUPPL. 1. American Diabetes Association,,* pp. S62-S69, Jan. 01, 2010.
　　　[http://dx.doi.org/10.2337/dc10-S062]

[2]　N. Sarwar, P. Gao, S.R. Seshasai, R. Gobin, S. Kaptoge, E. Di Angelantonio, E. Ingelsson, D.A. Lawlor, E. Selvin, M. Stampfer, C.D. Stehouwer, S. Lewington, L. Pennells, A. Thompson, N. Sattar, I.R. White, K.K. Ray, and J. Danesh, "Diabetes mellitus, fasting blood glucose concentration, and risk of vascular disease: a collaborative meta-analysis of 102 prospective studies", *Lancet,* vol. 375, no. 9733, pp. 2215-2222, 2010.

[http://dx.doi.org/10.1016/S0140-6736(10)60484-9] [PMID: 20609967]

[3]   M. Maniruzzaman, M.J. Rahman, B. Ahammed, and M.M. Abedin, "Classification and prediction of diabetes disease using machine learning paradigm", *Health Inf. Sci. Syst.,* vol. 8, no. 1, p. 7, 2020.
[http://dx.doi.org/10.1007/s13755-019-0095-z] [PMID: 31949894]

[4]   S. Shah, X. Luo, S. Kanakasabai, R. Tuason, and G. Klopper, "Neural networks for mining the associations between diseases and symptoms in clinical notes", *Health Inf. Sci. Syst.,* vol. 7, no. 1, p. 1, 2019.
[http://dx.doi.org/10.1007/s13755-018-0062-0] [PMID: 30588291]

[5]   Y. Saeys, I. Inza, and P. Larrañaga, "A review of feature selection techniques in bioinformatics", *Bioinformatics,* vol. 23, no. 19, pp. 2507-2517, 2007.
[http://dx.doi.org/10.1093/bioinformatics/btm344] [PMID: 17720704]

[6]   V. Kumar, and S. Minz, "Feature Selection: A literature Review", *Smart Computing Review,* vol. 4, no. 3, 2014.
[http://dx.doi.org/10.6029/smartcr.2014.03.007]

[7]   G. Chandrashekar, and F. Sahin, "A survey on feature selection methods", *Comput. Electr. Eng.,* vol. 40, no. 1, pp. 16-28, 2014.
[http://dx.doi.org/10.1016/j.compeleceng.2013.11.024]

[8]   V. Bolón-Canedo, N. Sánchez-Maroño, and A. Alonso-Betanzos, *A review of feature selection methods on synthetic data Knowledge and Information Systems Springer London,,* vol. 34, no. 3, pp. 483-519, Mar. 01, 2013.
[http://dx.doi.org/10.1007/s10115-012-0487-8]

[9]   M.F. Faruque, Asaduzzaman, and I.H. Sarker, "Asaduzzaman, and I. H. Sarker", *Performance Analysis of Machine Learning Techniques to Predict Diabetes Mellitus,* no. Apr, pp. 1-4, 2019.
[http://dx.doi.org/10.1109/ECACE.2019.8679365]

[10]   M. Jahangir, H. Afzal, M. Ahmed, K. Khurshid, and R. Nawaz, "An expert system for diabetes prediction using auto tuned multi-layer perceptron", *2017 Intelligent Systems Conference (IntelliSys),* London, UK, 2017, pp. 722-728.
[http://dx.doi.org/10.1109/IntelliSys.2017.8324209]

[11]   M. Li, X. Fu, and D. Li, "Diabetes prediction based on xgboost algorithm", *IOP Conf. Series Mater. Sci. Eng.,* vol. 768, no. 7, p. 072093, 2020.
[http://dx.doi.org/10.1088/1757-899X/768/7/072093]

[12]   R. Mirshahvalad, and N.A. Zanjani, "Diabetes prediction using ensemble perceptron algorithm", *2017 9th International Conference on Computational Intelligence and Communication Networks (CICN),* Girne, Northern Cyprus, 2017, pp. 190-194.
[http://dx.doi.org/10.1109/CICN.2017.8319383]

[13]   G.E.A.P.A. Batista, R.C. Prati, and M.C. Monard, "A study of the behavior of several methods for balancing machine learning training data", *SIGKDD Explor.,* vol. 6, no. 1, pp. 20-29, 2004.
[http://dx.doi.org/10.1145/1007730.1007735]

[14]   Haibo He, and E.A. Garcia, "Learning from imbalanced data", *IEEE Trans. Knowl. Data Eng.,* vol. 21, no. 9, pp. 1263-1284, 2009.
[http://dx.doi.org/10.1109/TKDE.2008.239]

[15]   R. Blagus, and L. Lusa, "Joint use of over- and under-sampling techniques and cross-validation for the development and assessment of prediction models", *BMC Bioinformatics,* vol. 16, no. 1, p. 363, 2015.
[http://dx.doi.org/10.1186/s12859-015-0784-9] [PMID: 26537827]

[16]   M. Maniruzzaman, N. Kumar, M. Menhazul Abedin, M. Shaykhul Islam, H.S. Suri, A.S. El-Baz, and J.S. Suri, "Comparative approaches for classification of diabetes mellitus data: Machine learning paradigm", *Comput. Methods Programs Biomed.,* vol. 152, pp. 23-34, 2017.
[http://dx.doi.org/10.1016/j.cmpb.2017.09.004] [PMID: 29054258]

[17]　A. Husain, and M.H. Khan, "Early diabetes prediction using voting based ensemble learning", *Commun. Comput. Inf. Sci.,* vol. 905, pp. 95-103, 2018.
[http://dx.doi.org/10.1007/978-981-13-1810-8_10]

[18]　A. Dinh, S. Miertschin, A. Young, and S.D. Mohanty, "A data-driven approach to predicting diabetes and cardiovascular disease with machine learning", *BMC Med. Inform. Decis. Mak.,* vol. 19, no. 1, p. 211, 2019.
[http://dx.doi.org/10.1186/s12911-019-0918-5] [PMID: 31694707]

CHAPTER 6

Empowered Internet of Things for Sustainable Development Using Artificial Intelligence

Pranali Gajanan Chavhan[1,*], **Namrata Nishant Wasatkar**[1] and **Gitanjali Rahul Shinde**[2]

[1] Vishwakarma Institute of information and Technology, Pune. (Maharashtra State), India

[2] Department of Computer Science & Engineering (Artificial Intelligence & Machine Learning), Vishwakarma Institute of Information Technology Kondhwa (Budruk), Pune – 411048, Maharashtra, India

Abstract: Everyone has been utilizing the Internet of Things in current years (IoT). Therefore, as the IoT has grown enormously, so too have concerns about Artificial Intelligence. Artificial intelligence (AI) is at the forefront of ubiquitous computing and is utilized to create intricate algorithms to safeguard networks and systems, including IoT devices. But to carry out cyber security assaults, hackers have learned how to make use of AI, and they have even started to deploy antagonistic AI. The goal of this research work is to comprehensively present and summarize the pertinent literature in these fields. It does this by compiling data from a few other surveys and research papers regarding sustainable development using AI, IoT, and attacks with and against AI. It also shows the relationship between IoT and AI.

Keywords: Artificial intelligence (AI), Cyber security Attacks, Energy management, Internet of things (IoT), Intelligent transportation systems (ITS), Smart irrigation, Water management using AI.

INTRODUCTION

The Internet of Things (IoT) has revolutionized the way we live and work by connecting everyday devices and facilitating communication between them. As the number of connected devices continues to grow, it is essential to ensure the security, efficiency, and reliability of IoT systems. Artificial Intelligence (AI) offers a wealth of opportunities for improving IoT, from enhancing security measures to optimizing performance. This study aims to explore various methods for securing, enhancing, and ensuring the reliability of IoT in the context of AI.

---

* **Corresponding author Pranali Gajanan Chavhan:** Vishwakarma Institute of information and Technology, Pune. (Maharashtra State), India; E-mail: pranali.chavhan@viit.ac.in

This will include an examination of current techniques and technologies, as well as an evaluation of their effectiveness and limitations. The goal of this research is to identify the most promising approaches for improving IoT with AI and provide insights for future work in this area.

The field of computer science known as AI is concerned with developing intelligent machines that can carry out tasks that ordinarily require human intelligence, such as visual awareness, speech recognition, decision-making, and language translation. Large datasets can be used to teach AI systems to recognize patterns, predict consequences, and then be programmed to respond accordingly. The goal of AI is to create systems that can perform tasks that would normally require human intellect and make decisions and perform actions that are not explicitly programmed. Some common examples of AI include virtual personal assistants like Siri and Alexa, recommendation systems used by streaming services, and self-driving cars.

AI offers several opportunities for improving the IoT in the following ways:

- Security: AI can be used to improve security in IoT systems by detecting and preventing cyber-attacks. For example, AI algorithms can identify anomalies in network traffic and take action to prevent potential security breaches [1].
- Performance Optimization: AI can be used to optimize the performance of IoT systems by analysing data and making predictions to improve efficiency. For example, AI algorithms can be used to predict which devices will consume the most power and adjust their usage accordingly [2].
- Predictive Maintenance: AI can be used to predict when IoT devices will fail and schedule maintenance accordingly. This can help reduce downtime and improve the overall reliability of IoT systems [1].
- Automation: AI can be used to automate many tasks in IoT systems, freeing up time for human operators and improving overall efficiency [3].
- Decision-Making: AI can be used to make decisions in IoT systems, for example, deciding which devices to turn on and off based on usage patterns.

In Fig. (**1**), AI offers a wealth of opportunities for improving IoT by providing new ways to enhance security, optimize performance, improve reliability, automate tasks, and make informed decisions.

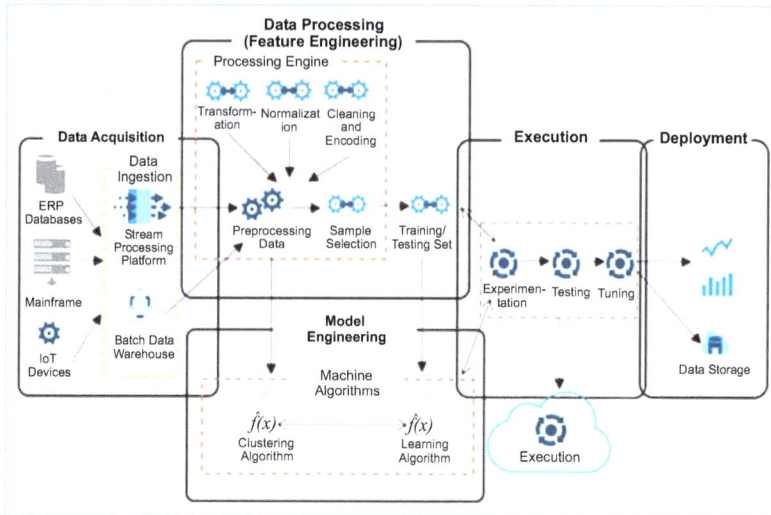

Fig. (1). Sustainable Security for the IoT Using Artificial Intelligence Architectures.

Artificial Intelligence

The ability of computers and other devices to carry out tasks that would ordinarily need human intelligence is known as AI, such as recognizing speech, understanding natural language, and making decisions [4].

An example of AI is a virtual personal assistant, such as Apple's Siri or Amazon's Alexa. These devices use Natural Language Processing (NLP) and machine learning algorithms to understand and respond to user requests for information, music, or other services. The more a user interacts with the virtual assistant, the more it learns about the user's preferences and behaviours, allowing it to provide a more personalized experience over time.

In Fig. (2), AI is used everywhere for example in self-driving cars, which use a combination of computer vision, machine learning, and sensor technology to understand and respond to their environment. These cars can detect obstacles, make decisions about the best route to take, and adjust their speed and trajectory accordingly, all without human intervention. As Artificial Intelligence is a broad field, the code will vary depending on the specific problem or task you want to solve with AI [3]. However, here in below Fig. (3) is a simple example in Python that uses a machine learning algorithm called a decision tree for classification:

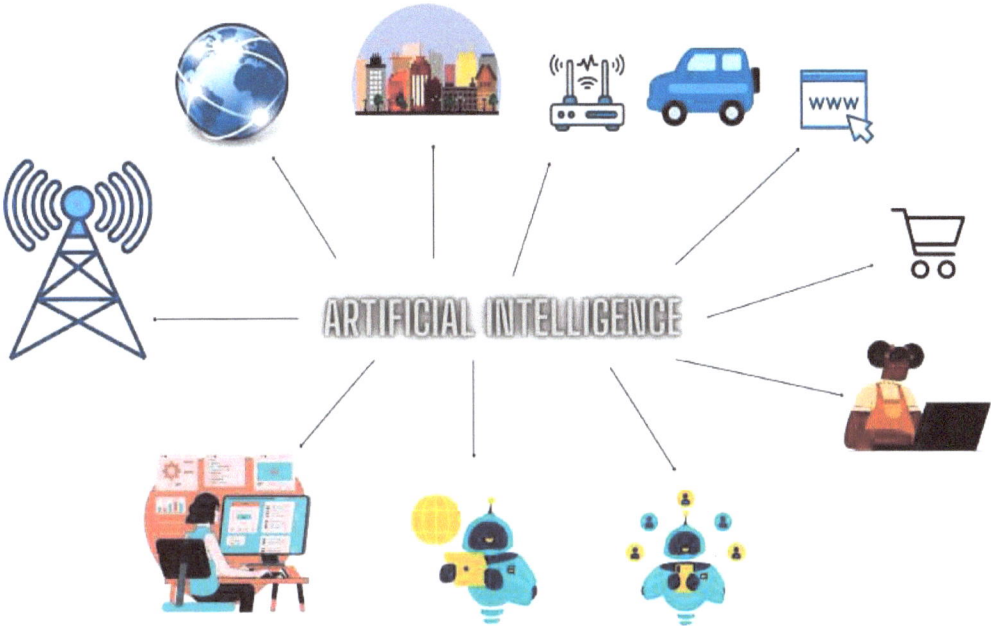

Fig. (2). Artificial Intelligence.

```
main.py
1    import pandas as pd
2    from sklearn.         import DecisionTreeClassifier
3    from sklearn.             import train_test_split
4    from sklearn.             import accuracy_score
5
6    # Load the data into a pandas dataframe
7    data = pd.      ("data.csv")
8
9    # Split the data into training and testing sets
10   train_data, test_data, train_labels, test_labels = train_test_split(data.     ("label", axis=1), data["label"], test_size=    )
11
12   # Train the decision tree classifier
13   clf = DecisionTreeClassifier()
14   clf.   (train_data, train_labels)
15
16   # Make predictions on the testing set
17   predictions = clf.      (test_data)
18
19   # Evaluate the accuracy of the classifier
20   accuracy = accuracy_score(test_labels, predictions)
21   print("Accuracy:", accuracy)
22
```

Fig. (3). Decision Tree Classification.

Significance of Artificial Intelligence

AI is a rapidly growing field that has the potential to transform many aspects of our lives. Here are some of the key ways in which AI is significant:

i. Automation of repetitive tasks: AI can automate many repetitive and routine tasks, freeing up time for humans to focus on more creative and strategic work. This can lead to increased productivity and efficiency.

ii. Improved decision-making: AI can analyze vast amounts of data and identify patterns that might be difficult for humans to see. This can help humans make better decisions by providing them with more complete and accurate information.

iii. Enhanced customer experience: AI can be used to provide personalized recommendations and improve customer service. For example, AI-powered chatbots can answer customer questions 24/7 and help resolve issues in real time.

iv. Healthcare advancements: AI can be used to analyze medical images, such as X-rays and MRIs, to help diagnose diseases more accurately and quickly. AI can also help researchers identify new treatments and cures by analyzing large amounts of medical data.

Advancements in scientific research: AI can help scientists process and analyze vast amounts of data, allowing them to make new discoveries and solve complex problems more quickly.

Improved safety: AI can be used in applications such as self-driving cars and drone navigation, to improve safety and reduce the risk of accidents.

Job creation: The development and deployment of AI systems are creating new jobs in fields such as data science, machine learning, and software engineering.

Benefits of AI

- Increased Efficiency: AI systems can perform tasks faster and more accurately than humans, leading to increased efficiency and productivity [3, 5, 6].
- Improved Decision Making: AI can analyze vast amounts of data and identify patterns, trends, and relationships, which can lead to more informed decision-making.
- Automation of Repetitive Tasks: AI can automate routine, repetitive tasks, freeing up human workers to focus on more creative and strategic activities.
- Personalization: AI can be used to personalize experiences, such as recommendations for products or services, based on individual preferences and behaviors.
- Improved Healthcare: AI can aid in the early detection of diseases and in the development of new treatments and therapies.
- Better Customer Service: AI-powered chatbots can provide 24/7 customer support, handling simple queries and freeing up human agents to deal with more complex issues.
- Enhanced Security: AI can be used for security purposes, such as identifying and stopping cyber threats and fraud.
- Environment and Resource Management: AI can be used to optimize resource usage and reduce waste, leading to a more sustainable and eco-friendly future.

Improving Sustainability in AI

Improving sustainability in AI involves considering the environmental impact of AI development, deployment, and usage. Here are some ways to improve sustainability in AI:

- Using energy-efficient hardware: AI models require a lot of computational power, and using energy-efficient hardware can reduce the amount of energy needed to train and run AI models. This can include using low-power processors, efficient cooling systems, and renewable energy sources.
- Reduce data center carbon footprint: Data centers that host AI models and data can consume large amounts of energy. Techniques like server consolidation, using energy-efficient cooling systems, and optimizing the utilization of resources can help reduce the carbon footprint of data centers.
- Develop sustainable AI models: Developing AI models that are optimized for energy efficiency can help reduce the carbon footprint of AI. This can include optimizing algorithms to require less computation, reducing the size of models, and using transfer learning to reduce the amount of data needed to train models.
- Promote reuse and sharing of models: Reusing and sharing AI models can help reduce the need to train new models from scratch, which can be resource intensive. Open-source AI models and libraries can encourage reuse and sharing.
- Encourage responsible AI usage: Encouraging responsible AI usage can also promote sustainability. This can include designing AI systems that are transparent, explainable, and ethical, and using AI to solve environmental problems, such as climate change.
- Develop eco-friendly AI applications: Creating AI applications that support sustainable practices can contribute to environmental conservation. Examples can include smart buildings, smart transportation systems, and waste management systems.
- Foster a sustainable AI community: Building a community that prioritizes sustainability can lead to better practices and knowledge sharing. This can involve engaging in discussions on sustainability, hosting events that promote sustainable practices, and collaborating with organizations that prioritize sustainability.

In summary, AI has the potential to bring about major advancements in many areas, from automation and decision-making to healthcare and scientific research. While there are also potential risks associated with AI, such as job displacement and privacy concerns, the overall impact of AI is likely to be positive and transformative.

IOT AND ITS SIGNIFICANCE

IoT refers to the network of physical devices, vehicles, home appliances, and other items that are embedded with electronics, software, sensors, and connectivity, which enables these objects to collect and exchange data. These connected devices are able to communicate with each other and with the internet, allowing for the seamless exchange of information and the automation of various tasks.

The significance of IoT lies in the ability to gather and analyze vast amounts of data from a large number of connected devices, which can provide insights and drive improvements in various industries. IoT has the potential to transform the way we live and work by creating smart homes, cities, and industries. For example, in a smart home, IoT devices can be used to control lighting, temperature, and security systems remotely, making our homes more comfortable and convenient. In healthcare, IoT devices can be used to monitor patients' vital signs remotely, improving the quality of care and reducing hospital readmissions. In the industrial sector, IoT can be used to improve supply chain management, reduce downtime, and optimize production processes.

IoT also has the potential to create new business models and revenue streams by providing companies with valuable data and insights. By analyzing the data generated by IoT devices, companies can gain a better understanding of their customers, operations, and market trends, which can lead to improved decision-making and increased efficiency.

Overall, IoT has the potential to significantly impact our daily lives and the way we do business, and its significance will only continue to grow as more devices become connected and technology advances.

ROLE OF AI IN IOT

The main role of IoT (Internet of Things) in AI (Artificial Intelligence) is to provide a vast amount of data for AI algorithms to process and analyse. This data can be used to improve the accuracy and performance of AI systems, and also to enhance the capabilities of IoT devices through the integration of AI algorithms.

IoT devices can generate data on various aspects of the physical world, including temperature, humidity, pressure, and other environmental conditions. This data can be analysed by AI algorithms to identify patterns, make predictions, and make decisions [5].

Additionally, IoT devices can be equipped with AI algorithms to perform tasks on the edge, reducing the need for data to be transmitted to the cloud for processing and analysis. This can improve the speed and efficiency of AI systems, and also diminish the amount of data that needs to be transferred, which can be particularly important in low-bandwidth or low-power environments [6].

Artificial Intelligence (AI) has the potential to revolutionize many aspects of society, including healthcare, transportation, education, and more. It allows machines to perform tasks that would normally require human intelligence, such as image and speech recognition, problem-solving, and decision-making. This can lead to increased efficiency, accuracy, and automation of certain processes, as well as new and innovative applications. However, there are also ethical and societal concerns related to AI, such as job displacement, privacy, and the potential misuse of AI systems. Overall, AI has the potential to greatly impact our lives, and it is important for society to carefully consider both its benefits and potential drawbacks as it continues to develop and advance [4].

Overall, IoT plays a critical role in AI by providing data for AI algorithms to process and analyse, and also by enabling the integration of AI capabilities into IoT devices.

AI has a significant impact on IoT in several ways:

- Data Collection: IoT devices generate vast amounts of data, which can be used as input for AI algorithms to improve their performance and accuracy.
- Intelligent Edge Devices: IoT devices can be equipped with AI algorithms to make them intelligent and capable of making decisions on the edge, reducing the need for data to be transmitted to the cloud for processing [3].
- Smart Infrastructure: IoT devices can be integrated with AI algorithms to create a smart infrastructure that can self-monitor, self-diagnose and self-heal, increasing efficiency and reliability.
- Predictive Maintenance: IoT devices can collect data on various parameters, which can be analysed by AI algorithms to predict when maintenance is required, reducing downtime and increasing efficiency.
- Enhanced Customer Experience: IoT devices can collect data on customer behaviour and preferences, which can be analysed by AI algorithms to personalize and improve the customer experience [1].
- Better decision-making: AI algorithms can analyse data from IoT devices in real-time and provide insights that can be used to make informed decisions, such as predicting maintenance needs, optimizing energy usage, and improving safety.
- Improved automation: IoT devices can be integrated with AI algorithms to

automate various tasks, such as controlling smart home devices, monitoring and managing industrial processes, and reducing waste in agriculture [7].

- Better services: AI-powered IoT systems can provide better services to users, such as personalized healthcare and smarter traffic management, by analysing and processing data from multiple sources.
- Enhanced security: IoT devices can collect and transmit sensitive data, which can be protected by AI algorithms that detect and prevent cyber-attacks and data breaches [1].
- Increased efficiency: IoT devices can collect and transmit large amounts of data, which can be analysed and processed by AI algorithms to improve decision-making and increase efficiency in various industries, such as healthcare, transportation, and manufacturing. The integration of IoT and AI has the potential to revolutionize various industries and improve our quality of life.

Overall, IoT and AI complement each other, and the integration of these technologies has the potential to revolutionize various industries and improve our lives in numerous ways.

SUSTAINABLE SECURITY FOR THE IOT USING AI

AI can play a critical role in ensuring sustainable security for the IoT [8]. AI-based security solutions can detect and prevent malicious attacks in real time, mitigate the impact of security incidents, and automate security management processes [1]. These solutions can be designed using various AI architectures, such as machine learning, deep learning, and neural networks. The use of these technologies can provide improved accuracy and speed in detecting security threats, reducing the likelihood of successful attacks, and improving overall security posture. However, it important to note that AI-based security solutions also have limitations and potential risks, including the need for robust data privacy protection and ethical considerations.

A General Pseudo-code for a Sustainable Security Solution for IoT using AI

INPUT: IoT device data, security threat information [4].

Process

1. Pre-process the IoT device data to format it for analysis.

2. Train the AI model using the pre-processed data and security threat information.

3. Implement the AI model on the IoT device or network.

4. Continuously monitor the IoT device or network data.

5. Use the AI model to analyse the data for potential security threats.

6. If a security threat is detected, take appropriate action

(Such as isolating the affected device, alerting security personnel, *etc.*)

7. Continuously update and retrain the AI model with new data and threat information.

OUTPUT: Secured IoT device or network.

A simple example of how to secure an IoT device using a password-based authentication system is shown in below Fig. (**4**):

```
source code
1   # Example code for password-based authentication for IoT device
2
3   # Store the correct password in a variable
4   correct_password = "secret_password"
5
6   # Prompt the user to enter the password
7   entered_password = input("Enter password: ")
8
9   # Compare the entered password to the correct password
10  if entered_password == correct_password:
11      # Grant access to the IoT device
12      print("Access granted")
13  else:
14      # Deny access to the IoT device
15      print("Access denied")
16  |
```

Fig. (4). IoT Device Authentication.

Simple example of code for securing an IoT device using the Transport Layer Security (TLS) protocol is shown in Fig. (**5**):

```
main.py
1   # Example code for securing an IoT device using TLS
2
3   import ssl
4   import socket
5
6   # Create a socket for the IoT device
7   s = socket.      (socket.     , socket.              )
8
9   # Wrap the socket with a TLS context
10  tls_context = ssl.                          (ssl.               )
11  tls_socket = tls_context.              (s, server_side=True)
12
13  # Bind the socket to a specific address and port
14  tls_socket.      (('localhost', 12345))
15
16  # Listen for incoming connections
17  tls_socket.      (1)
18
19  # Accept an incoming connection
20  conn, addr = tls_socket.        ()
21
22  # Communicate with the connected device securely using the TLS-wrapped socket
23  data = conn.      (1024)
24  conn.    (data)
25
26  # Close the connection
27  conn.    ()
28  |
```

Fig. (5). IoT device Security using TLS.

This example demonstrates the use of the TLS protocol to secure communication between an IoT device and another device. The SSL module provides support for Secure Socket-Layer (SSL) and Transport Layer Security (TLS) protocols. In this example, a socket is created, wrapped with a TLS context, and used to communicate with a connected device. The use of TLS ensures that the communication between the devices is encrypted and protected against network attacks.

DDoS (Distributed Denial of Service) Attacks

DDoS (Distributed Denial of Service) attacks are a type of cyber-attack that aims to disrupt the normal functioning of a website, network, or system by overwhelming it with a large amount of traffic. DDoS attacks can be categorized based on the following hierarchy [5]:

Types of Attack

a. Volume-based attacks: Flood the target with a high volume of traffic, overwhelming its network and causing it to become unavailable.
b. Protocol attacks: Exploit vulnerabilities in the communication protocols used by a system or network.

c. Application layer attacks: Attack specific applications or services running on a system or network.

Methods of Attack

a. Flooding: Overwhelm a target with a high volume of traffic.
b. Amplification: Use a botnet to amplify the attack traffic by many times.
c. Reflection: Reflect the attack traffic from another system or network to hide the attacker's identity.
d. Spoofing: Modify the source IP address of the attack traffic to hide the attacker's identity.

Source of Attack

a. Botnets: A network of infected devices used to launch DDoS attacks.
b. Server farms: Large, centralized servers used to launch DDoS attacks.
c. Individual devices: Single devices used to launch DDoS attacks.

ENERGY MANAGEMENT USING AI

Energy management is the process of monitoring, controlling, and conserving energy in a building or facility. AI has been increasingly used in energy management systems to optimize energy consumption, reduce costs, and minimize carbon emissions.

Here are some ways AI can be used in energy management:

- Predictive Maintenance: AI can be used to predict when equipment is likely to fail, enabling maintenance to be scheduled before a breakdown occurs. This can help prevent downtime and save energy by ensuring that equipment is running efficiently.
- Energy Optimization: AI can be used to optimize energy consumption by analyzing data from sensors and other sources to identify patterns and optimize energy usage accordingly. For example, AI can optimize lighting systems based on occupancy and daylight levels, or adjust HVAC systems to maintain a comfortable temperature while minimizing energy consumption.
- Demand Response: AI can be used to predict changes in energy demand and automatically adjust energy usage to match the available supply. This can help reduce peak demand and avoid the need for expensive standby generators.
- Renewable Energy Integration: AI can be used to optimize the integration of renewable energy sources into the power grid. By analyzing weather patterns and energy consumption, AI can predict when renewable energy sources will be

available and adjust energy usage accordingly.

• Energy Efficiency Analysis: AI can analyze energy usage data to identify areas of inefficiency and recommend changes to improve energy efficiency. For example, AI can analyze energy usage patterns in a building to identify areas of high energy consumption and recommend changes to improve efficiency.

In summary, AI can be a powerful tool for energy management, helping to optimize energy consumption, reduce costs, and minimize carbon emissions. By using AI to analyze energy data, identify inefficiencies, and optimize energy usage, organizations can achieve significant energy savings and reduce their environmental impact.

THE IMPACT OF THE IOT ON SUSTAINABLE WATER MANAGEMENT

IoT is having a significant impact on water use, by improving the efficiency and sustainability of water management.

When and Where to Irrigate with the Right Amount of Water Using IoT

Irrigation with the right amount of water can be achieved through the use of IoT technology. IoT-powered irrigation systems use sensors and algorithms to monitor soil moisture levels and weather conditions, and then adjust the amount and timing of water applied to crops accordingly [9].

The exact timing and location of irrigation depend on a variety of factors, including crop type, soil type, local weather patterns, and desired yield. However, IoT-powered irrigation systems can make these decisions more efficiently and accurately than traditional methods.

For example, sensors can be placed in the soil to measure moisture levels, and then send this data to a central system for analysis. Weather information can be gathered from online weather services, and then combined with soil moisture data to determine the optimal amount of water to apply [9].

Once the decision has been made, the IoT system can then activate the irrigation system, either through manual control or by automatically triggering the system based on set parameters. The system can also be programmed to adjust the amount of water applied based on real-time conditions, ensuring that the crops receive the right amount of water at the right time.

In summary, using IoT technology to control irrigation can help farmers apply the right amount of water to their crops at the right time, leading to improved yields, reduced water usage, and lower costs.

Here are some of the ways that IoT is changing the landscape of water use:

Smart Irrigation

IoT sensors and devices can be used to determine the ideal amount of water needed for irrigation that can be calculated using IoT sensors and devices that monitor soil moisture levels, weather patterns, and plant health. This helps to reduce water waste and improve crop yields [10].

Smart irrigation with AI involves the use of artificial intelligence algorithms to optimize irrigation systems, improve water use efficiency, and reduce waste.

Here's how it works:

- *Data collection*: IoT sensors and devices are used to gather data on soil moisture levels, weather conditions, and plant health. This data is then fed into AI algorithms for analysis.
- *Predictive modelling*: AI algorithms analyse the data to create predictive models of water requirements for different crops, based on factors such as soil type, weather conditions, and plant growth stage.
- *Irrigation scheduling*: Based on the predictive models, the AI algorithms determine the optimal times and amount of water needed for irrigation. This information is then used to schedule irrigation automatically.
- *Real-time monitoring*: IoT sensors and devices are used to monitor the soil moisture levels and weather conditions in real-time, providing ongoing updates to the AI algorithms to refine the predictive models.
- *Adjustment of irrigation*: If the soil moisture levels or weather conditions change, the AI algorithms adjust the irrigation schedule, accordingly, ensuring that only the necessary amount of water is used.

Smart irrigation with AI is a cost-effective and efficient way to manage water resources and improve crop yields. By using real-time data and predictive models, it helps farmers make informed decisions about irrigation, reducing water waste and improving water use efficiency.

Leak Detection

IoT sensors and devices can be used to detect leaks in pipes and other water systems. This helps to prevent water waste and reduces the cost of repairs. Leak detection in IoT refers to the use of Internet of Things (IoT) devices and technologies to detect and alert about leaks in various systems, such as plumbing, gas, or HVAC systems. The goal is to quickly identify and address the leak before it causes significant damage or waste [11].

IoT-based leak detection systems typically consist of a network of smart sensors that are placed in various locations throughout a system. These sensors can detect changes in pressure, temperature, or humidity that may indicate a leak. When a leak is detected, the sensors can send a real-time alert to a central control system or to the homeowner, allowing for a quick and efficient response.

Some examples of IoT-based leak detection systems include smart water sensors for plumbing systems, gas leak detectors for HVAC systems, and oil and fuel leak detectors for industrial and commercial applications.

The benefits of using IoT for leak detection include improved efficiency, cost savings, and increased safety. With real-time monitoring and alerts, leaks can be detected and addressed quickly, reducing the amount of water, gas, or other resources that are wasted. Additionally, early leak detection can help prevent significant damage to property and reduce the risk of hazardous situations, such as gas leaks.

- **Remote Monitoring**: IoT devices can be used to remotely monitor water usage, levels in reservoirs and wells, and water quality. This information can be used to make informed decisions about water management and ensure that water resources are being used sustainably.
- **Predictive Maintenance**: IoT devices can be used to collect data on water usage patterns, system performance, and equipment health. This information can be analyzed to predict when maintenance is required, reducing the cost of repairs and improving the efficiency of water management.
- **Water Allocation**: IoT sensors and devices can be used to monitor water levels in rivers, lakes, and aquifers to determine the availability of water resources. This information can be used to allocate water resources effectively, ensuring that they are used sustainably and efficiently.

Overall, the IoT is having a significant impact on water use by providing real-time data and insights that enable more efficient, sustainable, and cost-effective water management practices.

CLIMATE CONTROL SYSTEMS WITH AI

In the context of Artificial Intelligence, there are several tools that can be used to control climate:

- **Machine learning algorithms**: These algorithms can be trained on large datasets of climate data to make predictions and control climate-related systems.

For example, decision tree algorithms can be used to predict future climate patterns, and neural networks can be used to control HVAC systems.

- **Climate simulation models**: These models can be used to simulate the effects of different actions on the climate. For example, the Community Earth System Model (CESM) can simulate the interactions between the atmosphere, oceans, land surface, and sea ice to better understand the effects of climate change. Climate simulation models are computer models that simulate the behaviour of the Earth's climate system. These models use mathematical equations to describe the physical processes that control the climate, such as the transfer of heat and mass between the atmosphere, oceans, and land surface.

In the context of Artificial Intelligence, climate simulation models can be used to make predictions about future climate conditions, and to test the effects of different scenarios, such as changes in greenhouse gas emissions or land use.

There are several different types of climate simulation models, including:

General Circulation Models (GCMs)

These are the most comprehensive climate models, and are used to simulate global climate. GCMs use numerical methods to solve the equations that describe the physical processes that control the climate.

General Circulation Models (GCMs) are complex computer models used to simulate the Earth's climate. They are widely used by climate scientists to make predictions about future climate change and to understand the factors that drive global climate patterns [11].

Here is a simple example of a code in Python that can be used to simulate a GCM as shown in Fig. (**6**):

```
source code
 1
 2   #General Circulation Models (GCMs)
 3   import numpy as np
 4   import matplotlib.pyplot as plt
 5
 6   # Define parameters for the simulation
 7   timesteps = 1000
 8   latitude_steps = 180
 9   longitude_steps = 360
10
11   # Initialize the temperature field
12   temperature = np.zeros((timesteps, latitude_steps, longitude_steps))
13
14   # Set initial conditions
15   temperature[0, :, :] = np.random.    (latitude_steps, longitude_steps)
16
17   # Run the simulation
18   for t in range(1, timesteps):
19       for lat in range(latitude_steps):
20           for lon in range(longitude_steps):
21               # Update temperature based on previous state and any external forcing
22               temperature[t, lat, lon] = temperature[t-1, lat, lon] + np.random.    ()
23
24   # Plot the final temperature field
25   plt.imshow(temperature[-1, :, :], cmap='hot')
26   plt.colorbar()
27   plt.show()
28
```

Fig. (6). GCM Simulation.

Earth System Models (ESMs)

These models are similar to GCMs, but also include simulations of the Earth's biogeochemical cycles, such as the carbon and nitrogen cycles. ESMs are used to study the interactions between the climate and the biosphere.

- **Regional Climate Models (RCMs):** These models simulate the climate at a regional scale and are used to study the impacts of climate change on specific regions, such as cities or countries.
- **Climate-Chemistry Models:** These models simulate the interactions between climate and atmospheric chemistry and are used to study the effects of climate change on air quality and the ozone layer. The exact code for a climate simulation model will depend on the specific model and the programming language used. Climate simulation models can be written in a variety of programming languages, including FORTRAN, C, and Python. They often use large amounts of computing resources and can take several days or even weeks to run a single simulation.
- **Climate data analytics tools**: These tools can be used to process and analyze large amounts of climate data. For example, tools like Apache Hadoop and Apache Spark can be used to process data from multiple sources and extract

useful insights.

- **Climate control systems:** These systems can be used to directly control the climate. For example, smart HVAC systems can be programmed to adjust temperature and humidity levels based on the climate data they receive.

These are just a few examples of the tools that can be used in AI to control climate. The exact tools used will depend on the specific application and the goals of the project.

AI-IOT USE CASES

Here are a few examples of how AI and the IoT can be used together:

Smart Home Automation

In Fig. (**7**) Smart Home Automation, Lighting, temperature, and security are a few examples of the automated and controlled feature that AI-powered IoT devices can be utilised to automate [9]. The term "smart home automation with AI" describes the automation and control of numerous parts of a home using AI and IoT technologies. This can range from lighting and temperature control to security systems and home entertainment [12].

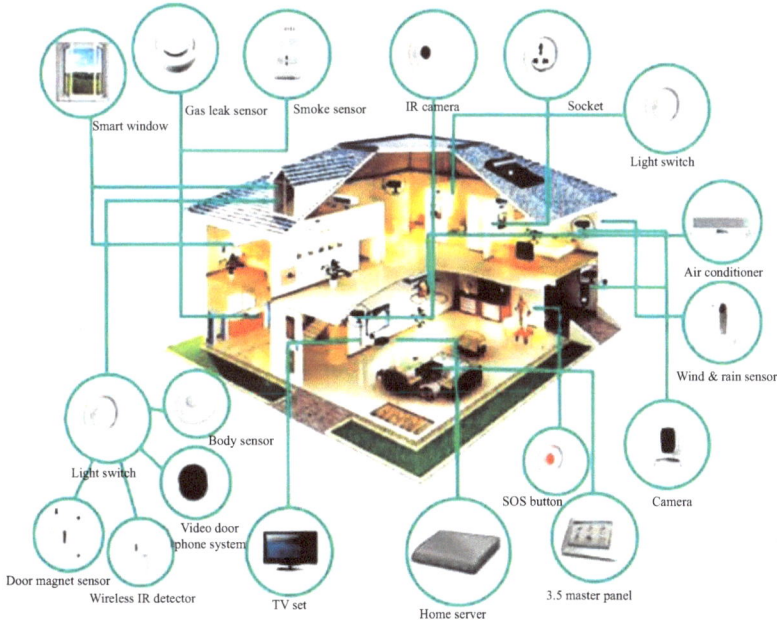

Fig. (7). Smart Home Automation.

One example of a smart home automation application with AI is a voice-controlled virtual assistant. This can be integrated into a home's existing devices and systems, allowing the homeowner to control and monitor their home using natural language commands. For instance, the homeowner can turn off the lights, change the temperature, or lock the doors using voice commands to a virtual assistant like Amazon's Alexa or Google Home.

Another example of a smart home automation application with AI is the use of smart sensors and devices that can automatically adjust, and control various systems based on the homeowner's habits and preferences. For instance, AI algorithms can learn the homeowner's preferred temperature and lighting settings, and automatically adjust these systems accordingly.

AI can also be used to enhance security in a smart home by integrating with surveillance cameras and other security systems. For example, AI algorithms can analyse footage from security cameras and detect unusual or suspicious behaviour, triggering an alert to the homeowner or security personnel.

Overall, the integration of AI into smart home automation systems can greatly improve the convenience and comfort of the homeowner, while also enhancing the security and energy efficiency of the home.

Intelligent Transportation Systems

AI and IoT can be used to improve traffic flow, reduce congestion, and increase road safety through connected vehicles and smart traffic management systems [13].

Smart and Sustainable Transportation

Smart and sustainable transportation using AI involves using advanced technologies to improve the efficiency of transportation systems while minimizing their environmental impact. Here are some ways AI can be used to promote smart and sustainable transportation.

Intelligent Traffic Management

AI can be used to optimize traffic flow, reduce congestion, and improve safety by analyzing traffic data in real time. This can be achieved through the use of smart traffic signals that adapt to changing traffic patterns, dynamic route guidance, and real-time incident management.

Intelligent Transportation Systems (ITS)

ITS involves the integration of various technologies like GPS, sensors, and cameras to provide real-time information about traffic and road conditions. AI can help in the processing and analysis of this data to provide recommendations to optimize transportation systems and enhance mobility. Intelligent Transportation Systems (ITS) with AI refers to the use of artificial intelligence to improve the efficiency and safety of transportation systems. AI can be used to gather, analyze, and interpret large amounts of data from various sources, such as sensors, cameras, and GPS devices, to provide real-time insights into transportation systems.

• One example of ITS with AI is connected vehicles, which use AI algorithms to communicate with other vehicles and infrastructure, such as traffic lights and road signs. This communication allows vehicles to optimize their speed and route, reducing congestion and improving road safety. For example, AI algorithms can analyse real-time traffic data to dynamically reroute vehicles to avoid congestion or accidents, improving travel times and reducing fuel consumption.

Autonomous Vehicles

AI-powered autonomous vehicles can reduce carbon emissions, improve safety, and optimize transportation networks. Self-driving cars, buses, and trains can reduce congestion, optimize routes and reduce fuel consumption.

Predictive Maintenance

AI can be used to predict and detect maintenance issues in transportation systems, such as road conditions, bridges, and public transportation. By identifying problems before they occur, transportation providers can prevent disruptions, reduce maintenance costs, and minimize environmental impact.

Ride-sharing and Carpooling

AI can help optimize ride-sharing and carpooling by matching commuters based on their location, destination, and route preferences. This can reduce the number of vehicles on the road and lower carbon emissions.

Smart Parking

AI can help optimize parking spaces, reduce the time it takes to find a parking spot, and reduce carbon emissions. Smart parking systems can help in locating available parking spots, reducing the time it takes to find a parking spot and reducing fuel consumption.

By implementing these AI-based solutions, transportation systems can become more efficient, sustainable, and environmentally friendly. Another example of IoT with AI is smart traffic management systems, which use AI algorithms to optimize traffic, flow in real time. For instance, AI algorithms can analyse traffic data to adjust traffic signal timings, prioritize emergency vehicles, and reduce congestion at intersections.

AI can also be used to enhance public transportation systems by optimizing schedules, routes, and resources. For example, AI algorithms can analyse passenger demand and real-time traffic data to optimize bus or train schedules, reducing waiting times and improving reliability.

Overall, the integration of AI into ITS can greatly improve the efficiency, safety, and sustainability of transportation systems, leading to a more connected and intelligent transportation network.

Predictive Maintenance

IoT sensors can collect data on the performance and usage of industrial equipment, which can then be analysed using AI algorithms to predict when maintenance will be needed [14].

Agricultural Monitoring

IoT sensors can be used to collect data on soil moisture, temperature, and other factors, which can then be analysed using AI algorithms to optimize crop growth and yields [15].

Healthcare Monitoring

IoT devices such as wearable fitness trackers and smart medical devices can collect health data, which can then be analysed using AI algorithms to provide personalized health insights and recommendations [16, 17]. IoT (Internet of Things) devices and technologies can be used in healthcare for remote monitoring of patients and to track and manage various health parameters such as heart rate, blood pressure, and blood glucose levels. IoT devices can also be used in wearables, such as smartwatches and fitness trackers, to track physical activity and sleep patterns. The collected data can then be sent to healthcare providers for analysis, enabling them to provide better care and improve patient outcomes. Additionally, IoT can also be used in smart homes to monitor elderly patients and people with chronic conditions, allowing them to live independently while ensuring their safety and well-being.

Energy Management

AI and IoT can be used to optimize energy usage in buildings, reducing waste and improving sustainability through smart energy management systems.

FUTURE OF IOT IN SUPPORT OF SUSTAINABILITY

The future of IoT in support of sustainability holds tremendous potential for reducing resource consumption and waste, improving energy efficiency, and mitigating the negative impacts of human activity on the environment. Some specific areas where IoT is expected to play a key role in promoting sustainability include:

Smart Energy Management

IoT devices can be used to monitor and control energy usage in homes, buildings, and factories. This can include smart thermostats, lighting controls, and energy management systems that automatically adjust energy usage based on occupancy, weather, and other factors [12].

Resource Conservation

IoT sensors can be used to track and manage the usage of resources such as water, gas, and electricity. This can help identify areas where resource consumption can be reduced, and help prevent waste by detecting leaks and other issues early.

Smart Transportation

IoT can be used to improve the efficiency of transportation systems, reducing emissions, and saving fuel. This can include smart traffic management systems that optimize traffic flow, and connected vehicles that communicate with each other to reduce emissions and conserve energy.

Sustainable Agriculture

IoT can be used to improve the sustainability of agriculture by monitoring soil moisture levels, weather patterns, and crop health. This can help reduce water usage, improve crop yields, and reduce the use of harmful pesticides and fertilizers.

Overall, the future of IoT in support of sustainability is expected to be characterized by increased integration and interconnectivity, with devices and systems working together to optimize resource usage, reduce waste, and promote sustainable practices. The impact of IoT on sustainability will be significant, and it will be an essential tool for achieving a more sustainable and environmentally friendly future.

CONCLUSIONS

AI and IoT are two interrelated technologies that are transforming the way we live and work. AI enables IoT devices to analyze and interpret the vast amounts of data they collect, while IoT provides the necessary infrastructure to gather and transmit that data. When combined, AI and IoT can create smart systems for sustainable development that can make decisions, automate processes, and offer personalized experiences. This integration is expected to revolutionize various industries such as healthcare, transportation, manufacturing, *etc.*

FUTURE SCOPE

AI is vast, and its impact is likely to be far-reaching and transformative. While there are also potential risks associated with AI, such as job displacement and privacy concerns, the overall impact of AI is likely to be positive, and it is likely to shape the world in significant ways in the coming years and decades.

REFERENCES

[1]   A. Ghosh, D. Chakraborty, and A. Law, "Artificial intelligence in Internet of things", *CAAI Trans. Intell. Technol.,* vol. 3, no. 4, pp. 208-218, 2018.
[http://dx.doi.org/10.1049/trit.2018.1008]

[2]   X. Shi, X. An, Q. Zhao, H. Liu, L. Xia, X. Sun, and Y. Guo, "State-of-the-art internet of things in protected agriculture", *Sensors,* vol. 19, no. 8, p. 1833, 2019.
[http://dx.doi.org/10.3390/s19081833] [PMID: 30999637]

[3]   L.M. Gladence, V.M. Anu, R. Rathna, and E. Brumancia, "Recommender system for home automation using IoT and artificial intelligence", *J. Ambient Intell. Humaniz. Comput.,* pp. 1-9, 2020.
[http://dx.doi.org/10.1007/s12652-020-01968-2]

[4]   P.H. Winston, *Artificial intelligence.* Addison-Wesley Longman Publishing Co., Inc., 1984.

[5]   S. Mishra, and A.K. Tyagi, *The role of machine learning techniques in internet of things-based cloud applications.* SpringerLink, 2022, pp. 105-135.
[http://dx.doi.org/10.1007/978-3-030-87059-1_4]

[6]   D. Airehrour, J. Gutierrez, and S.K. Ray, "Secure routing for internet of things: A survey", *J. Netw. Comput. Appl.,* vol. 66, pp. 198-213, 2016.
[http://dx.doi.org/10.1016/j.jnca.2016.03.006]

[7]   X. Shi, X. An, Q. Zhao, H. Liu, L. Xia, X. Sun, and Y. Guo, "State-of-the-art internet of things in protected agriculture", *Sensors,* vol. 19, no. 8, p. 1833, 2019.
[http://dx.doi.org/10.3390/s19081833] [PMID: 30999637]

[8]   C. Iwendi, S.U. Rehman, A.R. Javed, S. Khan, and G. Srivastava, "Sustainable security for the internet of things using artificial intelligence architectures", *ACM Trans. Internet Technol.,* vol. 21, no. 3, pp.

1-22, 2021.
[http://dx.doi.org/10.1145/3448614]

[9]   A. Salam, and A. Salam, "Internet of things in water management and treatment. Internet of Things for Sustainable Community Development: Wireless Communications", *Sens. Syst.,* pp. 273-298, 2020.

[10]   L. García, L. Parra, J.M. Jimenez, J. Lloret, and P. Lorenz, "IoT-based smart irrigation systems: An overview on the recent trends on sensors and IoT systems for irrigation in precision agriculture", *Sensors (Basel),* vol. 20, no. 4, p. 1042, 2020.
[http://dx.doi.org/10.3390/s20041042] [PMID: 32075172]

[11]   S.L. Grotch, and M.C. MacCracken, "The use of general circulation models to predict regional climatic change", *J. Clim.,* vol. 4, no. 3, pp. 286-303, 1991.
[http://dx.doi.org/10.1175/1520-0442(1991)004<0286:TUOGCM>2.0.CO;2]

[12]   V. Mani, G. Abhilasha, and S. Lavanya, "Iot based smart energy management system", *Int. J. Appl. Eng. Res.,* vol. 12, no. 16, pp. 5455-5462, 2017.

[13]   P. Goswami, A. Mukherjee, R. Hazra, L. Yang, U. Ghosh, Y. Qi, and H. Wang, "AI based energy efficient routing protocol for intelligent transportation system", *IEEE Trans. Intell. Transp. Syst.,* vol. 23, no. 2, pp. 1670-1679, 2022.
[http://dx.doi.org/10.1109/TITS.2021.3107527]

[14]   Y. Ran, X. Zhou, P. Lin, Y. Wen, and R Deng, "A survey of predictive maintenance: Systems, purposes and approaches", *IEEE Trans. Knowl. Data Eng.,.* vol. 21, no. 9, pp. 1263–1284, Sep. 2009, doi: 10.1109/TKDE.2008.239.

[15]   J. Jung, M. Maeda, A. Chang, M. Bhandari, A. Ashapure, and J. Landivar-Bowles, "The potential of remote sensing and artificial intelligence as tools to improve the resilience of agriculture production systems", *Curr. Opin. Biotechnol.,* vol. 70, pp. 15-22, 2021.
[http://dx.doi.org/10.1016/j.copbio.2020.09.003] [PMID: 33038780]

[16]   A.V.L.N. Sujith, G.S. Sajja, V. Mahalakshmi, S. Nuhmani, and B. Prasanalakshmi, "Systematic review of smart health monitoring using deep learning and Artificial intelligence", *Neuroscience Informatics,* vol. 2, no. 3, 2022. 100028.
[http://dx.doi.org/10.1016/j.neuri.2021.100028]

[17]   F. Ali, S. El-Sappagh, S.M.R. Islam, A. Ali, M. Attique, M. Imran, and K.S. Kwak, "An intelligent healthcare monitoring framework using wearable sensors and social networking data", *Future Gener. Comput. Syst.,* vol. 114, pp. 23-43, 2021.
[http://dx.doi.org/10.1016/j.future.2020.07.047]

CHAPTER 7

Digital Twin and Its Applications

Kiran Wani[1,*], Nitin Khedekar[1], Varad Vishwarupe[1] and N. Pushyanth[2]

[1] *Department of Mechanical Engineering, Symbiosis Institute of Technology, Symbiosis International [Deemed University], Maharashtra, India*

[2] *Department of Computer Science, University of Oxford, Oxford, United Kingdom*

Abstract: Digital twin technology is an important part of the industry 4.0 revolution. Digital twins is a concept of integrating different smart technologies including integration of data and digitization. The vision of the digital twin technology is based on the philosophy that any component, assembly, system, process, product, or even environment can be replicated in terms of form, functionality and several other parameters in a digital way throughout different phases of its lifecycle. The Digital Twin concept is based on the highly growing information and communication technologies alongside conventional methods for getting better interconnection and integration amongst all the entities involved in a particular phase of the product lifecycle. The Internet of things (IOT) and artificial intelligence (AI) are crucial parts of the Industry 4.0 revolution. IOT proposes to embed electronics, sensors, network connectivity and different software platforms with products. Better integration between the physical and digital world is achieved by a strong network infrastructure that facilitates remote sensing, monitoring and even controlling of connected systems. This technology provides users with many benefits such as increased efficiency, reduced downtime, improvement in precision and accuracy along with cost saving.

This chapter includes an overview of digital twin-enabling technologies and their applications. The applications range from Artificial Intelligence, Internet of Things (IoT) to manufacturing.

Keywords: Artificial intelligence, Digital twins, Internet of things (IoT), Machine learning.

INRODUCTION

As the world is moving towards building smarter products, the technological advancements required to achieve this have taken strides in recent days. Among them, in industry, the concept of digital twin has attracted a lot of attention world-

---

[*] **Corresponding author Kiran Wani:** Department of Mechanical Engineering, Symbiosis Institute of Technology, Symbiosis International [Deemed University], Maharashtra, India; E-mail: kiranwani2010@gmail.com

wide. It provides many advantages in the field of manufacturing like production and design, remote diagnostics, condition monitoring and operation in extreme conditions and services. It affects the design, structure and operation of the product. Digital twin majorly depends on accumulating data from sensing systems and presenting the data collected in real-time along with the modification and update with its physical model. With time, evolution is happening at a rapid pace, as is technology. The next generation technologies like advanced cloud computing, smart manufacturing, big data and AI are coming to the limelight, making life easier. As per several national manufacturing development strategies put forward like Industry 4.0, manufacturing based on cyber physical system (CPS) and industrial robotics is new. In order to bring such advancements to the industry, effective methods for maintenance, operation and monitoring are required. Also, to simulate plans or build what-if scenarios for the products, facilities, and processes we wanted to change before we actually put real-world resources behind, real-world implementation can be done with the promise of digital twins (DT).

From a temporal view point, there is a growing interest in DT and its evolution as shown in Fig. (**1**). As computing technology is developing day by day, CAD, CAM and CAE models are able to simulate the real-time changes in the virtual space. This prevents the spending of valuable resources and time by visualizing the data acquired from the models. After iterations, a final outcome can be decided based on the application and we may proceed with manufacturing.

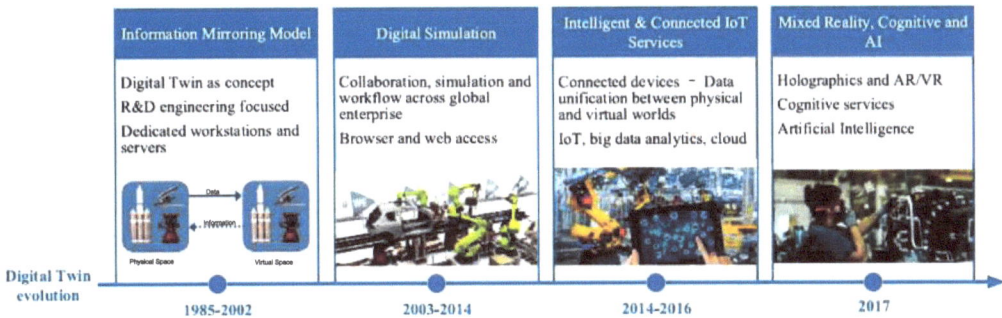

Fig. (1). Digital twin technology evolution with time [1].

The DT acts as a bridge between two spaces, that is the virtual space and physical space. By doing so, it eradicates the boundaries between them. The physical space is a real-life environment which involves several factors such as people, infrastructures and hardware with measurable properties such as mass, shape, size, *etc*. Each entity has its own positioning and follows physical laws and deals with uncertainty. The factors have their own physical functions and with proper organization, the tasks can be completed by considering the constraints on resources like time, cost quality, *etc.*

Augmented Reality (AR) and Virtual Reality (VR) are some of the technologies that can benefit from the implementation of a Digital Twin, due to the fact that it provides a virtual and realistic view of the environment in which the historical and real-time data flow is integrated with the human presence. However, considering the large amount of data and information in real-time that come from the Digital Twin model, it is difficult to provide users and operators with this information in an easy and intuitive way. In particular, AR does not replace the physical world but allows the user to see the physical world with overlapping virtual objects. Moreover, it gives users the opportunity to interact with the physical world to perform specific tasks or be alerted to possible dangers. The inclusion of these enabling technologies within Industry 4.0 implies their importance for modern factories. In general, an architecture that integrates the Digital Twin and AR/VR is composed of the following three main blocks:

A. Calibration: In order to obtain a clear and intuitive data visualization using AR devices, all the processing of historical data is as important as the data. In order to better manage the AR device, the 3D or 2D models must be perfectly aligned with the physical part. This process is called calibration.
B. Control process: The control process is a very important aspect for AR systems as it allows the user to interact with both the physical and the virtual part of the Digital Twin. After viewing the data in the increased process, users can use this information to support decision-making and directly control the physical part through the AR device.
C. Augmented process: The augmented process, through the AR devices, must provide users with an intuitive and clear AR view of the information coming from the Digital Twin. In practice, the AR device receives data from the virtual part, and after the calibration phase, it correctly presents this to the user.

Making use of the current technology, some challenges arise in using AR in the manufacturing sector. They can be summarized in four types:

1. Real-time data: There is a huge amount of real-time data exchanged between the manufacturing process, cloud and VR devices, and these have to be managed in order to support the users and operators in the correct way.
2. 3D and 2D modelling: Recognizing, tracking and following the target object(s) are extremely important for the quality of AR utilization.

3. Reliability: The manufacturing environment is dangerous, noisy and dirty, so the AR device has to be reliable and robust enough to carry out the tasks.
4. User cooperation: The manufacturing task can be done with the cooperation of multiple users and operators at the same time, so the VR infrastructure must be flexible enough to permit the data exchange between multiple devices.

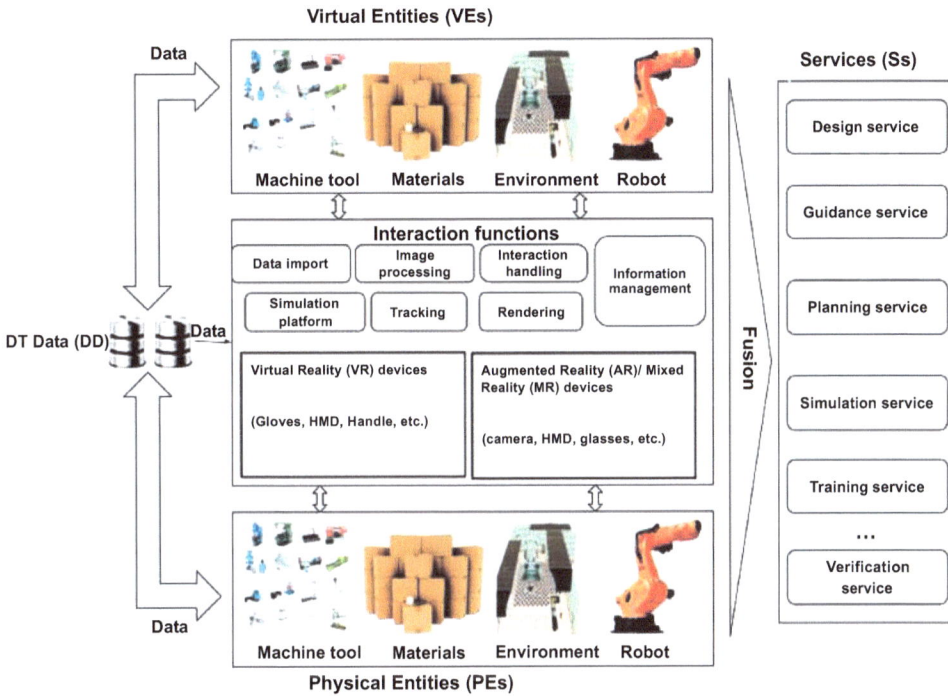

Fig. (2). Application framework of VR and AR in DT [2].

Based on the existing and potential applications of VR and AR in the DT, a framework that applies these technologies to the DT is proposed, as shown in Fig. (**2**). In the DT, the physical entities (PEs), virtual entities (VEs), DT data (DD), and services (Ss) are connected with each other. The PEs (*e.g.*, physical machine tool, robot, and materials) and VEs (*e.g.*, virtual machine tool, robot, and materials) are kept synchronous and interactive through advanced sensory devices. The DD can store and fuse data from both the PEs and VEs to provide valuable information for services. Based on this, the introduction of VR and AR can further enhance the interaction and fusion between the physical and virtual spaces, thus feeding users with higher quality services in the design, planning, guidance, and training. Due to the different characteristics of VR and AR, their roles in the framework are also different. With AR, gestures, operations, and positions of the PEs can be captured using devices such as data gloves, cameras, and RFIDs. Through image processing, tracking, and information rendering, virtual elements including virtual models from the VEs and insights from the DD can be superimposed on top of the corresponding PEs. The combination of PEs and virtual elements can be presented to the users *via* display devices, such as HMDs, iPads, and projectors. Meanwhile, haptic feedback can also be obtained through data gloves. In this way, a mixed environment where the PEs, VEs, and DD are tightly coupled with each other can be built to enhance the users' perception and understanding of the physical activities involved in the design, operation, and maintenance. Accordingly, corresponding services can be improved using an augmented display that feeds the users with precise virtual models and information as well as a familiar physical working environment synchronously.

DIGITAL TWINS

With the revolutionary industry 4.0 transformation wave, product design, development & product lifecycle management are changing their definitions and scopes with the inclusion of smart technologies driven by data and digitization. The vision of the digital twin technology is based on the philosophy that any component, assembly, system, process, product or even environment can be replicated in terms of form, functionality and several other parameters in a digital way throughout different phases of its lifecycle [1]. Although there is no universally accepted single definition of what a digital twin is, some researchers have tried to interpret it in various use cases ranging from multiple conceptualization cases in research and development to execution-based cases, such as smart manufacturing in the industry [3].

The Digital Twin concept is based on the highly growing information and communication technologies alongside conventional methods for having better interconnection and integration amongst all the entities involved in a particular phase of the product lifecycle. The Internet of things (IOT) and artificial intelligence (AI) are crucial parts of the Industry 4.0 revolution. IOT proposes to embed electronics, sensors, network connectivity and different software platforms with the product (product here refers to the considered entity). A more direct integration between the physical and digital world is achieved by a strong network infrastructure that facilitates remote sensing, monitoring and even controlling of connected systems [4]. This technology provides users with many business benefits such as increased efficiency, lesser downtimes, increase in precision and accuracy as well as savings in cost related to products and services [5]. All these benefits will be explained in detail later in this chapter.

The core functionality of the digital twin is the synchronization of the real-world system with a virtual replica by means of real-time monitoring/analysis of system parameters through information exchange using sensors and networking infrastructure. Communication generally works in a two-way manner [6]. Live continual inputs from real-life systems are monitored using physical sensors. The inputs are then fed to the digital replica in which they are analyzed and processed. The dynamics of the system are also accounted for in digital twin due to real-time connection and processing abilities. Based on processing, results from digital replicas are then communicated to the real-life system. Based on the results, the decision-making is done either manually or by means of automated logic built into digital twin itself. In this way, the process completes the loop. The Internet of Things (I.O.T) also includes features like cloud-based connectivity and storage for the continual working of this system in a closed loop as well as easy storage and retrieval of data at any point of time. In simpler terms, the digital twin can also be interpreted as a virtual simulation of real-world entities in real time with all dynamic considerations. Hence as explained earlier, this technology forms a prime part of Industry 4.0.

The first prime use case of the digital twin technology usage in research was by NASA during their "Apollo" program. The purpose of this DT was to mimic the life of a space vehicle by using different interconnected subsystem models in a series which would virtually represent different aspects and different subsystems of the actual vehicle in real life [7]. The model used sensor data as well as legacy data for better monitoring and processing for simulation. Since then, researchers in the aerospace sector started to adopt this technological philosophy in their research works.

After this, digital twin technology has been adapted and used in multiple fields of work. Depending on the area of work, the usage of digital twin was different. Many different industries are adopting this technology for their respective use cases due to a number of advantages that will be explained in detail subsequently [8].

During the initial phases, after the aerospace research and development sector, the DT technology was widely implemented for machine health monitoring and for preventive maintenance scheduling and planning. *E.g.*, In case of scheduled preventive maintenance of flights including crucial things such as engine maintenance, if the service interval between two successive maintenance is too short, this will result in safety hazards and potential accident risks with high severity. On the other hand, if service intervals are too short, this may result in an unnecessary increase in system downtime, huge maintenance costs as well as enormous loss due to non-operation of the flight. Both these things are unfavourable. Hence, for correct prediction of service scheduling call for optimized operation, different engine parameters like engine temperature, pressure, *etc.* can be monitored in real time using physical sensors and this data can then be fed into the digital twin which can process the same in real time to monitor machine health and give early alarms for potential failures based on legacy data fed to it in the background. In this way, DT can have huge benefits for crucial and costly operations of flights [9].

The other major usage of digital twin technology was observed to be for lifecycle monitoring of a physical entity and its response/performance predictions throughout lifecycle considering different dynamic effects of environmental parameters. Also, virtual simulation in real time assists in assessing the reliability of the physical entity throughout its lifecycle [10].

The use of digital replica in early phases of design and commissioning can also help user to identify potential issues during these phases. This yields in huge time and cost savings. Many cases consider digital twin as a simulation of system/process/service itself.

In today's date, DT technology is finding a place in design, simulation, testing and lifecycle management of many engineering products and processes. Some dominant examples may include exhaustive digital twin of production plant incorporated by Maserati, a renowned automobile manufacturer. The digital twin included real time monitoring and analysis of all the operations on the assembly line and aided in better decision making for planning and scheduling of different manufacturing operations and transactions. The result of implementing this technology was higher plant output with better quality management [11]. In other cases, a heavy construction equipment manufacturing company used digital twin technology to have a simulation of the gear train of their vehicles under operational loads to predict failure of the components during the actual usage. This can help the company to make decisions on the design, quality, and manufacturing as well as planning strategies for maintenance and warranty claim handling.

F1 and other competitive racing teams have also used DT technology in vehicle development for testing various sub-systems such as steering, suspension, powertrain based on their behaviours in real time on track. Physical sensors attached to these systems send data to the digital twin continually and based on this data, these systems can be analysed from different perspectives and optimized (tuned) for the track. DT technology saved a lot of time and costs involved in physical prototyping and testing iterations involved in development. DT technology is also finding its place in medical applications. Digital twins of prosthetic counterparts of the human body can be simulated first in the design phase based on physical world data and then designed to ensure correct functionality and reliability [12].

Smart town planning and power generation and conservation fields are also making use of DT technology for scheduling and management of power generation operations for optimum usage and maximum yield efficiency.

Hence, from the above examples, it is clear that digital technology has a wide range of usage areas.

Fig. (**3**) gives schematic representation of digital twin application cases along with their physical counterparts [13].

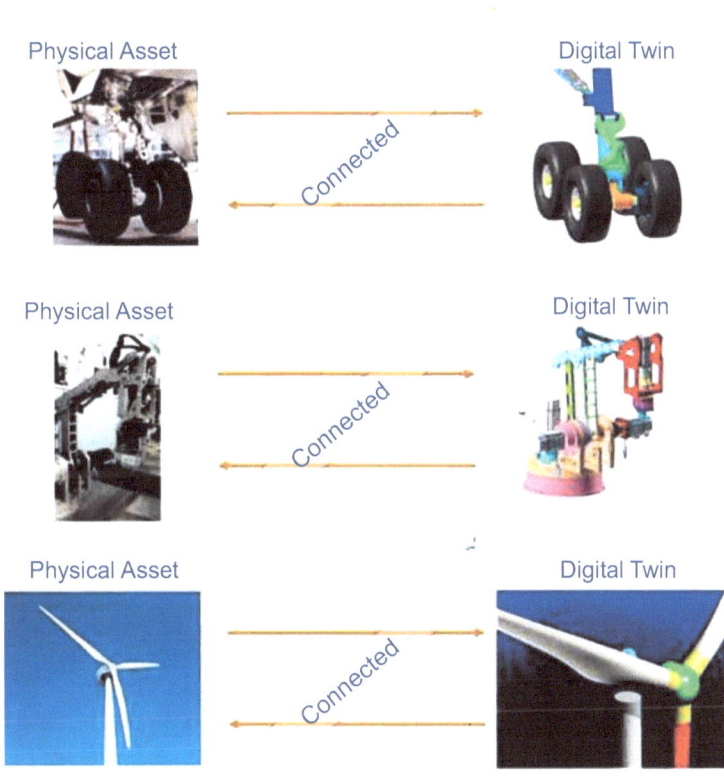

Fig. (3). Digital Twin Examples [13].

AUGMENTED REALITY

Augmented reality is one of the key technologies in Industrial 4.0; it allows the user to see the physical world, with the virtual objects composited with the physical world. It includes multiple sensory modalities, such as visual, auditory, haptic, somatosensory, and olfactory. AR technology usually has the following three characteristics: combining real and virtual worlds, interactive in real-time, and registered in three dimensions' space. It also has at least six classes of potential applications, including medical visualization, entertainment, manufacturing and maintenance, process planning, and military aircraft navigation and targeting [14].

Hardware for Augmented Reality

There are various types of hardware that can deliver Augmented Reality to users, and they can be divided into five major categories: Head-Mounted Displays (HMDs), Hand- Held Displays (HHDs), monitors, projectors, and 2D smart glasses. In general, there are four criteria to identify the features of AR hardware: mobility of the hardware, 3D-space spatially registration, the possibility of hands-free operation, and real-time data transmission. Table 1 below shows the summary of embedded features of each significant category. As shown in Table 1, HMDs are the only type of hardware that includes all these four features. In the manufacturing environment, HMDs have some distinct advantages compared with other types of hardware and traditional Human-Machine Interfaces (HMIs). Firstly, the mobility of HMDs can provide an intuitive interaction between the physical and virtual worlds from any position and angle inside the manufacturing environment. The operator can work more flexibly without staying in front of a particular machine or control panel for a long time. Secondly, the 3D-space spatially registration can help the AR hardware to recognise the relative position of the 3D environment and then integrate the virtual models correctly with the physical world. Thirdly, the possible hands-free operation for HMDs is extremely useful in the manufacturing environment. The operator can visualise and monitor the process of machines through HMDs. Furthermore, at the same time, they can also control the machines on the physical panels. These two processes can be achieved simultaneously without any interruption between each other. However, even if HMDs have all the critical features of the AR device, in different stages of manufacturing, other hardware may have their unique advantages for different tasks.

Table 1. Features of existing AR hardware.

-	HMDs	HHDs	Monitors	Projectors	2D Smart Glasses
Mobility	✓	✓	-	-	✓
3D Space Registration	✓	✓	✓	✓	-
Hands-free	✓	-	✓	✓	✓
Real-time data transmission	✓	✓	✓	✓	✓

VISUALIZATION OF THE DIGITAL TWIN DATA

The Digital Twin data are real-time data that reflect the physical counterpart. Digital Twin integrates and converges real-time and historical data to provide more useful information to the system. It eventually has the self-evolution ability to improve itself. Depending on the characteristics of the Digital Twin data, the visualisation of the Digital Twin data using AR requires the following five critical components as shown in Fig. (**4**): physical part, virtual part, calibration process, augmented process, and control process.

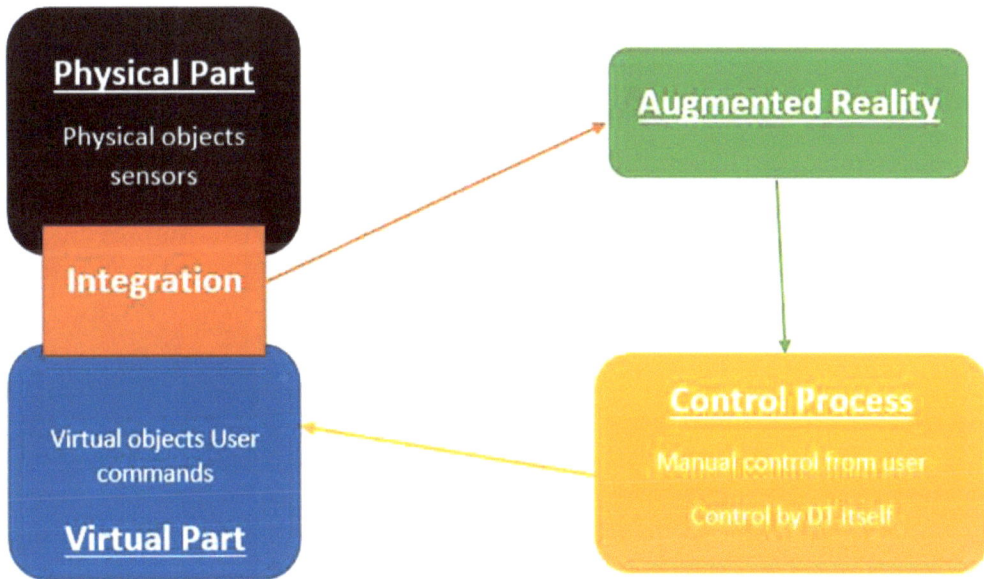

Fig. (4). Framework of visualizing digital twin data using AR.

Figure shows the framework of visualising the Digital Twin data by using AR. The physical part represents physical objects in the real world, it can be a part, a product, a machine or even an entire factory. In addition, all the data acquisition devices and sensors are also included in the physical part. The physical part is the base of this structure, all the other parts are aiming to analyse, utilise, and update the information from this part.

The virtual part in the figure cannot be described merely as the 3D model of the physical part, it is beyond the 3D model. 3D models are essential to represent the physical part in the virtual world. However, apart from this, all the real-time data collected from sensors, data acquisition devices, machines, and inputs from humans belong to the virtual part. Moreover, to achieve a comprehensive visualisation of a Digital Twin, all the historical data stored in the server are important to be treated as the virtual part.

In order to achieve the intuitive and flawless AR visualisation of Digital Twin, the 3D models in the virtual part need to be perfectly aligned with the physical part. This relies on the calibration process to accurately integrate these two parts. There are many calibration methods in AR, the most commonly used is the binary marker tracking method. In the physical part, the binary marker is placed in the physical world where the AR devices can visualise and recognise. In the virtual part, a cube is designed to align with the binary marker in the physical part. When the cube is perfectly aligned with the marker through the user's view, the calibration process is accurately done, the virtual world now is perfectly aligned with the physical world, which means all the 3D models in the virtual part can be overlaid onto their counterparts in the physical part.

Digital technologies increase the possibilities of communication, exchange and cooperation: between people, people and machines, and even between the machines or industrial objects themselves. With the aim of improving their processes and the performance of their operators, the manufacturing industry in future invests in new modes of technologies such as DT and AR.

REAL-TIME MONITORING

A variety of instruments are available for the measurement of sound as well as vibrations. The equipment to be used depends on the frequencies of interest, type of application, sensitivity and accuracy requirements, with other special requirements such as space and mounting constraints, *etc.* For measuring structure-borne vibrations, accelerometers are used. They also have different types, shapes, sizes and mounting methods depending on different application needs. In current experimentation, Tri-axial accelerometers (ADXL 345) are placed on the motors. These are also calibrated and used by referring manufacturer's catalog. For temperature and humidity measurement, DHT 22 sensors are being used and it is calibrated as per directions given by the manufacturer.

The monitoring of the manufacturing process in the factory has been around for a while. However, the digital twin provides real-time monitoring in a different and better way. First, digital twin integrates all the needed data with 3D models visually. Second, the digital twin fuses historical data, real-time data, and predicted data to track the past, monitor the present, and predict the future. Total elements of information perception technology, augmented reality technology, three-dimensional visualization monitoring technology, *etc.* are studied to implement digital twin for Real-time monitoring in the manufacturing phase. Digital twin for real-time monitoring is not just a presentation of current data and the status of physical objects, the high-fidelity model of digital twin also helps understand the situation and make optimization decisions.

DIGITAL TWINS USAGE & APPLICATIONS

Multiple interconnected processes in product design and development in an organization can be interfaced with each other and digital twins can be used to exchange the data from physical sensors to these processes. Some pectoral representations are also shown demonstrating the same [15].

During product design and development, many decisions are to be made which are interlinked with a further lifecycle of the product. As shown in Fig. (**5**) many things govern decision making including different design constraints, economic and market constraints, manufacturing feasibility, legacy data, *etc.*

In another patent, digital twin has been used to control and manage a wind turbine farm. The digital twin provides an interactive interface with all the turbines in the wind farm connected to it. The sensors connected to each of the turbines provide vital information including environmental information through the SCADA to the user. The turbine's current operating condition and optimum operating condition can be gauged and hence the decision can be made for achieving the best possible efficiency out of the power grid. Data also will help in health monitoring and fault diagnostics of the turbines and hence reduce the downtimes and maintenance costs [17].

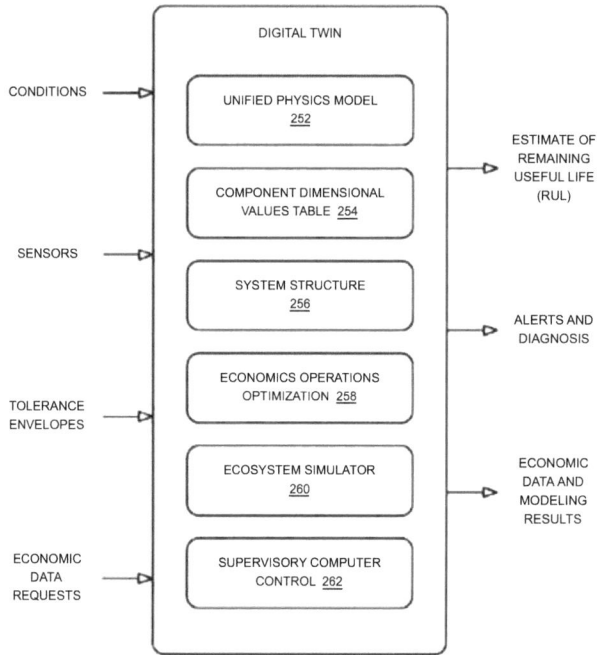

Fig. (5). Digital Twin usage example for actual decision making [16].

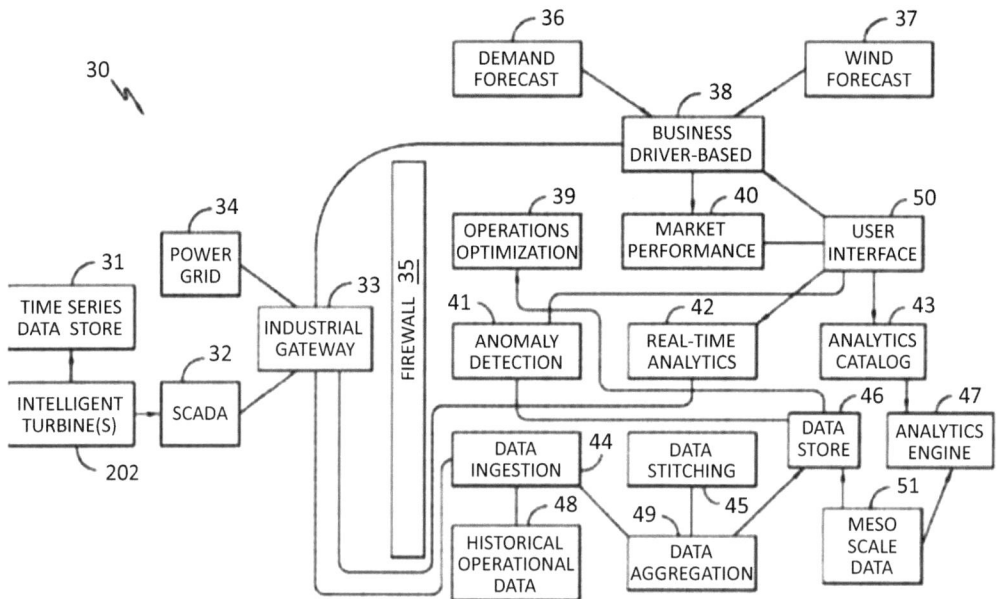

Fig. (6). Shows the system with digital twin integration and smart management [18].

The digital twin integration and smart management are explained in Fig. (**6**) Digital twin interfaced with remotely placed machines has huge benefits in multiple ways. The use case for preventive maintenance of remotely placed devices inter-connected to the server demonstrates the potential of this technology [19].

DT has huge potential and can be combined with other technologies such as cloud computing, Internet of Things and Augmented Reality (AI) and can be used in many ways for many different applications.

CONCLUSION

The basic idea of digital twin technology, its concept, subsystems, prime features, way of working, use cases and applications are understood with the help of an exhaustive literature review. Also, the project work revolves around monitoring the real-time data of operating conditions of the motor under different circumstances.

Further, for testing and experimentation, knowledge about different measurement tools and their correct usage as well as different parameters affecting test results is essential which is found in the literature. The input signals need to be processed and all the different operations in signal processing, their algorithms, and their effects on the signal should be known thoroughly to get proper results.

Literature also helped in demonstrating the possibilities of digital technology to benefit the user in multiple aspects of product and process design and development. It gives a base for the imagination of possibilities of technology use case. Other interactive software platforms as well as advanced technologies can also be used along with digital twin to develop smart and connected systems which truly adhere to the spirit of the Industry 4.0 revolution.

REFERENCES

[1] C. Qiu, S. Zhou, Z. Liu, Q. Gao, and J. Tan, "Digital assembly technology based on augmented reality and digital twins: A review", *Virtual Reality & Intelligent Hardware,* vol. 1, no. 6, pp. 597-610, 2019. [http://dx.doi.org/10.1016/j.vrih.2019.10.002]

[2] https://patents.google.com/patent/US20160247129A1/en

[3] Z. Zhu, C. Liu, and X. Xu, "Visualisation of the Digital Twin data in manufacturing by using Augmented Reality", *Procedia CIRP,* vol. 81, pp. 898-903, 2019. [http://dx.doi.org/10.1016/j.procir.2019.03.223]

[4] J.E. Hershey, F.W. Wheeler, M.C. Nielsen, C.D. Johnson, M.J. Dell'Anno, and J. Joykutti, *General Electric Co, 2017. "Digital twin of twinned physical system.", U.S. Patent Application,* 15/087,2017.

[5] J. Eargle, *The Microphone Book: From mono to stereo to surround-a guide to microphone design and application.* CRC Press, 2012.

[http://dx.doi.org/10.4324/9780080473468]

[6]   J. Wang, L. Ye, R.X. Gao, C. Li, and L. Zhang, "Digital Twin for rotating machinery fault diagnosis in smart manufacturing", Available from: https://www.researchgate.net/publication/329462066.
[http://dx.doi.org/10.1080/00207543.2018.1552032]

[7]   M. Sharma, and J.P. George, *George, "Digital Twin in the Automotive Industry: Driving Physical-Digital Convergence" TCS Design Services I M I 12 I 18 ,* 2017.

[8]   Sube Singh, Ankit Barde, and Biswajit Mahanty, *M. K. Tiwari "Digital Twin Driven Inclusive Manufacturing Using Emerging Technologies" IFAC PapersOnLine 52-13,* pp. 2225-2230, 2019.

[9]   F. Tao, J.f. Cheng, Qi. Qinglin, Z. Meng, He. Zhang, and Sui. Fangyuan, "Digital twin-driven product design, manufacturing and service with big data", *Int. J. Adv. Manufac. Technol.,* vol. 94, pp. 3563-3576, 2018.
[http://dx.doi.org/10.1007/s00170-017-0233-1]

[10]   Qi. Qi, *Tianliang Hu, Nabil An., Ang Liu, Yongli Wei, Lihui Wang, A.Y.C. Nee, "Enabling technologies and tools for digital twin..*
[http://dx.doi.org/10.1016/j.jmsy.2019.10.001]

[11]   V. Dygalo, And. Keller, and Al. Shcherbin, *Principles of application of virtual and physical simulation technology in production of digital twin of active vehicle safety systems..*
[http://dx.doi.org/10.1016/j.trpro.2020.10.015]

[12]   Z. Song, and A.M. Canedo, *Siemens Corp. "Digital twins for energy efficient asset maintenance.",* U.S. Patent Application, 15/052,2016.

[13]   Q. Qi, and F. Tao, "Digital twin and big data towards smart manufacturing and industry 4.0: 360 degree comparison", *IEEE Access,* vol. 6, pp. 3585-3593, 2018.
[http://dx.doi.org/10.1109/ACCESS.2018.2793265]

[14]   J. Lee, B. Bagheri, and H-A. Kao, "A Cyber-Physical Systems architecture for Industry 4.0-based manufacturing systems", *Manuf. Lett.,* vol. 3, pp. 18-23, 2015.
[http://dx.doi.org/10.1016/j.mfglet.2014.12.001]

[15]   Z. Zhou, J.M. De Bedout, J.M. Kern, E. Biyik, and R.S. Chandra, *General Electric Co Energy optimization system. U.S. Patent.,* 2013. 8,359,124.

[16]   A.M. Lund, K. Mochel, J.W. Lin, R. Onetto, J. Srinivasan, P. Gregg, J.E. Bergman, K.D. Hartling, A. Ahmed, and S. Chotai, *General Electric Co, "Digital twin interface for operating wind farms.,* 2018. U.S. Patent 9,995,278.

[17]   Y. Cai, B. Starly, P. Cohen, and Y.S. Lee, "Sensor Data and Information Fusion to Construct Digital-twins Virtual Machine Tools for Cyber-physical Manufacturing", *Procedia Manuf.,* vol. 10, pp. 1031-1042, 2017.
[http://dx.doi.org/10.1016/j.promfg.2017.07.094]

[18]   http://images.huffingtonpost.com/2016-05-13-1463155843-8474094- AR_history_timeline.jpg

[19]   R. Magargle, L. Johnson, P. Mandloi, P. Davoudabadi, O. Kesarkar, S. Krishnaswamy, and A. Pitchaikani, "A simulation- based digital twin for model-driven health monitoring and predictive maintenance of an automotive braking system", *Proceedings of the 12th International Modelica Conference* Prague, Czech Republic Linköping, University Electronic Press, pp. 35-46, 2017.
[http://dx.doi.org/10.3384/ecp1713235]

CHAPTER 8

Ontology Based Information Retrieval By Using Semantic Query

Rupali R. Deshmukh[1,*] and **Anjali B. Raut**[2]

[1] *Department of Computer Science & Engineering, H.V.P. M's COET, Amravati, Maharashtra, India*

[2] *Computer Science & Engineering, H.V.P. M's COET, Amravati, Maharashtra, India*

Abstract: The volume of data is increasing quickly in the modern day. Effective information retrieval techniques are needed to extract important facts from such a large collection of information. As a result, retrieval of information is the process of gathering valid data from a variety of sources. The majority of the time, information is retrieved from the internet using search queries. The aim of this research is to explore various issues existing in information retrieval techniques and to propose new techniques to overcome existing challenges in the field of Information retrieval.

Modern information retrieval methods have been examined, and it was discovered that they do not take semantic keyword knowledge into account when returning results. The semantic web is a development of the internet that enables computers to comprehend human inquiries in terms of their intent and produce pertinent responses.

This research mainly focuses on Ontology-Based Information Retrieval which can support semantic similarity and retain the view of an approximate search in a document repository using machine learning techniques. Further, this research works explores an adaptive update model for retrieving the information and proposes a semantic search model for the given user query. The objective of ontology-based semantic web information search is to increase the accuracy, precision and recall of user queries.

Keywords: Information retrieval, Machine learning, Ontology, Semantic web, Semantic query expansion.

INTRODUCTION

Huge data is generated in an integrated environment from multiple sources. The generated data is housed in a repository. The need to retrieve context-specific rel-

* **Corresponding author Rupali R. Deshmukh:** Department of Computer Science & Engineering, H.V.P. M's COET, Amravati, Maharashtra, India; Tel: 8275389793; E-mail: drupali1604@gmail.com

Sonali Mahendra Kothari, Vijayshri Nitin Khedkar, Ujwala Kshirsagar and Gitanjali Rahul Shinde (Eds.)

evant data is a challenging need of the time. Information Retrieval (IR) is becoming a more popular technique due to the tremendous growth of data resources on the internet in many forms. The main motive of the IR system is to discover the relevant information and documents that fulfill the requirements of the user. As searching the documents through the internet has become an imperative part of people's life, there is a great demand for obtaining such documents from a huge source of information which are appropriate to the information referred. Searching for information and documents from Web repositories through search engines gives many times irrelevant pages. This is because of the fact that search engines solve queries based on text pattern matching. This may sometimes output relevant as well as matched but irrelevant information.

Semantic web technology plays a significant role in retrieving relevant information. The semantic search tries to understand the user intention and improves the search accuracy and in turn appears in the searchable data space. Ontology plays a vital role in Semantic Web Technology. The component of the Semantic Web referred to as Ontology provides a common understanding of a particular term along with its relationship with the other terms in the query, where, the adaptive ontologies represent both the search domain and the user domain. This will reflect the search domain's ability to adjust to domain evolution semi-automatically. The obtained data in ontologies were used to strengthen the semantics of submitted queries as well as online data.

Likewise, the system automatically uses the chosen ontologies to enrich the produced query in accordance with the query enrichment criteria. Based on web data found in the graphs that validate the enriched query, the domain ontology is modified. The vision of the semantic Web proposes a situation where the information and administrations on the Web can be semantically translated and handled by machines to encourage human utilization. The semantic Web depends vigorously on the formal ontologies that structure basic information with the end goal of far reaching and transportable machine understanding. Semantic Web innovation depends on metaphysics as an instrument for displaying a conceptual perspective of the genuine and relevant semantic examination of documents.

Accordingly, the accomplishment of the semantic Web will be subject to the expansion of ontologies, which requires quick and simple designing of philosophy and evasion of a learning procurement bottleneck. However, there are certain challenges to which knowledge can or should be formalized.

The main purpose of this study is to propose an ontology-based information retrieval model that can retain the perception of an estimated search in a document repository and permit semantic query expansion similarity. In addition, this research investigates the creation of rank-based simultaneous history and knowledge update models and offers an adaptive update model for gathering information as well as a semantic query expansion model for the specified user query. Accuracy, precision, and recall are to be strengthened by ontology-based semantic query expansion and web information search.

Historical Background

Information Retrieval (IR) is the science and technology of efficiently allowing interested parties to obtain data from a repository of information. In information retrieval (IR), the task is to select information resources in vast repositories and satisfy customers' queries that reflect information needs. As things like text, image, audio, or a combination of all these, information resources are represented.

The basic aspects of the IR process are shown in Fig. (**1**). The user represents required information using query syntax during the conceptualization phase of IR. Only a minimal presentation of information complexity is required in the query. In practice, the user approximates the requirement for the inquiry by expressing numerous instances of the standout demand qualities, resulting in a set of terms that are tied to some coordinating terms. This frequently results in retrieval ambiguities, making it the major supply for the revision process.

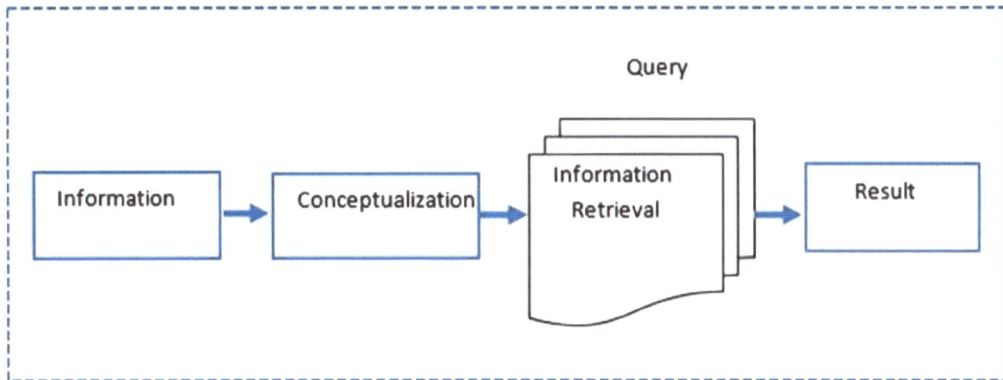

Fig. (1). Basic Information Retrieval Process.

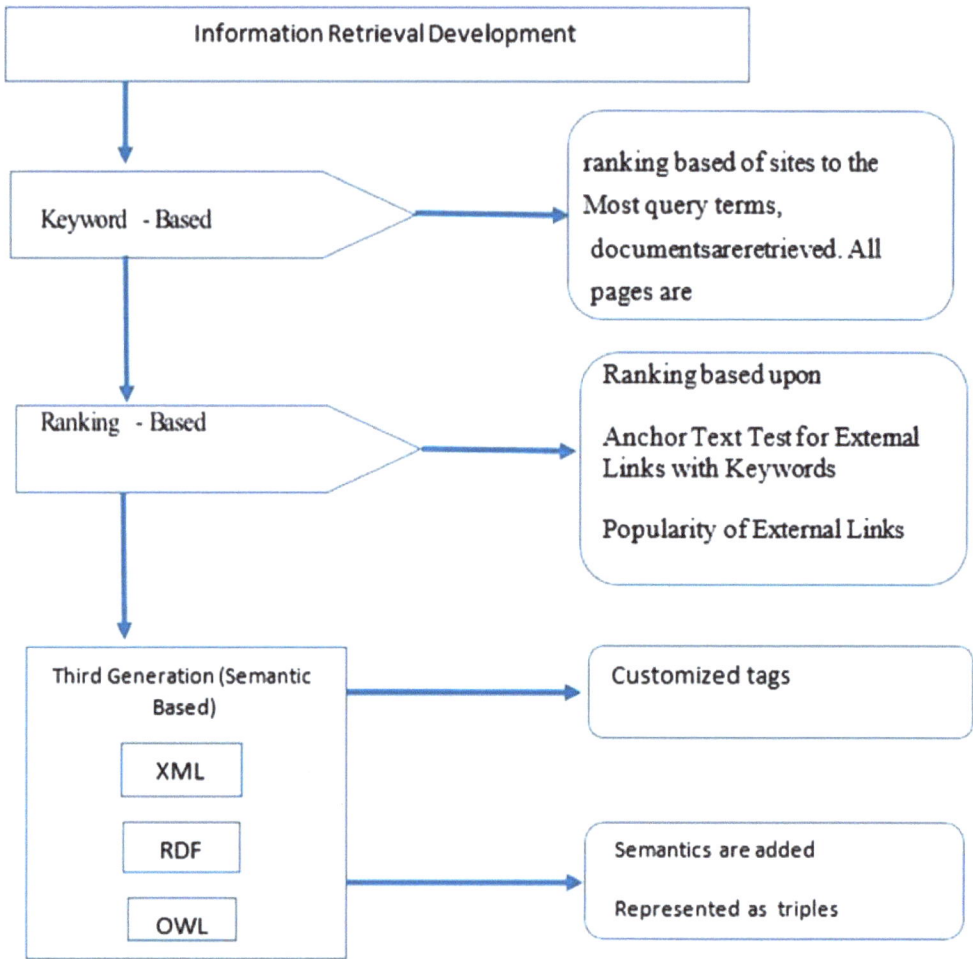

Fig. (2). Evolution of Information Retrieval.

Growth of Information Retrieval

Due to the papers' improved availability, IR issues have gained increasing attention. Based on a user query, IR selects pertinent documents from a documents' collection. Fig. (2) depicts the progression of IR, with the 3rd generation IR processing performed in accordance with different semantic related requirements such as Metadata (XML), Resource Description Framework (RDF), and Web Ontology Language (OWL) [1]. This approach blends increased relevancy models with the scalability of internet search engines.

Ontology

An ontology is a statement of an abstract that provides a purposefully reduced picture. An ontology is referred to as a collection of conceptual terminologies used for representation. The link between concepts describes the target reality. Domain-dependent and generic approaches are used to build ontologies. Ontologies are distinct knowledge resources that range from simple concept taxonomies, like domain hierarchical structures, to sophisticated formal systems, like embedded ontologies. These resources have reasoning capabilities that enable new knowledge to be inferred from previously automatic classification, and knowledge is validated through consistency checks. From a set of available resources, IR extracts information resources pertinent to the information required. Due to the growth of the Web, contemporary graphical user interfaces, and mass storage devices, IR has seen a significant change over time. An ontology is a description of terminology that is appropriate to a specific field or subject. To be more specific, vocabulary does not fit that definition of ontology.

However, vocabulary captures such terms conceptually. Ontology concepts are not conceptually altered when they are changed from one language to another, such as from French to Hindi. A body of knowledge utilizing representation vocabulary that describes a domain, often one of the common senses, is referred to as an ontology. The structure of knowledge employing while representation vocabulary offers terms to explain facts in a certain domain, that vocabulary is a collection of information regarding a specific domain. The structure of Knowledge is clarified *via* ontological analysis. The core of a domain's knowledge representation system is that domain's ontology. No specific vocabulary is used to represent knowledge in the absence of ontologies or conceptualizations that underlie knowledge. Effective ontological investigation of the field/domain is the first stage in developing a knowledge representation system and terminology. Incoherent knowledge bases are the product of weak analysis. An ontology is a commonly used phrase to describe semantic networks of connected information components, which is a hierarchy of concepts with properties and relations.

An ontology, which emphasizes knowledge sharing and agreement on its representation, offers a vocabulary of classes and attributes to characterize a domain. For instance, an ontology for computer applications might comprise classes like Software, Document, and Person as well as relationships like Software produces Documents, and Software Depends on the Software and Person that created the Document. A network of nodes that are characterized and connected by classes and attributes that are defined in shared ontologies will subsequently be used to describe services and contents. Thus, for example, a virtual organization may structure its contents by defining instances of applications, developers, papers, *etc.* once an ontology for computer applications has been formed.

An effective method for obtaining information from ontologies available as background knowledge to create similarity measures or learn features for machine learning models is ontology embedding. In these situations, ontologies are employed as the basis of a similarity function or a machine learning model.

MOTIVATION

The motivation for this research comes from the increase in the difficulty of searching for vast amounts of information on the Web. Multiple definitions for some terms in the paper cause complications. Thus, offering ontology-based similarity undoubtedly aids in developing successful clustering in accordance with user requirements. This study aims to define a model for particle swarm optimization-based ontology-based annotation and clustering. This study focuses on how to employ ontology-based annotation techniques to enhance document grouping. By collecting documents from the same cluster based on query vector matching to the cluster, clustering preserves related documents in a single group and speeds up the IR process. Using an optimal clustering algorithm with annotated weights will increase the quality of the result.

This method's notion is built on relationships and concepts that were taken from the articles and it consists of three major steps: firstly, ontology-based annotation is used to extract the concepts and their relationships from the document. Next, the corpus is ontology-indexed, and finally, an optimized technique is used to identify the best clusters.

LITERATURE REVIEW

Numerous research works that compare various semantic web characteristics have been described in the literature. An important area of research is ontology learning, which aims to make it easier to create new domain-specific ontologies with the least amount of work.

Ontology Approach to Web Content Mining [2]. For ontology learning, text-mining algorithms are employed to extract pertinent concepts and concept instances from domain sources. Numerous methods have been developed by authors to identify relationships between these ideas [3].

OWL supports overlapping classes and properties as well as complement and disjoint functional properties. For ontology specification, OWL can be utilized [1]. Executing the RDQL query against the knowledge base results in a list of tuples instances satisfying the query. As a result, documents that have been annotated with these occurrences are found, ranked, and displayed [4]. Information Retrieval (IR) research is now undergoing a number of changes that aim to broaden the field's scope in order to accommodate both the newest technological advancements and emerging needs [5]. With the spread of the Net and varied user demographics of search engines, which could be considered the new frontier of IR, a new major issue called the semantic web has emerged in terms of unique demands [6].

In [7], Document processor and document retrieval are the two components that make up the design and implementation of the information retrieval system. The query conversion module widens the initial query on its synonyms, hypernyms, and senses while carrying out semantic processing in accordance with user requests. The information retrieval paradigm now includes an ontology server that tags and indexes the retrieval sources using ontologies. Of queries is used by the retrieval agent module to locate the information source.

In a study [8], semantic query expansion is used to enlarge the recommended framework inquiries, which are then tested on different search engines like Google, Yahoo, Bing, and Exalead, these are four of the most widely used search engines. Precision, Mean Average Precision (MAP), Mean Reciprocal Rank (MRR), R-precision, and Number of documents retrieved are the performance measures employed. The search engines on the Web focus on accuracy. Based on the suggested framework, all of the KPIs have improved by about 10%. On different search engines, precision before the query expansion ranges from 0.75 to 0.81, whereas precision after the query expansion ranges from 0.85 to 89. After query expansion, the number of documents returned has nearly improved by 1/1000.

A study [9], provides an ontology-based automatic semantic Web service synthesis technique with the purpose of resolving the issue of semantic heterogeneity in web service descriptions. This approach sees web services as a triple set. Domain ontologies are used to label input and output parameters, category ontologies are used to identify service domains, and WordNet synonym sets are used to label matched scopes. This strategy aids in combining new Web services while also making use of the existing data of web service composition.

Additionally, the technique can have a single output with one or more input parameters.

Dahab *et al.* [10], offered a general overview of query expansion-based information retrieval models together with usage examples and a description of implementation techniques. To help the reader understand the key concept behind query expansion (QE) approaches like Kullback-Leibler Divergence (KLD) and the candidate expansion terms based on WordNet, toy examples with data are given. The information retrieval technique used in the course, spectral analysis, takes proximity into account.

Archana P. R. *et al.* [11], suggested a system that fetches the data using ontology-based semantic augmentation. The user can get the desired outcome. The suggested system is a search engine that effectively retrieves data. Natural language query submission is simple for a novice user, which makes this system friendly. A semantics-based search offers effective tools for understanding user requirements. This system attempts to function for a specific domain and can be expanded to encompass the whole knowledge base of several domains. This could include designing a system that can combine different ontologies. Here, the content that was collected can be ranked according to its relevance. A lexical database for the English language called Word Net is also made to improve the query, imported into the system.

Salah-dine *et al.* [12], discussed the topic of creating ontologies combining the two quickly expanding topics of semantic web and web mining, or semantic web mining. Web mining is the application of data mining tools to examine the usage, structure, and content of web resources. The Semantic Web is the second generation of the World Wide Web, enhanced with data that can be processed by computers to aid users in their jobs. This can aid in the discovery of both global and local structure "models" or "patterns" within and between Web pages, as well as ontology extraction, the automatic or semi-automatic creation of ontologies that includes extracting the terms from the relevant domain and the connections between those terms, and encoding them with an ontology language for convenient retrieval.

Terms from the respective domain, as well as the connections between them are identified, and codified using an ontology language to make retrieval simple. Ontology construction is incredibly labor- and time-intensive when done manually, hence automation is highly desirable. This paper provides an overview of the current intersection of the two fields and explores how a more complete integration would be beneficial.

Sylvie Ranwez *et al.* [13] presented a hybrid IRSs' usage of various methods to blend the document scores from the two techniques and rank documents in accordance with both points of view.. They explain a different combination that is implemented in a hybrid IRS specifically designed for retrieving scientific articles and somehow still view these two approaches as competitors. By using their conceptual indexing, relevant papers are found and then subdivided to highlight passages that would be of particular interest to users.

In another study [14], a novel, a comprehensive, semantic search model that builds on the traditional IR paradigm, addresses the issues brought on by the big and diversified Web, and combines the benefits of keyword and semantic search. A novel rank fusion strategy that lessens the negative effects of knowledge sparsity on the still-emerging SW is another addition, as is the creation of a large-scale assessment benchmark based on TREC IR evaluation criteria that permits a complete comparison of IR and SW approaches. Our semantic search model yielded equivalent and superior performance results, according to experiments.

Sangita S. Modi [15], in order to help e-learners fulfill their educational requirements, provide a model of individualized credit-based suggestion. Today's retrieval algorithms, however, can now also recover material that is stored in media like video, digital pictures, scanned and online handwriting, genetic data, music, audio snippets, and hypertext [16-18]. In addition, there are numerous cross- lingual IR techniques that can handle the vast majority of human languages [19].

The program's objectives include developing an algorithm for the implementation of a recommendation system and conducting usability testing on learners to improve their online learning experience.

Another study [20] proposed a domain ontology-based information retrieval model for computer crime evidence using a structured approach. This model accepts user-provided natural language input for evidence retrieval requirements. The mapping of retrieval terms to knowledge is accomplished by determining the correlation and similarity between words and ontology topics. On this basis, user forensics needs' query semantic extension is further fulfilled. The experimental findings demonstrated that the suggested evidence retrieval approach outperformed the typical information retrieval method's keyword matching, searching terms of retrieval outcomes.

A study [21], proposed a technique for community evolution analysis based on the development of key phrases. The community's topic is represented through the primary keywords. In addition to being more effective at recognizing community evolution, determining the evolution relationship using the core keywords is also better suited for extensive analyses of community evolution, which takes less time.

A study [22] presented an ontology-based method rather than a traditional keyword-based approach to creating and implementing new representation IR systems. This representation enhances document retrieval's recall and precision. The usefulness of the suggested approach is demonstrated by experiments conducted on the ontology-based approach and the keyword-based approach.

ISSUES IN INFORMATION RETRIEVAL

The key issues with IR models are the selection of a search vocabulary, search strategy formulations and information overload. The main issues identified with Information Retrieval model may be summarized as follows:

- Only full matches are obtained. The query is only used to obtain documents that perfectly match it. Therefore, in order for users to create successful queries for a wide range of documents, effective retrieval depends on their domain knowledge [17].
- The papers you retrieve are not ranked.
- The Boolean model either retrieves an excessive number of documents for a given big set of documents, or it retrieves extremely few documents.
- Term weights are not used in the model. A term is regarded the same whether it appears more than once or only once in a document [18].
- To resolve the limitation arising due to strict Boolean expression over terms, an extended Boolean retrieval model was proposed which utilizes additional operators like term proximity operators. This result shows some improvements over the Boolean model. To overcome the issue of an exact match as in Boolean Model, Fuzzy Set Model was proposed which considers the correlations among index terms and degree of relevance between queries and docs can be achieved. But it does not take into account the frequency of a term in a document or a query.

- The vector-based model of information retrieval addresses the issue of partial fetch matches and the lack of a method for rating the retrieved documents, but index terms are thought to be independent of one another. The semantics of the query or the document are not represented by this model. Additionally, massive document collections come at a great expense in terms of computing.

The area that has not yet been thoroughly examined or that has just recently been weakly explored is also considered as the study literature's missing component or components. This category could include factors or conditions related to the population or sample (size, kind, location, *etc.*), research methodology, data collection and/or analysis, or other study factors. There are the following research gaps:

1. Data collections and the information retrieving approach.

2. Feature extractions and selections for machine learning models.

3. Finding the best Machine learning model for retrieving the information from Semantic Web using an Ontology-based approach.

4. Improve the overall accuracy, precision and other parameters for information retrieval.

The majority of the materials on Web are huge, unstructured text. Finding relevant information to a user query is a challenging undertaking because standard information retrieval techniques are no longer appropriate for the massive amounts of text data that are being generated. It is challenging to create efficient analysis queries and extracting useful information from the documents.

One of the biggest issues in information retrieval is using domain knowledge and semantics to carry out efficient information retrieval. The study provided frameworks for sharable domain ontology-based information retrieval. A semantic knowledge representation is made through semantic annotation of the documents. The user query's semantic descriptors can then be compared to those of the annotated documents to conduct document retrieval. The objective is to extract pertinent data from the corpus using ontology. The new instance is created by the ontology population, which also causes the document to be semantically annotated. Using an ontology-based similarity metric, the method infers the semantic relatedness between the documents. The outcomes demonstrate that a domain ontology-based information retrieval system can outperform keyword-based systems in terms of results.

AIM

We require a test collection made up of three items in order to assess information retrieval effectiveness in a conventional manner:

A group of documents.

A set of information demands that can be expressed as queries for testing.

For each query-document pair, a series of relevant decisions are made, and these decisions are frequently categorized as either relevant or not relevant. The major objective of this research project is to develop and put into practice a novel method that can extract pertinent features from a variety of textual documents, ranging from fully unstructured plain text to semi-structured data.

It is critical to understand that traditional IR is a well-established and researched field. It should be supplemented rather than replaced by a semantics-enhanced approach to information retrieval. The semantic-enhanced one can benefit from the methods created for traditional IR research.

Simply said, the semantic query expansion or improved retrieval approach, which incorporates background knowledge with explicitly stated semantics, can aid in the development of intelligent search applications. The author has determined the driving force behind a framework for semantically enhanced information search and retrieval based on some of the shortcomings of traditional IR methodologies. The following are the goals of the current study:

PROPOSED RESEARCH METHODOLOGY

This work uses IDF to extract characteristics from the ontology representation of web contents. Then, using GA, the best features are chosen. The next step is to train a machine learning technique to categorize web pages. A few of the factors utilized for web page URL-based classification include baseline, URI components, length, precedence, orthographic traits, and sequential features [23 - 26]. The available contents of the web pages are not utilized in this manner. IDF, stemming, and stopping words are a few of the features employed based on the content that is accessible.

Inverse document frequency is the best feature used for web page classification.

IDF is high for rarely used words and low for frequently used phrases. Based on a common vocabulary and taxonomy, ontology is used to express the things or concepts and the relationships between them. In this work, semantic query expansion and maintaining the semantics of the online material are done using an ontology-based representation.

GA reduces the dimension of the features for effective categorization. The new strategy's architecture is provided in Fig. (**3**).

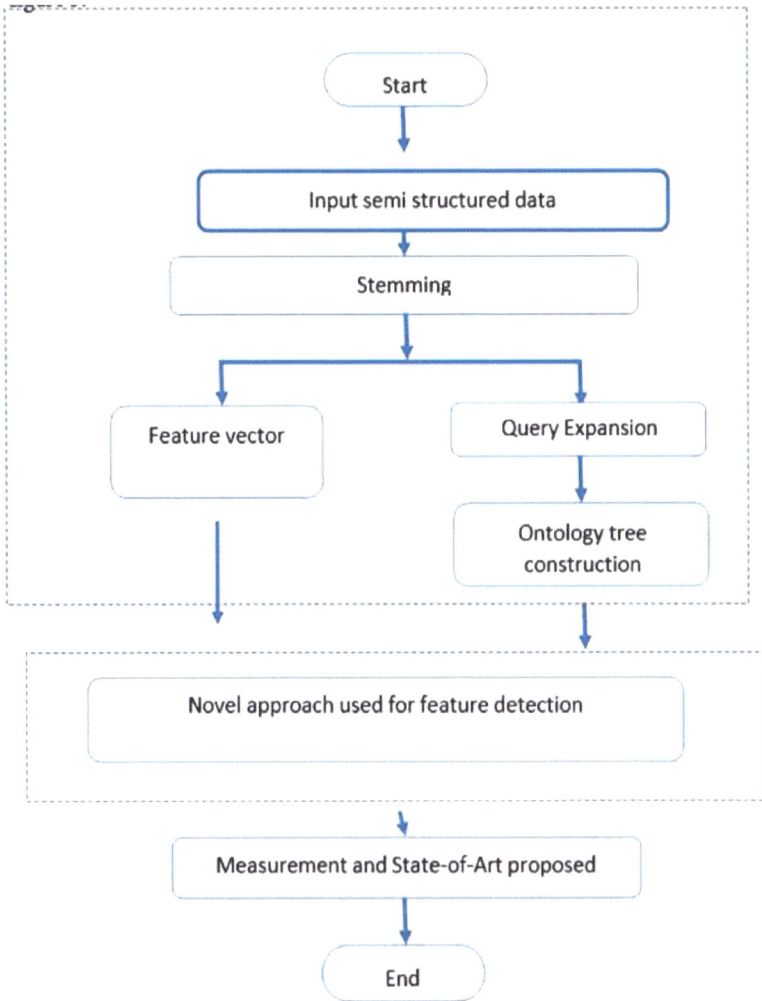

Fig. (3). Work Flow.

The practical application of this research is to leverage ontologies' knowledge to match objects and queries. With an emphasis on using machine learning techniques on the characteristics retrieved from ontology and NLP ideas, the usage of ontologies poses a number of issues. In natural language, many words can signify many things depending on the situation and context. Therefore, creating web directories, categorizing websites, and researching topic-specific searches are all beneficial. Most content management and retrieval tasks include classifying the content as a crucial component.

CONCLUSION

This research mainly focuses on Ontology Based Information Retrieval which can support semantic similarity and retain the view of approximate search in document repository using machine learning techniques.

REFERENCES

[1]   J. Maheswari, and G. Karpagam, "A conceptual framework for ontology- based information retrieval", *Int. J. Eng. Sci. Technol.,* vol. 2, no. 10, pp. 5679-5688, 2010.

[2]   M. Hazman, S.R. El-Beltagy, and A. Rafea, "Survey of ontology learning approaches", *Int. J. Comput. Appl.,* pp. 36-43, 2011.
[http://dx.doi.org/10.5120/2610-3642]

[3]   H. Luong, S. Gauch, and Q. Wang, "Ontology learning using wordnet lexical expansion and text mining", http://cdn.intechopen.com/pdfs/38914

[4]   D. Vallet, M. Fernández, and P. Castells, An ontology-based information retrieval model.*The Semantic Web.* Research and Applications Springer Berlin Heidelberg, 2005, pp. 455-470.

[5]   E. Sanchez, *Fuzzy Logic and the Semantic Web.* Elsevier: Amsterdam, the Netherlands, 2006.

[6]   D. Kraft, G. Bordogna, and G. Pasi, Fuzzy set theory. In: Encyclopedia of library & information sciences, 4th Edition. John D. McDonald & Michael Levine-Clark (eds.). Taylor & Francis, pp.1618-1622.

[7]   Binbin Yu, "EURASIP journal on wireless communications and networking", 2019:30.
[http://dx.doi.org/10.1186/s13638-019-1354-z]

[8]   S. Jain, K.R. Seeja, and R. Jindal, "A fuzzy ontology framework in information retrieval using semantic query expansion", *Int. J. Informa. Manag. Data. Insig.,* vol. 1, no. 1, p. 100009, 2021.
[http://dx.doi.org/10.1016/j.jjimei.2021.100009]

[9]   S. Sharma, A. Kumar, and V. Rana, "Ontology based information retrieval system on the semantic web: semantic web mining", *International Conference on Next Generation Computing and Information Systems (ICNGCIS),* 2017.
[http://dx.doi.org/10.1109/ICNGCIS.2017.21]

[10]   F. Arman Rasool, "Trends and issues in modern information retrieval", *J. Adv. Sci. Technol.,* vol. III, no. IV, 2012.

[11]   M. Dahab, S. Alnefaie, and M. Kamel, *ATutorial on information retrieval using query expansion.* SpringerLink, 2018, pp. 761-776.
[http://dx.doi.org/10.1007/978-3-319-67056-0_35]

[12]   P. R. Archana, T. P. Nisha, and S. Leya Elizabeth, "Semantically enhanced information retrieval system", *Int. J. Innov. Technol. Expl. Eng. (IJITEE),,* vol. 9, no. 5, 2020.

[13]   K. Salah-ddine, "Mining the Web for learning ontologies: state of art and critical review",

[14]   S. Ranwez, B. Duthil, M-F. Sy, J. Montmain, and P. Augereau, "How ontology-based information retrieval systems may benefit from lexical text analysis", Oltramari, Alessandro; Vossen, Piek; Qin, Lu; Hovy, Eduard. New Trends of Research in Ontologies and Lexical Resources, Springer, pp.209-230, 2013, Theory and Applications of Natural Language Processing, 978-3-642-31781-1. hal-00797143.
[http://dx.doi.org/10.1007/978-3-642-31782-8_11]

[15]   M. Fernández, I. Cantador, V. López, D. Vallet, P. Castells, and E. Motta, "Semantically enhanced information retrieval: An ontology-based approach", *J. Web Semant.,* vol. 9, no. 4, pp. 434-452, 2011.
[http://dx.doi.org/10.1016/j.websem.2010.11.003]

[16]   S. Sangita, "Web page classification using WSD and YAGO and Ontology", *Proceedings of the International Conference on Communication and Electronics Systems (ICCES 2018),* IEEE Xplore Part Number: CFP18AWO-ART; ISBN:978-1-5386-4765-3.

[17]   N.J. Belkin, and W.B. Croft, "Information filtering and information retrieval", *Commun. ACM,* vol. 35, no. 12, pp. 29-38, 1992.
[http://dx.doi.org/10.1145/138859.138861]

[18]   K. Gao, Y. Wang, and Z. Wang, "An efficient relevant evaluation model in information retrieval and its application", Available from: http: //doi.ieeecomputersociety.org/10.1109/CIT.2004.1357300

[19]   F. Arman Rasool, "Trends and issues in modern information retrieval", *J. Adv. Sci. Technol.,* vol. III, no. IV, 2012.

[20]   X. Chi, "The information retrieval model for computer crime evidence based on domain ontology", *2019 12th International Symposium on Computational Intelligence and Design (ISCID),* Hangzhou, China, 2019, pp. 45-49.
[http://dx.doi.org/10.1109/ISCID.2019.10093]

[21]   X. Zhang, X. Li, S. Jiang, X. Li, and B. Xie, "Evolution analysis of information retrieval based on co-word network", *2019 3rd International Conference on Electronic Information Technology and Computer Engineering (EITCE),* Xiamen, China, 2019, pp. 1837-1840.
[http://dx.doi.org/10.1109/EITCE47263.2019.9094904]

[22]   F. Ramli, S.A. Noah, and T.B. Kurniawan, "Ontology-based information retrieval for historical documents", *2016 Third International Conference on Information Retrieval and Knowledge Management (CAMP),* pp.55-59, 2016.
[http://dx.doi.org/10.1109/INFRKM.2016.7806335]

[23]   N. Vanjulavalli, and A. Kovalan, "Multi-layer perception for web page classification based on Tdf/Idf ontology based features and genetic algorithms", *J. Theor. Appl. Inf. Technol.,* vol. 57, no. 3, pp. 347-353, 2013.

[24]   S. Sharma, A. Kumar, and V. Rana, "Ontology based information retrieval system on the semantic web: Semantic web mining", *International Conference on Next Generation Computing and Information System,* 2017.
[http://dx.doi.org/10.1109/ICNGCIS.2017.21]

[25]   W. Alromima, I. F, R. Elgohary, and M. Aref, "Ontology-based query expansion for arabic text retrieval", *Int. J. Adv. Comput. Sci. Appl.,* vol. 7, no. 8, pp. 223-230, 2016.
[http://dx.doi.org/10.14569/IJACSA.2016.070830]

[26]   H.K. Azad, and A. Deepak, "Query expansion techniques for information retrieval: A survey", *Inf. Process. Manage.,* vol. 56, no. 5, pp. 1698-1735, 2019.
[http://dx.doi.org/10.1016/j.ipm.2019.05.009]

CHAPTER 9

Paradigm Shift of Online Education System Due to COVID-19 Pandemic: A Sentiment Analysis Using Machine Learning

Prajkta P. Chapke[1,*] and **Anjali B. Raut**[1]

¹ Department of Computer Science & Engineering, H.V.P.M's, C.O. E.T., Amravati, India

Abstract: The COVID-19 epidemic has completely altered the environment and every aspect of every individual. The most affected part is the education system and the stakeholders associated with it. Organizations are currently being forced to adapt and alter their strategies in response to the new situation created by the COVID-19 epidemic. The proposed study gathers tweets on online schooling from social media sites like Twitter and Facebook comments in order to conduct a thorough sentiment analysis (SA) during the epidemic. The current study utilizes techniques for natural language processing (NLP) and machine learning (ML) to extract subjective data, establish polarity, and identify how people felt about the educational system prior to and following the COVID-19 crisis. The first step in the proposed study is to retrieve tweets using Twitter APIs before they are ready for rigorous preprocessing. One filtering method is Information Gain (IG). We will identify and examine the latent causes of the unpleasant feelings. We'll look at the machine-learning classification algorithm at the end. The proposed model will analyse the perceptions of people about the online educational system during COVID-19.

Keywords: COVID-19, Machine learning, Natural language processing, Online educational system (OES), Pandemics, Sentiment analysis.

INTRODUCTION

The Internet has developed over the past 20 years from being almost non-existent to being the biggest, most accessible database of knowledge ever made. It has changed the way people communicate, transact business, shop, socialize, and approach information and education. Education is becoming more accessible than ever because of online learning, which is revolutionizing the way traditional

* **Corresponding author Prajkta P. Chapke:** Department of Computer Science & Engineering, H.V.P.M's, C.O. E.T., Amravati, India; E-mail: prajkta.chapke@rediffmail.com

Sonali Mahendra Kothari, Vijayshri Nitin Khedkar, Ujwala Kshirsagar and Gitanjali Rahul Shinde (Eds.)

classes are administered. It is much more than just a fresh method of distance education.

Online education is a style of instruction where students use their personal computers to access the internet. Over the past 10 years, many unconventional students, such as those who choose to continue working full-time or raising families, have become more and more interested in online graduation and courses. The host university's online learning portal frequently provides online academic and graduation programs, some of which use digital technologies.

Schools, training facilities, and institutions of higher education have been forced to close in the majority of countries as a result of the COVID-19 lockdown and social isolation tactics. There has been a paradigm shift in how educators deliver high-quality education using a range of online channels. Online learning, distance learning, and continuing education have emerged as the panaceas for this unprecedented global epidemic, notwithstanding the challenges that both teachers and students must overcome. Both learners and teachers may experience a completely different learning environment when switching from traditional face-to-face learning to online learning, yet they are forced to adjust because there are few or no other options. Through a variety of online channels, the educational system and instructors have accepted "Education in Emergency," forcing them to use a system for which they are not ready.

E-learning resources have been essential in facilitating student learning while universities and schools have been closed due to the pandemic. Staff and student preparation must be assessed during the transition to the new changes and supported appropriately. Learners who have a fixed mindset find it difficult to adapt and alter to a new learning environment, in contrast to students who have a growth mentality.

The survey by the Chicago Community Networks Study included not only a series of questions on organizational characteristics but also a roster of organizations identified by the research team and by locals as contributing to community development work in each organization's neighbourhood [1]. India is not an exception to the difficulty of online learning for both students and teachers worldwide. Online courses have had a greater detrimental effect on a small percentage of students. Most teachers who taught English were unpaid during the shut-down of the school; embassies rejected offering student visas; and new teachers were not appointed by the school [3]. People are now using social media to express their emotions as a result. In order to examine the emotional current of Indian instructors and learners in light of these issues, this study will employ machine learning (ML) on Twitter tweets.

Technology will have a significant impact on education in the upcoming years. The Internet of Things (IoT) is reaffirming its critical role in the context of information and communication technologies and societal advancement. Institutions may improve learning outcomes with the use of IoT by offering more open learning opportunities, increasing operational effectiveness, and collecting real-time, actionable insight into student performance.

To our knowledge, this is the initial research to look at how COVID-19 has affected India's educational system using data from social media. Research will commonly use the social media sample approach. This study provides a helpful data analysis of the feelings at this point by assessing the emotions and the shift in positive and negative polarity throughout time.

HISTORICAL BACKGROUND

Social Network Analysis

Social Network Analysis (SNA) is a demonstrative strategy to reveal the connections inside an informal community that are likely to lead to further associations. It incorporates an arrangement of strategies and instruments to give a visual picture of the interpersonal organization and acts like an" authoritative X-beam" into the casual workings of a gathering of individuals. The essential spotlight is on the connections between individuals as opposed to the characteristics of the people [2].

Impact of Social Networks

Just one click away, the thoughts are shared with other people, paving the way to start a new journey in a new world. This technology is used for many other purposes, but communication is the main one and still persists. A new bond is created with common friends and similar people. It seems to be the perfect tool for those who admire each other, but some are worried about the impact of these social networking sites. There are two types of attitudes and impacts —positive and negative —that are realized by the users [3]. The impacts are mainly classified as follows:

- Positive Impact
- Negative Impact

Positive Impact

There are numerous good points that support social networks' continued use by many users. Expressing the facts about ourselves is a major positive motivation. This helps one understand us by analyzing our likes and dislikes. Uploading favorite songs, posting new pictures that have been taken recently, updating cover photos, and showing outfits are some examples of positive impacts. People could reduce their embarrassment when using the internet rather than in person. So, users feel it is easy to express feelings on sites like Facebook, Twitter, and WhatsApp, *etc*. This helps people study and learn about their personal lives and the feelings of other people by just checking their pages. The page holds information regarding their likes and dislikes, phone number, friends, relationship status, and everything else. During a busy work schedule, this helps them to entertain themselves, share their feelings, and reduce mental stress. Also, it becomes a home where many friends and family members can always interact and chat with each other, especially when they are far away from home or live in another country. A friend of friends is a way for people to make new connections and communicate with us.

Negative Impact

Modern people don't have negative thoughts regarding this social networking site because they are addicted to modern technology. But the problem persists when it comes to privacy and security. If private information is disclosed to others and misused, then users face many problems. Another problem called cyberbullying or cyberharassment mainly happens through electronic means. Bullying is done behind a screen so that it cannot be effectively stopped or noticed when it actually happens. Only reporting about the bully can help stop it, and victims may be frightened too.

Characteristics of Social Networks

Social networks have several characteristics that explain their important and valuable features. By understanding them, one can know their unique features as compared to other websites. The common characteristics of social networks have great advantages, and some of these are free web space, building profiles, free web addresses, uploading content, chat clients, building conversations, e-mail, and creating pages. For differentiating a social network from regular websites, five core characteristics are observed, as follows [4].

User-based

A single person would often change the content of websites, which was subsequently read by online users, before the advent of social networks like Twitter, Facebook, LinkedIn, and others. The information flow is actually updated in a single direction, and the writer or webmaster determines the direction of future updates. But on online social networks, the user himself updates their own profile, which they created. Unless any person updates new information, the empty forums, chat rooms, and applications are not used by the network. Hence, Internet users are much more dynamic with social networks as content and conversations are populated on the network and discussions can be seen by them.

Interactive

This is another type of feature or characteristic that social networks possess in the modern world. So, it does not contain only forums or chat rooms but also applications for games that can be played with other users, such as poker, chess, and many more. A tournament is also held for challenging groups of friends, and this makes them interact with each other. This entertainment application gives you fun when you connect with other users or friends, which makes it a pastime.

Community-driven

This concept is used and thrives on social networks. Some common hobbies and beliefs are followed by groups of people, who form a community, create a page to hold those group members, and follow some principles regarding this particular community. Nowadays, online social network users hold lots of communities and sub-communities, particularly to connect people from high schools, colleges, and welfare associations. This helps many people find new friends and also connect with people they haven't met for a long time or lost contact with.

Relationships

Previous versions of websites did not give preference to relationships, which became the main part of today's social network. The more relationships there are between the network and people, the more establishments gravitate toward the center of the network. Online social networks are a strong and powerful way to bring people together. It may not be realized that updating some notes on the page could spread the content to contacts and sub-contacts in a huge way.

Emotion Over Content

This is also a unique characteristic of today's online social networks. No matter what happens, it easily reaches out to friends A great deal of support is provided to those who are emotionally affected.

Growth and Development in Sentiment Analysis

People are always curious about other people's opinions and thoughts. With the internet, more and more people have used services on the internet to voice their opinions. With the help of social media platforms like Facebook, LinkedIn, and Twitter, it is now possible to automate and identify how the general public feels about a specific subject, news item, product, or brand. The opinions gleaned through such services may be worthwhile. It is possible to analyze and show accumulated data sets in a way that makes it simple to determine whether the online mood is positive, negative, or neutral.

As a fine-grained sentiment classification problem, aspect-based sentiment analysis (ABSA) has gained more popularity in recent years. It is focused on determining the sentiment score of specific components instead of focusing on how polarized the sentence's sentiments are. For instance, in a review of research on the subject of education, "I find it difficult to understand the course, even though the teacher is knowledgeable and he is very serious when teaching," the instructor also incorporates the course's difficulty as two components. Two features of the linked sentiment polarity are separate. To accomplish SA tasks, it is necessary to understand how to identify an aspect and its associated sentiment word. Deep neural networks have greatly outperformed conventional ML algorithms in a variety of NLP tasks, yet end-to-end deep learning systems are usually rigid. For instance, NN often struggles to identify the truly connected features of the emotion-expressing words when the text has many aspects and sentimental words. This has led to the suggestion of attention-based neural networks, which have performed astonishingly well in NLP processes. In 2016, Wang *et al*. [5] proposed that, *via* a NN and an attention mechanism, in order to produce a sentence representation of the aspect, the target aspect was inserted behind each word in a sentence. The aspect information was then used to classify the sentences using the neural network's results. Ma *et al*. [6] presented that the target aspect was embedded behind each word in a sentence using NN and an attention mechanism to produce a sentence representation of the aspect. The aspect information was then used to classify the sentences using the neural network's results. Liu *et al*. [7] provided a novel methodology for executing user SA in context. The model takes into account several semantic relevance facets as well as the impact of tweet context data. Li *et al*. [8] employed a transformation network to classify sentiments with a specific aim in mind. They held the opinion that certain context-specific keywords typically define the sentiment polarity of a target. This notion aligns with the notion of local attention. However, due to the complexity of human language, there isn't a consistent guideline for choosing important words in a phrase. Moreover, the local focus is likely to be excessive, forcing the network to focus heavily on a single phrase or even skip the area that contains the most vital information.

CONTRIBUTION IN THE AREA OF RESEARCH

This research work proposes a sentiment classification of tweets regarding the online education system before and after the COVID-19 crisis and an opinion analysis for the online education system by utilizing supervised machine learning algorithms. It begins with a new proposed method for sentiment analysis. Sentiment analysis in the online education system is performed by combining NLP and ML algorithms. An empirical comparison has also been made to understand the clear view of sentiment analysis by utilizing supervised learning algorithms. Furthermore, many others were used to improve the accuracy of the tweets that were provided. A classification method that integrates two or more algorithms is called an ensemble. For all the algorithms employed, the mode value is determined depending on the vote reference. In this research, various machine learning algorithms will be combined. Thus, the proposed method will show more accuracy than the existing algorithms. Finally, an examination of the different calculations utilized in Twitter for sentiment analysis will be made. This research work mainly focuses on sentiment analysis using machine learning algorithms.

Institution Involves in Area & Research

AI-based sentiment analysis systems utilise NLP and machine learning to discover topics, themes, and categories inside sentences in order to determine (as a positive number, negative number, or zero) sentiments. Large banks can evaluate customer sentiment concerning their brand or products *via* AI-based sentiment analysis technologies in an attempt to enhance customer experiences. Recently released AI-based systems were divided into over 77 different categories in our analysis of the banking industry's vendor landscape and capability map.

The defence of social participation does not imply a constant public deliberation on all the subjects, imposing on the citizens a permanent and exclusive involvement in the public sphere, because the important thing is that people deal with the central questions and that the fundamental information is available [9].

Trends in the Area of Development

Different ways and several techniques have developed in the day-to-day life of social networks. Several categories have emerged, and a new trend shows the ultimate usage of social networks [10]. Some trending topics have emerged so far in social networks, such as social television, mobile evolution, and social sharing.

Changing Prospective

To interact with human emotions, social networking programs need to be smarter. Facebook is one of the most popular social networking websites. Through uploading status updates, images, videos, and other content, individuals connect and share their accomplishments, emotions, thoughts, observations, and most likely, emotions. By working together in domains like cognitive psychology and human psychology, the goal can be achieved while integrating a camera with deep learning computing technology, real-time face image detection and recognition, facial expression analysis, and activity recommendations based on experimental findings. The goal is to create a bridge between humans and computers that can interact intelligently [11].

Industrial Trends and International Trends

Sentiment analysis provides ways to improve the product's quality, and it also helps the user make a purchasing decision. It is considered necessary to maintain a positive interaction with customers, and the best approach to doing this is to reduce the gap between what is required and what is offered. Companies that use sentiment research methods should consider the following: Sentiment analysis can reflect the various emotions expressed by a product's users. For instance, if a beverage brand releases a new drink and wonders about the success rate, it will probably feed the tool with the information on the new drink that was gathered from several authorized response sites. The method has the potential to interpret and organize this chunk of data into meaningful, accessible, and functional data. The organization can understand whether or not the study of the instrument desires the beverage produced. Comparisons and even the words that were most commonly used to describe the object should also be illustrated. The organization will either bring in improvements or proceed with the product, depending on this data. To determine the admiration of their brand among the alternatives present on the market, businesses may use sentiment analysis. The research on Careem and Uber's usage carried out by separate analyzers is an obvious illustration of this. According to a study conducted in 2017 by the social media analytics company Crimson Hexagon, Careem, which launched in the Middle East in 2012, received 108% more input than Uber, located in the United States, which launched in the region in 2013 and received 827% more feedback in 2014. This may give the impression that consumers prefer Uber to Careem. However, a closer examination is provided through emotion analysis in action, which reveals that, in contrast to Uber, the positive response is just 4% more than the negative [12]. The service company can only face recognition if what they deliver is what they say. They need to provide the difference between what the customers are asking for and what the manufacturers are giving them to do so. Opinion assessment can be applied to determine the viewpoint of the consumer. Sentiment analysis really does have the ability to help businesses flourish by identifying the emotions conveyed along with the positive or negative statements in online reviews. A good example of this is the 2013 report by Klout, which emphasises the fact that the service sector is facing more negative feedback than the retail sector. If torn down further, the airlines' extremely poor reviews are compared to those of the auto sector. Further examination of airline industry research reveals that Spirit, Delta, and United customers have extremely pessimistic outlooks. At the same time, Air Mauritius, Sun Country, and Thomas Cook are very positive. In essence, this knowledge is important for these businesses to realise where the service deficit can be reduced [13]. This market relies solely on forecasts, and investors must ensure that they pay for the correct shares. To achieve financial benefits, a large number of instinctive and judicial decisions are made. The basic business theory is what is practiced in capital markets:

Bigger Risk = Bigger Returns.

Many variables influence stock prices, and it is also difficult for buyers to choose the correct moment to purchase or sell these stocks. SA completes the task of comprehending the attitudes and sentiments of the clients according to the views posted on numerous social media platforms or the internet in general. This makes use of the Sensex points from the accumulated opinions, which show the buyers' optimism or disapproval, to decide what to sell. There are two techniques in which this method operates: one path is where the emotion is not considered, although instead the changing average is determined. In comparison to this, we have two paths to evaluate the change in the stock market by the emotion and the moving average [14].

MOTIVATION

Everybody's daily lives have been impacted by COVID-19. The education sector is one of the areas most affected by COVID-19. As a result of this instability, the pandemic's influence on educational systems around the world has been minimal, which has resulted in substantial adjustments to how education is delivered. The proper comeback to this is the Internet and online courses [2, 3]. However, the transformation of classrooms to online ones hasn't been without issues. Some issues with online teaching platforms are outlined in a study [4]. In order for authorities to use the insights from social media sentiment mining to instantly make decisions based on data, there is a vital need for rescrach concerning distance learning that is ready for practice.

LITERATURE REVIEW

Social networking sites (SNS) will change just as quickly in the technological age and probably end up looking a little different than they do right now. Social media platforms still have one fundamental component that enables users to create profiles inside a system, communicate with other users of that system, and browse other users' profiles. A faint glimmer of social networking started in the 1980s, and many people think that the phenomenon of social networking started in the late 1990s. Specific networks are specialized for mobile internet browsing, while social networks can also be accessed through mobile social applications. Facebook's social network has over 1.86 billion active monthly members, making it the market leader in terms of reach and scope. Since its inception, the website has influenced the social media landscape and is now a crucial topic when addressing user privacy and defining the difference between a private and public online self. Social networking services offer opportunities for sharing user-generated content, such as images and videos, in addition to allowing users to connect beyond local or social borders.

The research work delineates the effect of the digital divide on online education. Expanded and autonomous learning options are provided by technology. There are still many impoverished metropolitan areas with unskilled labour, young people with low education levels, and few resources. The lack of access to knowledge and training for high-tech professions is the main factor contributing to the digital divide.

Information and communication technologies have revolutionized the way we learn for over a decade. Web 2.0 technologies enhanced the path of teaching and learning. By using the internet more often for learning-related activities, discussion forums, *etc.*, learners are producing a lot of unstructured data. Comments, reviews, and discussion forums are extremely important to the instructor in this digital age. It is challenging for the instructor to comprehend the learner's thinking. The size of data to be analyzed is humongous. It can be done through different knowledge-mining techniques. Data and text mining techniques are emphasized to focus on enhancing the learner's abilities. Comments, reviews, feedback, and discussion forum contents are used to perform the analysis. Sentiment Analysis (SA), otherwise known as opinion mining, is a part of education data mining and is used by many researchers to express their ideas.

Education data extraction helps analyze the state of the instructor and learner to provide a better platform.

Sentiment analysis is made possible by natural language processing (NLP), which enables a variety of text mining techniques to identify and extract people's views, attitudes, and emotions (Shah and Siddiqui, 2018). Conducting sentiment analysis in the area of education is the main topic of this section. This paper's major goal is to reflect the state-of-the-art classification, models, algorithms, and applications of sentiment analysis (SA) in the field of education. Related research publications are also discussed. Many scientists have used various sentiment analysis models and methods. However, researchers mostly concentrate on using Naive Bayes (NB) and Support Vector Machines (SVM) to analyse user sentiment [15].

Tools such as Weka [16] and Rapid Miner are primarily used for sentiment analysis. SA uses text analysis, CL (computational linguistics), and NLP to find out the emotions from the raw data. It provides an illustration of how information from various disciplines can be merged to produce correct analysis, including statistics, linguistics, engineering, and other relevant fields. SA grasped the attention of many types of research by showing its potential for information retrieval, reviews, and blogs, and by making it easier to gather user thoughts from their remarks on discussion forums.

The ability to determine the polarity of the information at the phrase, viewpoint, or archive level is crucial for sentiment categorization. The given record should be categorised as either good, neutral, or negative, depending on how the statement is expressed. The final goal is to anticipate the meaning of the given statement and transform it into valuable insights. The given data can be classified into two categories: actualities and conclusions. Articulation of the target substances, properties, and occasions are the actualities, and the emotional connections belong to conclusions that portray the decision of the individuals, sentiment towards the substances, evaluations, and their properties [17].

In a study [18], we identified the effects of the pandemic on classrooms, learners, and educators in both qualitative and quantitative ways. In order to detect distinct topical pain points appearing during this era, they sampled emotion and stress on learners and instructors using applied ML algorithms and a new Twitter database particular to SK (South Korea) in the epidemic. They utilized cutting-edge, open-source, geofenced data on learners and teachers' opinions in SK that is being made usable to other researchers to determine polarity and sentiment trends over the epidemic timeline, as well as the main motivators of the feelings. Additionally, comparing Text Blob and VADER, the most popular pre-trained sentiment analysis methods, using statistical significance tests In the end, examine how people's emotions towards the pandemic changed in terms of pessimistic attitudes towards having access to study materials, online support groups, attending classes, and creativity, as well as negative attitudes towards mental stress, job loss, student relativeness, and overburdened institutions.

In another study [19], it was proposed to address the core issue of sentiment analysis known as the sentiment polarity categorization challenge. With thorough process descriptions, a general procedure for emotional polarity classification is presented. Online product views gathered from Amazon.com were the source of the data for this study. Sentence-level categorization experiments and review-level classification experiments were conducted with promising outcomes. Finally, we also provide a preview of our next sentiment analysis work.

In a study [20], we used an unsupervised learners' understanding model created for synchronous tutorial discourse in MOOC forums. The study used a clustering method to assemble posts that were similar, liken the clusters with manual annotations by MOOC researchers, and further qualitatively investigated clusters. This study is the first step in automating discourse analysis and mining on a large scale to better enhance students' learning in asynchronous conversation.

A study [21] provided research on students' attitudes regarding the course and its components to model their emotional behavior over time and, ultimately, ascertain whether and how this affected their overall performance. In order to improve the educational process, the combined understanding of the aforementioned strategies can be used by instructors to give students useful information on the structure and substance of their exchanged messages, the trends in their interactions, and the orientation of their moods. In another study [22], we analyzed the state and constraints of employing cloud technologies in e-learning environments and suggested a cloud-based service that would assess and promote students' learning and give teachers recommendations for augmenting resources and platforms. In a study [23], at a self-financed university in Hong Kong where Moodle and Microsoft Team are the primary teaching technologies, the critical factors in defining the approval of undergraduate students (N = 425) from various departments using ERL were investigated. All multiple regression and ML models demonstrated enhanced accuracy when comparing their predictive accuracy before and after the application of random forest recursive feature reduction, with elastic net regression having one of the highest accuracies (65.2 percent explained variance). In a study [24], the study uses ML with NLP algorithms to extract personal information, establish polarity, and identify feelings. The effects of COVID-19 on students and educators by analyzing and summarizing data collected from Twitter using machine learning with sentiment analysis to analyze emotions and also identifying key topics *via* qualitative analysis have been examined by using a novel geo-fenced dataset on student and educator opinions within South Korea [25].

RESEARCH ISSUES

SA is typically focused on determining a speaker's or writer's viewpoint on a point or covering contextual polarity. Aspects of the author's view may include their affective state (*i.e.*, their emotional state at the time of writing) or intentional emotional communication (*i.e.*, the author's intended emotional impact on the reader). The World Wide Web receives tremendous amounts of data every day that are generated *via* social networks, blogs, and other media. This enormous amount of data includes highly important opinion-related information that may be utilised to the advantage of enterprises and other areas of the commercial and scientific industries. Sentiment analysis is necessary because it is impossible to manually track and extract this essential information. Sentiment analysis is the practise of removing feelings or viewpoints from internet reviews that users have posted about a given topic, region, or product. To extract subjective information from source data, TA (text analytics), computational linguistics, and NLP are all applied. It groups the emotions into positive and negative categories. As a result, it establishes the speaker's or writer's broader view of the topic in question.

GAP IN RESEARCH

The area that has not yet been adequately studied, or the gap, is also referred to as the missing piece(s) in the study literature. Population or sample (size, type, location, *etc.*), research methodology, data collection and/or analysis, or other study factors or conditions could all fall under this category. The following research gaps have been identified:

1. Large numbers of emotive features are needed for sentiment analysis research. Therefore, it is crucial to choose elements that accurately describe internet reviews.

2. Because English has a distinctive manner of expressing sentiment due to the different language structures, it is impossible to simply apply the n-gramme elements that define English online reviews to English ones.

3. Due to computational constraints, many high-quality features cannot be included because of noise and redundancy in the feature space. Feature extraction techniques have been used for sentiment analysis since document frequency (DF) approaches have reached an advanced stage in obtaining feature subsets.

PROBLEM STATEMENT

- From the literature survey, it is found that very little work has been done in the field of sentiment analysis of the changed education system due to COVID-19.
- The present system uses SA, which is known as opinion mining, to find subjective information like opinions, attitudes, and sentiments conveyed in text using automated methods.
- The basic issue is that emotion extraction is a highly domain-specific procedure instead of just being generic. To get meaningful results, a person's vocabulary, language, and resources should be domain-relevant.
- Sentiment analysis plays an important role in finding the polarity of acceptance or rejection of the changed education paradigm by educationalists, institutes, students, and educators.
- So, the problem has been chosen to find the polarity of sentiments for decision-makers in the education system using machine learning algorithms.

Aim and Objectives

Aim

1. Conducting systematic research for sentiment analysis and classifying the polarity based on the user tweets.

2. The main aim of this research is the classification of the opinion's polarity, which entails determining whether the viewpoint is favourable, unfavourable, or neutral towards the user's tweet.

3. Improve the accuracy level of sentiment analysis and classification.

Objectives

This research aims to identify suitable techniques for sentiment analysis using machine learning by developing a prototype as a proof of concept. The findings from this research will be used to practically further research in the field of sentiment analysis for the educational system during COVID-19. Therefore, the specific objectives of this project are as follows:

1. To explore the polarity of learner and educator attitudes towards online learning during COVID-19 using sentiment analysis.

2. To analyze the trends and paradigm shift of online education platforms due to COVID-19 using machine learning.

3. To analyze sentiments regarding the changed way of education from the learner's and educators' perspectives.

4. To provide statistical analysis from the dataset.

IMPLICATIONS

The implication of this research work is sentiment classification about the polarity of tweets regarding the online education system before and after the COVID-19 crisis and opinion analysis for the online education system by utilising machine learning algorithms. In this research, we will design the framework for sentiment analysis and analyse the polarity of user tweets. We will use user tweets about educational systems before and after COVID-19.

EXPECTED RESULT

- The expected outcome is to identify suitable techniques for sentiment analysis using machine learning by developing a prototype as a proof of concept. The findings from this research will be used to practically further research in the field of sentiment analysis for the educational system during COVID-19.
- Proposed a sentiment classification about the polarity of tweets regarding the online education system before and after the COVID-19 crisis and opinion analysis for the online education system by utilising various supervised algorithms.
- An empirical comparison has also been made to understand the clear view of sentiment analysis by utilising supervised learning algorithms.
- It is expected that the proposed model will show more accuracy than the existing algorithms.

CONCLUSION

The proposed model will give sentiment classification of tweets regarding the online education system and opinion analysis for the online education system by utilising various machine learning-supervised algorithms.

REFERENCES

[1]   S. Nuez, and Yu. Audrey, "Examining the structure of organisational relationships using social network analysis", *Reflections on Methodology,* 2018.

[2]   Z. Ping, L. Fudong, and S. Zheng, "Thinking and practise of online teaching under the COVID-19 epidemic", *IEEE 2nd International Conference on Computer Science and Educational Informatization (CSEI).,* 2020.Xinxiang, China

[3]   J. Li, and C. Li, "Exploration and practise of the teaching pattern of skill-oriented courses in the

context of online home schooling", *15th International Conference on Computer Science & Education (ICCSE).,* 2020.Delft, Netherlands

[4]   X. Feng, "A brief discussion about the impact of coronavirus disease 2019 on teaching in colleges and universities of china", *International Conference on E-Commerce and Internet Technology (ECIT).,* 2020.Zhangjiajie, China

[5]   Y.Q. Wang, M.L. Huang, X.Y. Zhu, and L. Zhao, "Attention-based LSTM for aspect-level sentiment classification", *Proc. 2016 Conf. Empirical Methods in Natural Language Processing,* pp. 606-615, 2016.Austin, TX, USA
[http://dx.doi.org/10.18653/v1/D16-1058]

[6]   D.H. Ma, S.J. Li, X.D. Zhang, and H.F. Wang, "Interactive attention networks for aspect-level sentiment classification", *Proc. 26th Int. Joint Conf. Artificial Intelligence,* pp. 4068-4074, 2017.Melbourne, Australia
[http://dx.doi.org/10.24963/ijcai.2017/568]

[7]   B. Liu, S. Tang, X. Sun, Q. Chen, J. Cao, J. Luo, and S. Zhao, "Context-aware social media user sentiment analysis", *Tsinghua Sci. Technol.,* vol. 25, no. 4, pp. 528-541, 2020.
[http://dx.doi.org/10.26599/TST.2019.9010021]

[8]   X. Li, L.D. Bing, W. Lam, and B. Shi, "Transformation networks for target-oriented sentiment classification", *Proc. 56th Annu. Meeting of the Association for Computational Linguistics,* pp. 946-956, 2018.Melbourne, Australia
[http://dx.doi.org/10.18653/v1/P18-1087]

[9]   D. José Silva Oliveira, P. Henrique de Souza Bermejo, J. Roberto Pereira, and D. Aparecida Barbosa, "The application of the sentiment analysis technique in social media as a tool for social management practises at the governmental level", *Brazil. J. Publ. Administ. Rio de Janeiro,* vol. 53, no. 1, pp. 235-251, 2019.

[10] V. Kaushal, and M. Patwardhan, "Emerging trends in personality identification using online social networks: A literature survey", *ACM Trans. Knowl. Discov. Data,* vol. 12, no. 2, pp. 1-30, 2018.
[http://dx.doi.org/10.1145/3070645]

[11] K. Abdullah Ayub, "Sentiment analysis: A research perspective", *I. J. Scienti.Tech. Res.,* vol. 10, no. 2, 2021.

[12] G. Bisht, "Sentiment analysis and industrial growth", *EEO,* vol. 19, no. 4, pp. 2810-2823, 2020.
[http://dx.doi.org/10.17051/ilkonline.2020.04.764649]

[13] P. Deulgaonkar, "Uber vs. Careem: Which is most talked about in the Middle East?", Availanle from:https://www.arabianbusiness.com/uber-vs-careem-which-ismost-talked-about-in-the-m-ddle-east--665326.html

[14] G. Hu, "Analysing users' sentiment towards popular consumer industries and brands on Twitter", *IEEE International Conference on Data Mining Workshops (ICDMW) IEEE.,* 2017.

[15] S. Dhineshkumar, "Design, synthesis and biological evaluation of novel thiosemicarbazone-indole derivatives targeting prostate cancer cells", *Eur J Med Chem.,* vol. 210, p. 112970, 2017.

[16] A.E. Hassanien, M.F. Tolba, M. Elhoseny, and M. Mostafa, "The international conference on advanced machine learning technologies and applications (AMLTA2018)", cario, Egypt, 2018.

[17] M. Hall, E. Frank, G. Holmes, B. Pfahringer, P. Reutemann, and I.H. Witten, "The weka data mining software", *SIGKDD Explor.,* vol. 11, no. 1, pp. 10-18, 2009.
[http://dx.doi.org/10.1145/1656274.1656278]

[18] K. Asha, and T. Devi, "Study on mining emotions from literature: A method using computers to extract opinionated knowledge nuggets", *Int. J. Emerg. Technol. Adv. Eng.,* vol. 2, no. 8, pp. 91-94, 2012.

[19] X. Fang, and J. Zhan, "Sentiment analysis using product review data", *J. Big Data,* vol. 2, no. 1, p. 5,

2015.
[http://dx.doi.org/10.1186/s40537-015-0015-2]

[20]   Aysu. Ezen-Can, Kristy. Elizabeth Boyer, Shaun. Kellogg, and Booth. Sherry, "Unsupervised modelling for understanding mooc discussion forums: A learning analytics approach", *LAK '15: Proceedings of the Fifth International Conference on Learning Analytics And Knowledge.,* pp. 146-150, 2015.

[21]   V. Kagklis, A. Karatrantou, M. Tantoula, C.T. Panagiotakopoulos, and V.S. Verykios, "A learning analytics methodology for detecting sentiment in student fora: A case study in distance education", *E. J. Open, Distance and E-Learning,* vol. 18, no. 2, pp. 74-94, 2015.
[http://dx.doi.org/10.1515/eurodl-2015-0014]

[22]   Z. Taoufiq, R. Chiheb, R. Faizi, and Abd. El Afia, "Cloud computing and sentiment analysis in E-learning systems", *2nd International Conference on Cloud Computing Technologies and Applications (CloudTech).,* 2016.Marrakech, Morocco
[http://dx.doi.org/10.1109/CloudTech.2016.7847695]

[23]   I.M.K. Ho, K.Y. Cheong, and A. Weldon, "Predicting student satisfaction of emergency remote learning in higher education during COVID-19 using machine learning techniques", *PLoS One,* vol. 16, no. 4, p. e0249423, 2021.
[http://dx.doi.org/10.1371/journal.pone.0249423] [PMID: 33798204]

[24]   M.M. Ali, "Arabic sentiment analysis about online learning to mitigate COVID-19", *J. Intell. Syst.,* vol. 30, no. 1, pp. 524-540, 2021.
[http://dx.doi.org/10.1515/jisys-2020-0115]

[25]   I.D. Aiyanyo, H. Samuel, and H. Lim, *Effects of the COVID-19 pandemic on classrooms: A case study on foreigners in south korea using applied machine learning sustainability.,* vol. 13, no. 9, p. 4986, 2021.*Sustainability,* vol. 13, no. 9, p. 4986, 2021.
[http://dx.doi.org/10.3390/su13094986]

CHAPTER 10

Image Processing for Autonomous Vehicle Based on Deep Learning

Tanvi Raut[1], **Ishan Sarode**[1], **Riddhi Mirajkar**[2,*] and **Ruchi Doshi**[3]

[1] *BTech-Information Technology, Vishwakarma Institute of Information Technology, Pune, India*

[2] *Faculty, Vishwakarma Institute of Information Technology, Pune, India*

[3] *University of Azteca, Chalco de Díaz Covarrubias, Mexico*

Abstract: The automation industry is rapidly growing and coming up with new and improved techniques for reducing time and efforts. One such example is the autonomous cars which are said to be the future of the automobile industry since they would be driver less, very efficient and relieve the stress of daily commuting [1]. Advances in technology using the AI and deep learning techniques help in improving the safety of the passengers and also in minimizing the efforts of the driver. For the study of autonomous vehicles, a lot of data needs to be collected, some of which include warning signals, speed limits, obstacles, collision avoidance, *etc*. This paper shows how IoT devices *i.e.* cameras and LiDAR sensors help in data collection, how deep learning is a solution, and how image recognition methods that use deep learning can help in object or any obstacle detection. An image processing algorithm based on deep learning is proposed in which the image perception can be made by an optical camera communication technique that can be used for collecting the data. Hence it will highlight how deep learning is used in the field of image processing or image recognition.

Keywords: Autonomous driving, Camera, CCD, LiDAR, Convolution neural network(CNN), Deep learning, Image processing, Lane detection, LED area detection, Machine learning, Object detection, Vehicles, YOLO.

INTRODUCTION

Modern day cars are equipped with technology that assist drivers to avoid drifting into adjacent lanes, making unsafe lane changes, brake automatically if a vehicle stops ahead, and warn drivers of vehicles behind them and various other things. All of these features use a combined effort of software and hardware to help iden-

---

* **Corresponding author Riddhi Mirajkar:** Faculty, Vishwakarma Institute of Information Technology, Pune, India; E-mail: riddhi.mirajkar@viit.ac.in

Sonali Mahendra Kothari, Vijayshri Nitin Khedkar, Ujwala Kshirsagar and Gitanjali Rahul Shinde (Eds.)

tify certain safety risks. Autonomous cars are vehicles capable of driving without human input by sensing the environment and making decisions based on the conditions. The car can travel to any place a traditional car can go and drive with experience [2].

Levels of Autonomous Driving

Autonomous driving is classified into 6 different levels. This classification is done based on the amount of control that the computer or the AI has over the car or the amount of input that is required from the driver. Fig. (**1**) shows a representation of the different levels of autonomous driving based on the input required by the users.

Level 0 – The work is done by humans and there is no role of the computer.

Level 1 – The work is mostly done by a human and only the acceleration is done by the computer.

Level 2 – The ADAS (Advanced Driver Assistance System) can handle tasks like steering and acceleration, but human monitoring is required at all times.

Level 3 – The ADAS can perform driving tasks in limited areas, but human input is required in cases where the computer fails and asks the driver to regain control.

Level 4 – The ADS (Advanced Driving System) can perform all driving tasks independently in which human attention is not required.

Level 5 – Involves complete automation in which all the work is done by the vehicle in all conditions and requires no human attention or input.

Camera vs LiDAR: The Better Hardware for the Detection of Vehicles

LiDAR technology utilizes light pulses to detect and gauge the distance and range of objects, similar to how radar uses radio waves. This information is then used to inform the actions of self-driving vehicles, such as applying the brakes to avoid collisions. Additionally, LiDAR systems can generate 3D maps of the surrounding environment by emitting thousands of pulses per second and using on-board software to process the resulting data. These maps provide a comprehensive, 360 degree view that enables self-driving cars to navigate various road conditions.

LEVELS OF DRIVING AUTOMATION

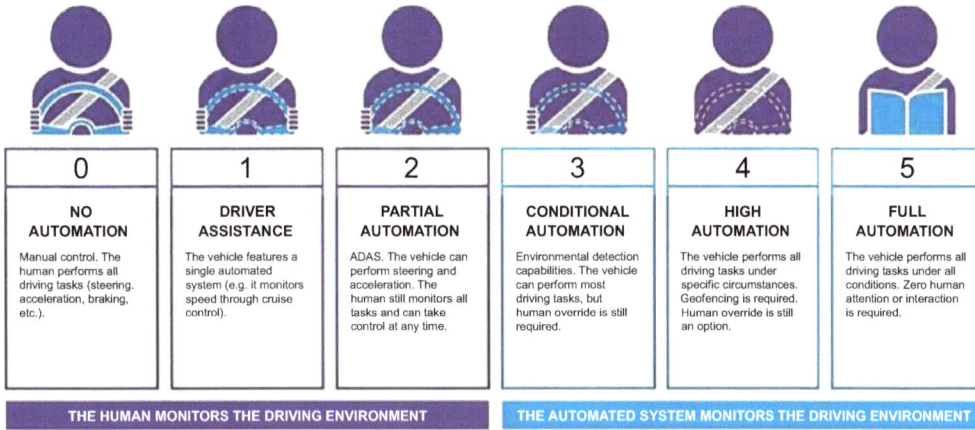

0	1	2	3	4	5
NO AUTOMATION	**DRIVER ASSISTANCE**	**PARTIAL AUTOMATION**	**CONDITIONAL AUTOMATION**	**HIGH AUTOMATION**	**FULL AUTOMATION**
Manual control. The human performs all driving tasks (steering, acceleration, braking, etc.).	The vehicle features a single automated system (e.g. it monitors speed through cruise control).	ADAS. The vehicle can perform steering and acceleration. The human still monitors all tasks and can take control at any time.	Environmental detection capabilities. The vehicle can perform most driving tasks, but human override is still required.	The vehicle performs all driving tasks under specific circumstances. Geofencing is required. Human override is still an option.	The vehicle performs all driving tasks under all conditions. Zero human attention or interaction is required.

THE HUMAN MONITORS THE DRIVING ENVIRONMENT   **THE AUTOMATED SYSTEM MONITORS THE DRIVING ENVIRONMENT**

Fig (1). The 6 distinctive levels of autonomous driving.

Cameras on self-driving vehicles utilize visual data captured by the optics in the lens to inform the on-board software about the surrounding environment. With advances in computer vision algorithms and neural networks, these cameras are capable of identifying various objects and utilizing this information to guide the actions of the vehicle, such as avoiding collisions, slowing down in the presence of traffic, and safely changing lanes. Additionally, cameras may utilize OCR (Optical Character Recognition) technology to interpret and read text from road signs and other written materials. Table **1** gives a detailed difference between the two systems.

Table 1. Distinction between Camera and LiDAR System.

Camera	LiDAR
The camera has better advantages at visual recognition and working with AI to identify objects on the road.	LiDAR plots a virtual map in real time which gives it more precision while determining distance between objects.
The camera also has the capability to utilize OCR and read road signs.	Since LiDAR uses radio waves, it cannot read road signs.
Cameras are more reliable when used as visioning systems as they are good at imaging.	LiDAR's reliability is affected by wavelength stability and detector sensibility.
Cameras lack range to detect objects and weather conditions like fog can hamper this range further.	LiDAR systems have a better range since it relies on radio waves and harsh weather conditions like fog do not affect its capabilities.
Cameras are less expensive and compact to fit.	LiDAR is on the expensive side and looks bulky on the vehicle.

The integration of LiDAR and other IoT sensors, such as cameras, has the potential to significantly enhance public safety in self-driving vehicles. As the capabilities of these systems, particularly in regard to object identification and decision-making, continue to improve through the use of advanced AI techniques such as machine learning and neural networks, it is possible that LiDAR may become redundant. The ultimate goal of self-driving technology is to minimize accidents caused by human error, and the effectiveness of these systems in achieving this goal will depend on the accuracy and reliability of their software. Ultimately, the quality of the software and its ability to accurately analyze data and make informed decisions may be the key factor in determining the safety of self-driving vehicles on the roads.

CHALLENGES FACED BY AUTONOMOUS VEHICLES

- Lidar and Radar – The equipment cost for lidar and radars is very high. The radar works on the principle of detecting reflections of radio waves from nearby objects but when there are multiple cars on the road using the same technology, the car may not be able to distinguish between the radio waves causing interference [3].
- Road conditions – Road conditions are highly unpredictable and vary from place to place. The difference ranges from a marked and smooth broad highway to an unmarked and highly deteriorated street with potholes.
- Weather conditions – Weather is another factor that may cause failure in autonomous driving systems. The system should be able to work even in a snow-filled road with no markings visible.
- Traffic conditions and laws – Autonomous cars may require driving along other autonomous cars as well as other human beings. There are often cases of people breaking traffic and the system should react to such situations in a timely manner.
- Accident liability – The question arises in case of autonomous driving of who will be held liable in case of an accident, the manufacturer, or the driver. Especially with a few level 5 prototypes with no steering wheel for the driver to regain control in case of an accident.

LITERATURE SURVEY

The object detection is represented by Abhishek Gupta [4] *et al*. who applied LIDAR-SLAM fusion. LIDAR-SLAM is used to eliminate obstacles like less visibility, absence of adequate light or uneven movement of vehicles. This method applies different spatial resolutions which are incorporated with the missing data. Optical technology is used to enhance the detection of upcoming obstacles. A set of cameras known as the time of flight and monocular are used for mapping, and various other purposes. This is implemented by using compressed 3D visual sensing devices. These devices detect glare from dangerous road situations along with a panoramic view of the background and for the location and detection of objects, spectral processing is used.

The represented work for the detection of LED regions using a deep learning-based image processing algorithm is proposed by Trong Hop-Do [5] *et al.* It is employed in the detection of LED regions. A CNN model is used to extract the image. The extracted feature vector is used to output the LED region's top-left, top-right, bottom-left, and bottom-right corners in the input image. In addition, interpolation on these four points is used to improve the accuracy of the LED region's detected bounding box. Intersection over Union (IoU) is used to evaluate detection accuracy. It can be implemented through VOCC systems because of the high-level efficiency and accuracy of the model. The results show that the proposed algorithm has a high level of accuracy, a short processing time, and a high level of robustness when detecting LED regions.

The algorithm that consists of an intelligent kernel with an SLFN core predictor and EHF task scheduler algorithm was proposed by Gomatheeshwari Balasekaran [6] *et al.* The algorithm is based on Iot related autonomous vehicles. They have developed two learning algorithms namely LW_DNN and SLFN. To predict the multicore like "4L1b, 8L0b and 8Lb "they have used a single-layer feedforward network (G.B. Hung 2006). For the initial stage comparison, they have adopted the DNN network. On selective and required processors, synthetic workloads are executed which are proposed by the resource predictor. Up to 96.3 to 98% of accuracy is achieved for synthetic workloads.

A deep learning algorithm for object detection for a Safe Autonomous Driving is proposed by Khan Muhammad [7] *et al.* It consists of a regression neural network for traffic management executed with the help of a 3D object detection framework implemented by applying the deep CNN model for the prediction of objects, location, and relative boxes, along with the implementation of a mathematical model for object localization.

Implementation of deep learning for the application of Lane Detection with the help of a Canny Detection operator for edge detection along with Hough Transform was proposed by Aditya Singh Rathore [8]. They implemented Gaussian Blur for image smoothening. The displayed image from the camera showed lane lines in colored format which can be used in autonomous vehicles for efficiency and driving accuracy.

Hironobu Fujiyoshi [9] *et al.* published a paper in 2019 by implementing an application of a Convolution Neural Network, an aspect of deep learning in the field of image processing for Autonomous vehicles. With the help of CNN, obstacles in the image, categorization of objects based on prior given names and detection of the signals on the road can be procured. CNN-based models are best when it comes to multiple object detection.

IMAGE RECOGNITION BASED ON DEEP LEARNING

Image recognition is one the tasks in which deep learning excels. An image is processed and is categorized into pre-defined classes, so image recognition software can define what's depicted in an image and differentiate between one object and another. There are several tasks that the computer vision performs such as image classification with localization, object detection, object (semantic) segmentation, and instance segmentation.

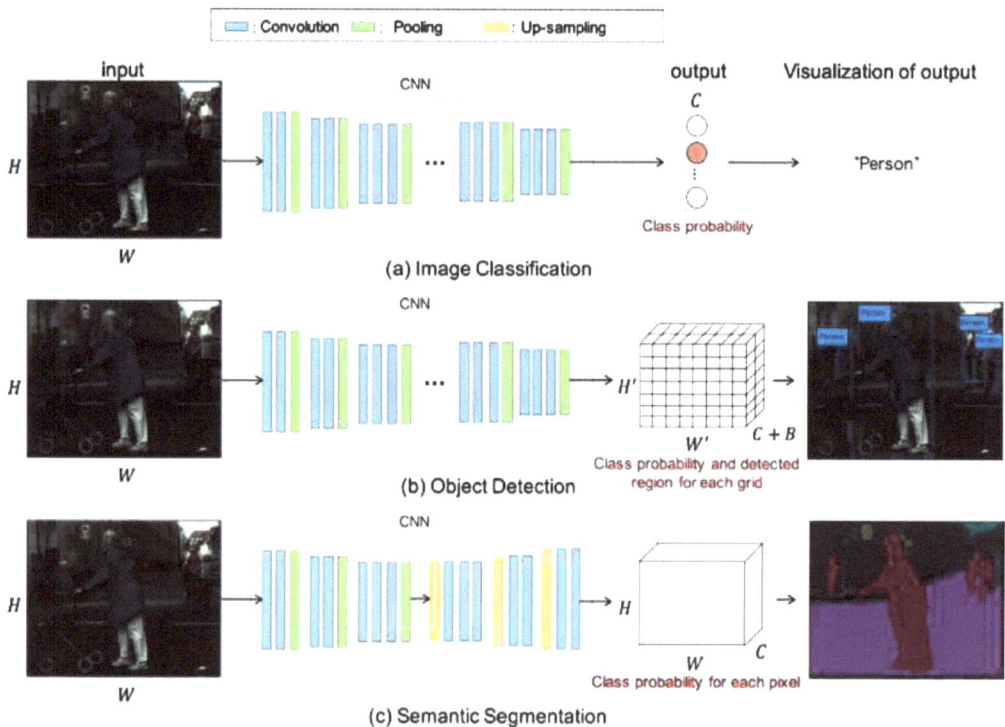

Fig. (2). Example of image classification, object detection, semantic segmentation.

All of these tasks are necessary in autonomous driving as it relies heavily on the computer vision to recognize the surroundings of the car in order to take necessary actions. It is crucial that the system distinguishes between the objects accurately and is fast enough to have time to react. Along with this, the distance of the object from the car is also important.

There are various algorithms for image classification and object detection, but convolutional neural network (CNN) is one of the best algorithms for deep learning in the analysis of an image [10]. The representation of image classification, object detection and semantic segmentation is depicted in Fig. (**2**).

CNN is a machine learning algorithm that takes an input image, assigns importance to the various objects that are present in the image and is capable of differentiating one from the other.

All CNN consists of an input layer or the input image, an output layer that contains binary or multi-class labels and hidden layers consisting of convolution layers, rectified linear unit (ReLU) layers, pooling layers and a fully connected CNN [11]. Refer to Fig. (**3**) to illustrate the complete CNN process.

The three major layers are defined as follows:

- Convolutional layer: Each input neuron is connected to the next hidden layer in a typical input layer but in a CNN, only a small region of the input layer connects to the next hidden layer.
- Pooling layer: The pooling layer summarizes the presence of features in feature maps and reduces the dimensionality of feature maps.
- Fully connected layer: These are some of the last layers in a CNN. The output from a pooling layer is flattened and then inputted into the fully connected layer.

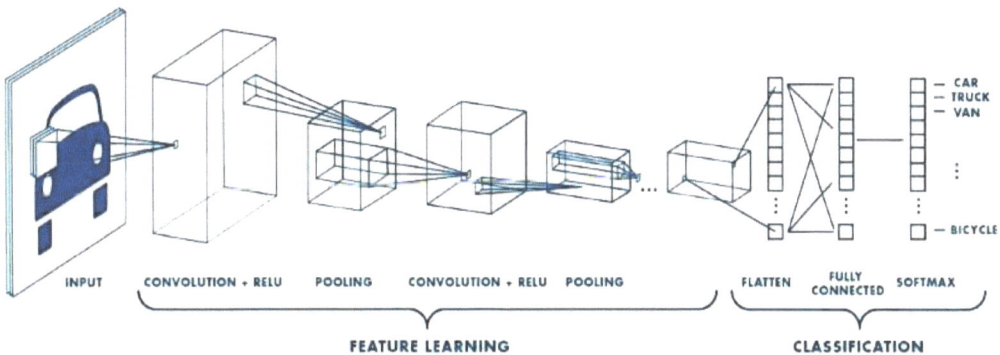

Fig. (3). CNN process from input to output.

Advantages of CNN Over Traditional Algorithms

- The main reason for CNN is that feature engineering is no longer required. We need to spend so much time on feature selection before CNN (algorithm for features extraction). When we compare handcrafted features to CNN, CNN performs better and has higher accuracy. It covers both local and global issues. It also learns different characteristics from images.
- Simple feedforward neural networks do not detect any order in their inputs. If you shuffled all of your images in the same way, the neural network would perform the same way it did when trained on non-shuffled images.
- CNN, on the other hand, employs image local spatial coherence. Because adjacent pixels are meaningful when combined, using convolution on patches of adjacent pixels can significantly reduce the number of operations required to process an image as shown in Fig. (**4**). This is also known as local connectivity. Each map is then filled with the result of the convolution of a small patch of pixels slid across the entire image with a window.
- There are also pooling layers, which reduce the image size. This is possible because we keep spatially organized features like images throughout the network, so downscaling them makes sense in the same way that reducing the size of the image does. A vector cannot be downscaled on classic inputs because there is no coherence between the input and the one next to it.
- They can be treated as backbone function approximators that can be implemented as visual/audio feature extractors for downstream applications that need to reason about image/audio data. They closely resemble mammal visual cortex and there are neuroscientific links between biological visual cortex and artificial CNNs.

SYSTEM ARCHITECTURE

Autonomy in self-driving cars is achieved by the collection of data on public roads. Vehicles that are used for this purpose have a wide range of sensors and cameras around the car and data from these sensors are stored on a local disk or on a cloud storage. This data is then used to train various models and algorithms for autonomy including motion estimation, vehicle detection, and pedestrian detection. Driving on public roads in real-life situations for the evaluation of performance and refinement of technology is important for the future of self-driving cars. In autonomous cars, good accuracy is set at 100% and accuracy less than that may lead to accidents. This data consists of a wide array of weather and traffic conditions, road markings, intersections, turns, curve roads, zebra crossings, pedestrian behaviors, and other vehicle behaviors and this increases the size of the data to hundreds of terabytes.

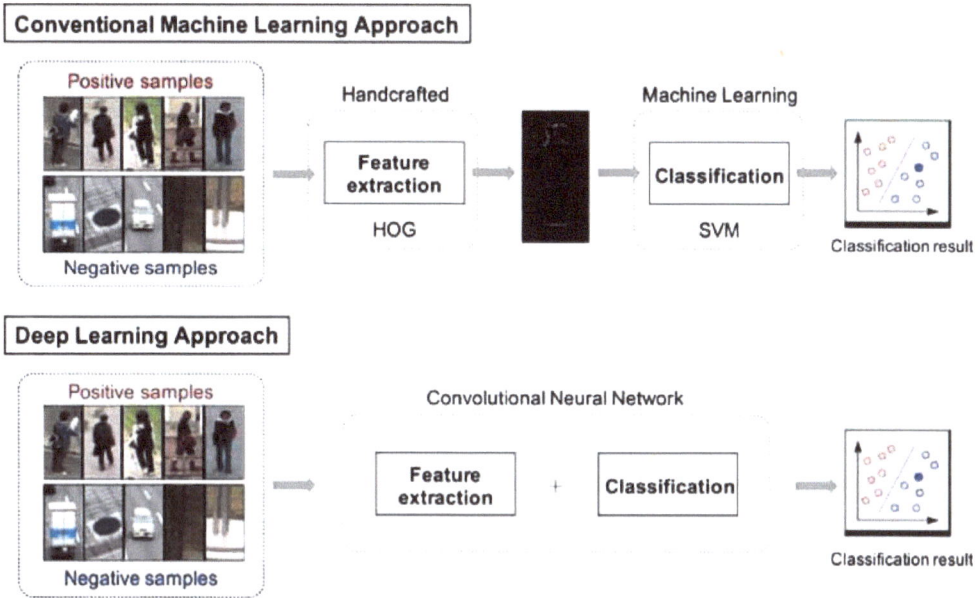

Fig. (4). Difference between conventional machine learning and deep learning [9].

The Vehicle Optical Camera Communication (VOCC) is elaborated in Fig. (**5**). The cameras placed on the hoods of cars capture the light emitted by the brake LED of a car in front. The data is captured in video format and each frame is processed individually to obtain information. This information is used for various purposes as vehicle type, speed, position, future behavior, direction, *etc.*

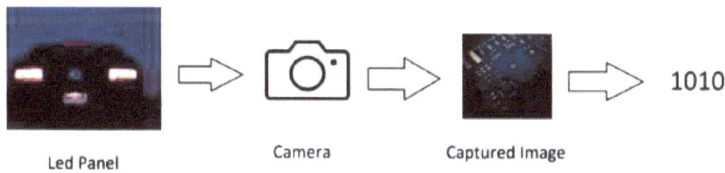

Fig. (5). Data collection system.

Proposed Algorithm

Deep learning's evolution in the last decade has resulted in assistance in many areas of computer science, particularly computer vision. Many new deep-learning algorithms have been discovered and proposed to solve this problem. There are several effective deep learning algorithms available to solve object detection. Each algorithm has its own set of advantages and disadvantages. The algorithm proposed uses deep learning for LED light region detection. Fig. (**6**) describes the algorithm architecture. A CNN (Convolutional Neural Network) forms the backbone of the algorithm to extract features from the image. Specifically, we use Xception. After that, by performing regression on the extracted area vector of the LED light, we take four points top-right, top-left, bottom-left, and bottom-right. Lastly, we apply interpolation on the four points for higher accuracy of the LED light bounding box.

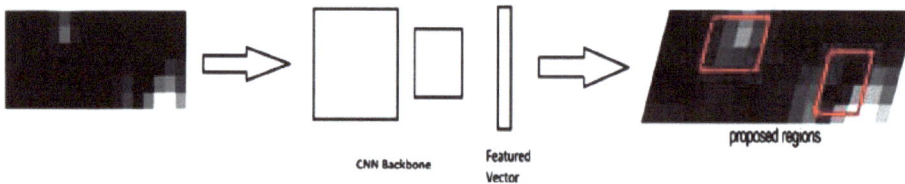

Fig. (6). Proposed architecture.

Object Detection

Object detection is a crucial task in autonomous vehicles as the vehicle must be aware of the surroundings in order to react to them within sufficient time [12].

A fixed CCD camera captures images of the road. The properties of the CCD array, such as the pixel size and the number of pixels in the image sensor, provide important information for determining the position of objects in an image. When an object is captured in an image, its position is represented by the pixel coordinates of the CCD array. By using the known properties of the CCD array, such as the physical dimensions of each pixel, it is possible to calculate the real-world coordinates of the object in three-dimensional space. By analyzing the pixel information of an object's shape and size, it is possible to determine its orientation and distance from the camera.

There are various algorithms for object detection:

- OverFeat – Released in 2013, OverFeat performs object recognition, detection, and localization at the same time. It is one of the most successful algorithms. OverFeat is 8 layers deep and is based on the idea of producing detection boxes at multiple scales and combining them together into high-confidence predictions.
- Fast R-CNN – Focuses on accuracy while having moderate speeds. It uses the shared computation per region proposal to speed up prediction time and training of the model.
- VGG16 – It is a 16- and 19-layer model which was created as an improvement to the OverFeat algorithm in object classification and detection by effects of an extreme layer depth. It set new benchmarks in localization and classification.

You Only Look Once (YOLO)

YOLO uses CNN to detect objects in real time and uses a single forward propagation to move forward in a neural network while detecting objects [13]. The entire prediction on the image is done in one single algorithm run. This improves the speed of recognition significantly and it provides high accuracy with less background errors. The algorithm also has learning capabilities that allow it to learn representations of objects and apply them.

The image is divided into grids, refer to Fig. (**7**). Each grid has a defined size S*S and every grid is of equal dimensions. Every grid detects objects that appear in those grids.

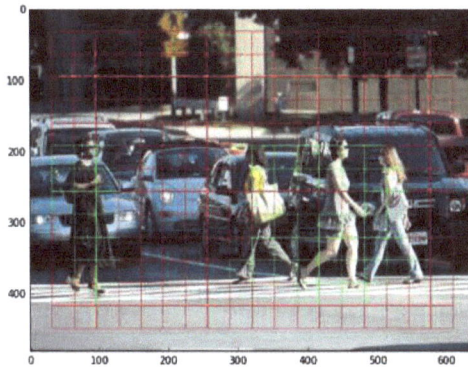

Fig. (7). Image divided into grids.

A bounding box is drawn over the grids which contain an object in them. A bounding box is an outline that highlights an object in an image, each bounding box has height (bh), width (bw), class, center (bx, by). Each grid cell is responsible for producing bounding boxes and their confidence scores. Fig. (**8**) displays bounding boxes on an image and its symbols.

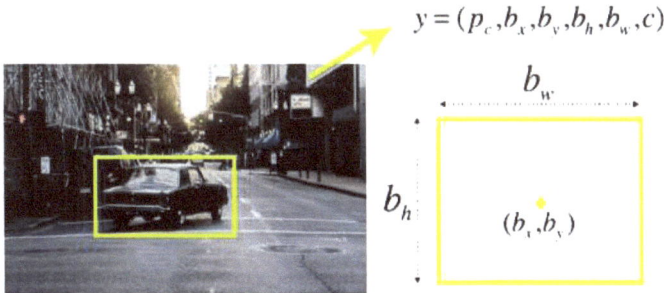

$$y = (p_c, b_x, b_y, b_h, b_w, c)$$

Fig. (8). Bounding boxes and its symbols.

Intersection over union (IOU) is used to provide an output box that completely borders the object, as shown in Fig. (**9**).

Fig. (9). Representation of Intersection over union (IOU).

If IOU is equal to 1, then the predicted box and real box are the same, this removes all the unnecessary boxes that are not equal to the real ones. Fig. (**10**) represents the combination of all the techniques applied on the given image. The final detection will consist of unique boxes that surround the objects.

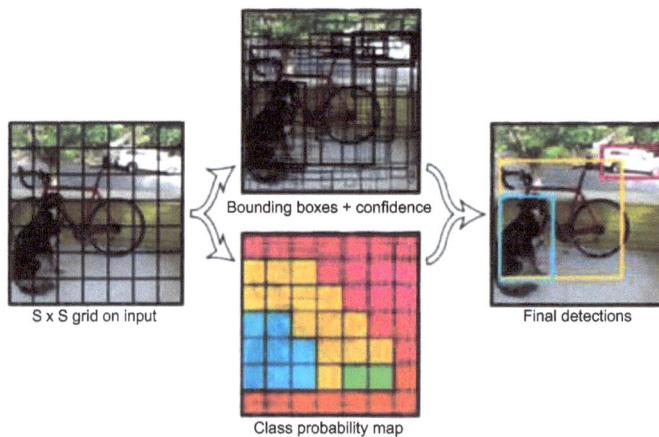

Fig. (10). Combination of all the techniques [9].

Lane Detection

Traffic accidents are common in the world. The lanes help in the identification of roads and their usage. Single white lines are seen which are used to regulate traffic. In general, highways are divided by dividers and have multiple lanes dedicated to two-wheelers, four-wheelers heavy, and four-wheelers non-heavy. These various lanes aid in the smooth operation of road traffic.

The Lane Detection system is an important system when it comes to the development of autonomous vehicles. The road image of parallel lane detection is shown in Fig. (**11**). As an autonomous vehicle, its basic requirement is of a computer vision system model which perceives and detects lanes in any given weather conditions. Given that the lane detection problem is a multi-feature detection, it can be solved with the help of many machine learning techniques [14].

The frequently detected distortions that lead to errors in image processing are due to object shadows, brake marks of tires, and breakage of lane lines on the road. To avoid these distortions, we propose using a CCD Camera which provides a distortion-free digital output with high-quality images. These cameras are also cost-effective so they can be easily implemented in mass-production cars as well.

A fixed CCD camera captures images of the road. The obtained color image is then converted into a grey scale image to reduce the processing time and make pixel intensity identification easier. Hough detection is used for image analysis of the obtained image. The edge detector then detects the edges and filters out only the necessary parts of the images. Edge detection is used to improve the detection of curves and road edges. Edge detection captures the brightness seen in the image at the image's curves and edges. The parabolic model is used for curved paths. Both have matched boundaries.

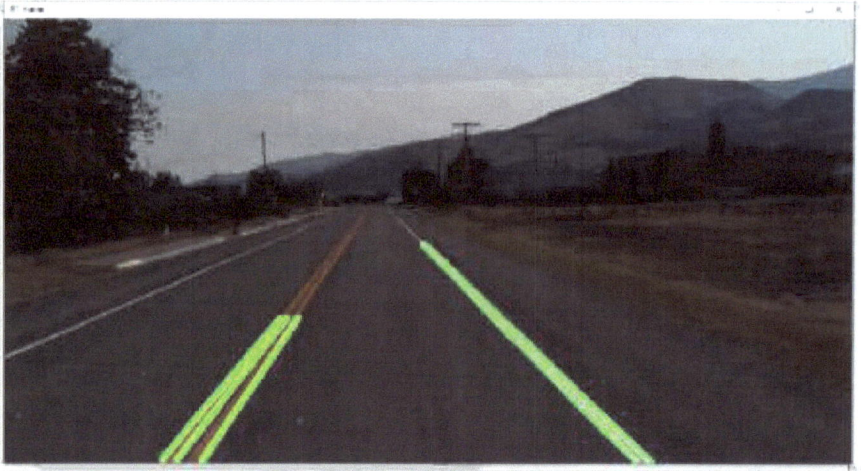

Fig. (11). Parallel Lane detection [8].

• Gaussian Blur

In order to smoothen and reduce noise distortion in the image, the Gaussian blur method is used. It preserves low spatial frequency and reduces negligible details from the obtained image. The procedure is to convolve the obtained image with Gaussian Kernel. To smoothen the image, all pixels where noise distortion occurs are to be adjusted according to the neighboring pixels. Hence the kernel (of numbers) is run along the pixels of the obtained image and the pixels are adjusted based on the weighted average calculated from the neighboring pixels.

• Canny Detection

In Fig. (**12**), we can see that a canny edge detection technique is applied after the image is smoothened. A canny edge detector uses a multi-stage algorithm to detect a variety of edges in images [15]. An image is a matrix consisting of rows and columns. As image can have a 2D representation, therefore the height of the image captured is measured in terms of y-axis and the width of the image is measured in terms of x-axis. The derivatives of x and y axis are taken into consideration by the Canny edge detector. A bilateral filter is applied which actually smoothens the image. Hence more optimized and accurate results are procured.

Fig. (12). Represents an image after Canny Edge detection is applied [8].

• Hough Transformation

Hough detection is applied as it is a feature detection technique in image processing and computer vision. It identifies lanes on roads along with the shape of the roads. It uses image coordinates in an equation and then votes are considered.

Y = mX + C Equation 1 (Polar coordinates are used as 'm' can tend to zero.)

From equation 1, Y is the intercept and 'm' is the slope of the given line which is then plotted as a single dot in the Hough Space. On consideration, there are various lines which pass through this particular dot with different values of the slope. But there is one line that will surely pass through two points. That line passing through both the points having the slope m and C values will be the intersection point in the Hough Space. The Hough Space is represented in a grid format for a better identification of the lines. The slope and y value of a line are represented in the format of a bin present in the grid. A vote is cast for each point of intersection in a Hough Space. The line with the maximum votes is considered. Below is a visual representation of the Hough transform when applied.

Graphical representation of Hough transform by the replacement of Cartesian coordinates with polar coordinates.

$$r = x.cos\, cos\, \theta + y.sin\, sin\, \theta \qquad (1)$$

$$y = -cos\theta\, sin\theta\,.x + r\, sin\, sin\, \theta \qquad (2)$$

Normal representation of points over a graph is shown in Fig. **13** (b-1):

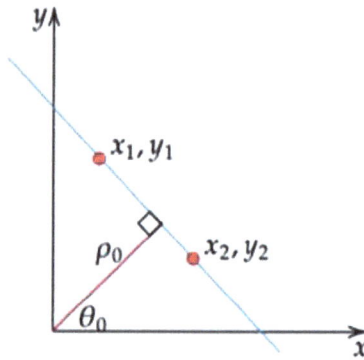

Fig. (13). (b-1) Normal representation of points.

Fig. **14** (b-2) shows the representation after Hough Transform is applied:

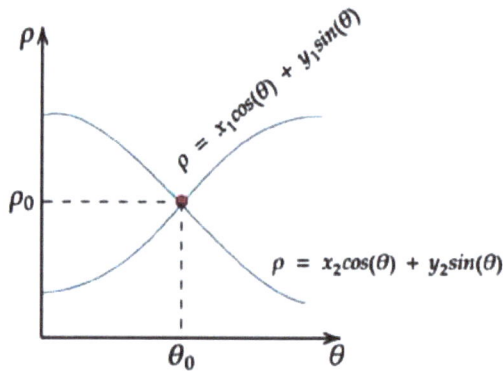

Fig. (14). (b-2) After effect of Hough Transform.

Transformation of two points into a Hough Space is shown in Fig. **15** (b-3), where it is represented by Hough Space lines which depict all the lines that can pass through these points.

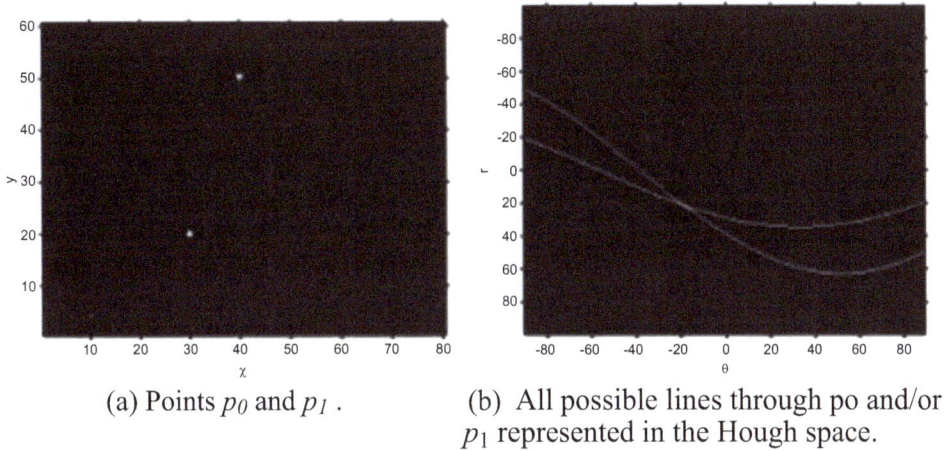

(a) Points p_0 and p_1.

(b) All possible lines through po and/or p_1 represented in the Hough space.

Fig. (15). (b-3) Transformation of two points.

Conversion of such obtained points into a proper visible line based on the votes casted is shown in Fig. **16** (b-4):

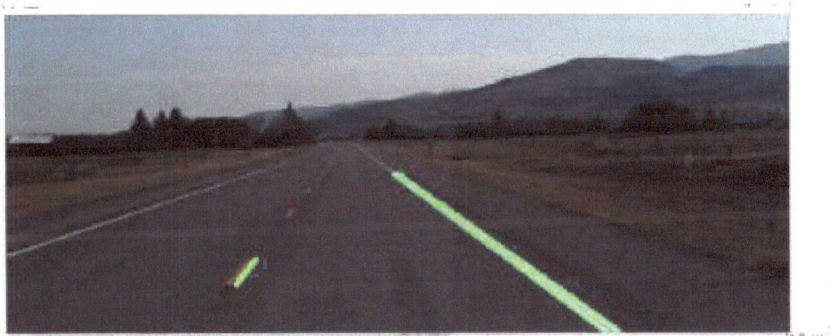

Fig. (16). (b-4) Hough Transform.

CONCLUSION

In this paper, image resolution along with deep learning is applied to autonomous driving vehicles. As the number of accidents due to vehicles increases globally, autonomous driving seems a safer option, but advancements need to be made in the way cars detect their surroundings for faster response time. We have proposed algorithms related to object detection and lane detection using CCD Cameras. We also state how these cameras would be helpful in detecting the lanes and objects with high quality while keeping the cost in check.

Object detection is one of the crucial aspects of autonomous driving and the model used for object detection must be able to classify between various objects efficiently. Convolution Neural Network (CNN) provides a combination of both efficient accuracy and quick response time. Thus, supporting the objective of the paper. The 3 algorithms proposed in the paper have a combination of accuracy along with a faster response time, but further study would be required to determine which algorithm fits the best.

One of the basic requirements in autonomous vehicles relies on accuracy lane detection with the help of computer vision models. We have proposed an algorithm that aims towards higher precision as required for the autonomous vehicle to operate effectively. This algorithm consists of Gaussian Blur, Canny Detection and Hough transformation. Further study would be required to gain the practicality of the above proposed algorithms to draw an accurate conclusion regarding their efficiency and accuracy.

REFERENCES

[1]   J. Liu, "Survey of the image recognition based on deep learning network for autonomous driving car", 2020 5th International Conference on Information Science, Computer Technology and Transportation (ISCTT), Shenyang, China, 2020, pp. 1-6, doi: 10.1109/ISCTT51595.2020.00007.

[2]   N. M. Tahir, U. I. Bature, M. A. Baba, K. A. Abubakar, and S. M. Yarima, "Image recognition based autonomous driving: A deep learning approach",

[3]   Y. Tian, K. Pei, S. Jana, and B. Ray, "Deep Test: Automated testing of deep neural network driven automated cars", 2018 IEEE/ACM 40th International Conference on Software Engineering (ICSE), Gothenburg, Sweden, 2018, pp. 303-314.

[4]   A. Gupta, A. Anpalagan, L. Guan, and A. S. Khwaja, "Deep learning for object detection and scene perception in self-driving cars: Survey, challenges and open issues", vol 10, 2021.

[5]   Trong Hop-Do, Ngan-Ling Nguyen, Hoang-Thong Vo, Than-Binh Nguyen, and Thanh Vu Khanh Ngo, "Deep learning based image processing for proactive data collecting system for autonomous vehicle", 2021 21st ACIS International Winter Conference on Software Engineering, Artificial Intelligence, Networking and Parallel/Distributed Computing (SNPD-Winter), Ho Chi Minh City, Vietnam, 2021, pp. 253-256, doi: 10.1109/SNPDWinter52325.2021.00062.

[6]   G. Balasekaran, S. Jayakumar, and R. Pérez de Prado, "An Intelligent task scheduling mechanism for autonomous vehicle using deep learning".

[7]   K. Muhammad, A. Ullah, J. Lloret, J. del Ser, and H. C. Victor, "Deep learning for safe autonomous driving: Current challenges and future directions", IEEE Transactions on Intelligent Transportation Systems, vol. 22, no. 7, pp. 4316-4336, 2021, doi: 10.1109/TITS.2020.3032227.

[8]   A.S. Rathore, "Lane detection for autonomous vehicles using OpenCV library".

[9]   H. Fujiyoshi, T. Hirakawa, and T. Yamashita, "Deep learning-based image recognition for autonomous driving".

[10]   Mi-Hwa Song, "Implementation of low cost autonomous car for lane recognition and keeping based on deep neural network model".

[11]   T. Xu, Z. Zhang, X. Wu, L. Qi, and Yi Han, "Recognition of lane changing behaviour with machine learning".

[12]   Yan. Zhou, S. Wen, D. Wang, Ji. Mu, and I. Richard, "Object detection in autonomous driving scenarios based on an improved faster R-CNN".

[13]   A. Boukerche, and Xi. Ma, "Vision based autonomous vehicle recognition: a new challenge for deep learning based systems".

[14]   Jiy. Jhang, T. Deng, F. Yan, and W. Liu, "Lane detection model based on spatio-temporal network with double convolutional gated recurrent units", IEEE Transactions on Intelligent Transportation Systems, vol. 23, no. 7, pp. 6666-6678, 2022, doi: 10.1109/TITS.2021.3060258.

[15]   S. Fernandes, D. Duseja, and R. Muthalagu, "Application of image processing techniques for autonomous cars".

CHAPTER 11

Applications of AI and IoT for Smart Cities

A. Kannammal[1,*] and **S. Chandia**[1]

[1] *Department of Computing (Decision and Computing Sciences), Coimbatore Institute of Technology, Coimbatore, Tamil Nadu-641014, India*

Abstract: Due to the rapid increase in urban population, the today's life of every citizen undergoes drastic changes. For the betterment of human life, Government of India had decided and announced the development of smart cities *i.e* the cities to be developed with all modern facilities in which people can use the internet for their daily activities. Smart city development would heavily depend on the Internet of Things (IOT) which combines three important aspects of Internet such as people-people interaction, people-objects interaction, and objects-objects interaction. Artificial Intelligence (AI) is another technology that provides the city equipped with efficient systems for security, safety, parking, *etc*.

The applications of AI enable IoT in smart cities that are discussed in this chapter such as Smart Home, Smart Healthcare, Smart Water, Smart Grid and Energy, Smart Transport, and Real Estate investment. Section 12.1 gives an introduction about the chapter that includes an introduction to Smart City, IoT and integration of AI and IoT. Section 12.2 discusses the potential use cases of AI and IoT in smart cities. Smart Home use case that includes smart management of equipment and human activity recognition is discussed. It also discusses Smart Healthcare which includes the fitness-tracking system, glucose-level monitoring system, body-temperature monitoring system, stress detection system, and oxygen-saturation monitoring system. Smart Infrastructure is also discussed which includes Smart Water, Smart Grid and Energy, and structural health monitoring. Smart Transport is also discussed in this chapter which includes the Vehicle Infrastructure Pedestrian (VIP), Smart Parking System (SPS) and Automated Incident Detection system (AID). The final section concludes the chapter by discussing the challenges in the smart city environment and future enhancements.

Keywords: Artificial intelligence, Internet of things, Smart city, Smart healthcare, Smart infrastructure, Smart home, Smart transport, Smart water.

---

* **Corresponding author A. Kannammal:** Department of Computing (Decision and Computing Sciences), Coimbatore Institute of Technology, Coimbatore, Tamil Nadu-641014, India; E-mail: kannammal@cit.edu.in

Sonali Mahendra Kothari, Vijayshri Nitin Khedkar, Ujwala Kshirsagar and Gitanjali Rahul Shinde (Eds.)
All rights reserved-© 2023 Bentham Science Publishers

INTRODUCTION

Due to the complexity of the ecosystem such as increased population, climatic variations, pollution, scarcity of resources, heavy traffic, poor infrastructure *etc.,* cities have become unorganized. So, there is a need for using technology as a solution to all these issues. This paved the path for the development of smart cities [1]. By utilizing all the city resources, the quality of life should be improved and operational cost should be reduced. A smart city can be defined by various characteristics as shown in Table **1**. Each characteristic is defined based on the key aspects of the city.

Table 1. Characteristics of a Smart City.

Characteristics	Factors
Smart Environment(Natural Resources)	Smart Energy
	Smart Air, Water, Land, and waste Management
	Environmental Protection
Smart Society(Quality of Life)	Smart Health and Education
	Smart Safety and Security
	Smart Housing
	Smart Cultural Facilities
Smart Government(Governance)	Smart Public and Social Services
	Smart Participation in decision-making
Smart Economy(Infrastructure, Technology and Environment)	Smart Industry and Business
	Smart Tourism
	Smart Payment and Banking
Smart Mobility(Transport and ICT)	Local accessibility
	Innovative and Safe Transport Systems
	Availability of ICT-infrastructure

Internet of Things

The Internet of Things (IoT) is an interconnected system of physical items that are distinctively addressable and has various degrees of sensing and processing capabilities. Its main feature is to make the devices communicate through the internet as their common platform. The broad areas which are covered by IoT are the industrial sector, health sector, smart cities, security, agriculture, and emergencies among many others.

AI-Enabled IoT

AI is considered the science of agent design. By associating intelligence with the agent's behavior, a human-like mind without a human-like brain is acknowledged [2]. When the integration of Artificial Intelligence (AI) and the Internet of Things (IoT) is implied for a city, then the city is considered to be smart. Many practical innovations have been produced in such cities in almost all sectors [3]. By utilizing all the city resources, the quality of life is improved and operational cost is reduced. The major role of IoT is connecting the various digital and analog devices through the Internet with its unique identifier while the role of AI is to focus on devices making decisions through learning from their data and experience [4].

POTENTIAL USE CASES OF AI AND IOT IN SMART CITIES

Smart Home

The smart home is one of the inevitable components of a smart city. Gartner defines a smart home as "Smart Homes consist of a set of devices and services that are connected to each other and to the internet and can automatically respond to pre-set rules, be remotely accessed and managed by mobile apps or a browser, and send alerts or messages to the user(s) [5]."

IoT facilitates the interaction between connected household equipment and people, and integrating AI with it makes this interaction intelligent and smart. Industry giants like Amazon, Samsung, Apple, Google, *etc.* have leveraged this to offer smart home platforms that integrate well with third-party applications. Fig. (**1**) illustrates how IoT can be set up from the rooftop to the garage, which facilitates reduced carbon emission, energy consumption, and cost benefits along with other benefits. IoT environment is set up using a variety of sensors like motion, hydraulic, chemical, ambient, electric, identification, biosensors, and presence used for detecting motion, measuring liquid level and flow, physical quantities, electrical power, near field communication, health parameters, and presence of objects, respectively.

AI and IoT are combined together to provide effective solutions to daily household routines by collecting and analysing data through sensors and interactions [6]; for example, water leakage prevention, temperature control in rooms and water tanks, water usage monitoring, air quality control, automatic on/off of fans, lights, and air conditioners, recording of TV programs of user's taste, detection of trespassers, people behaviour monitoring, *etc.* As a smartphone is an essential component of a smart home, the user can easily monitor from a remote, control and interact with devices and get smart responses as well. Integration of a security system in a smart home lets the user prevent threats and security at check.

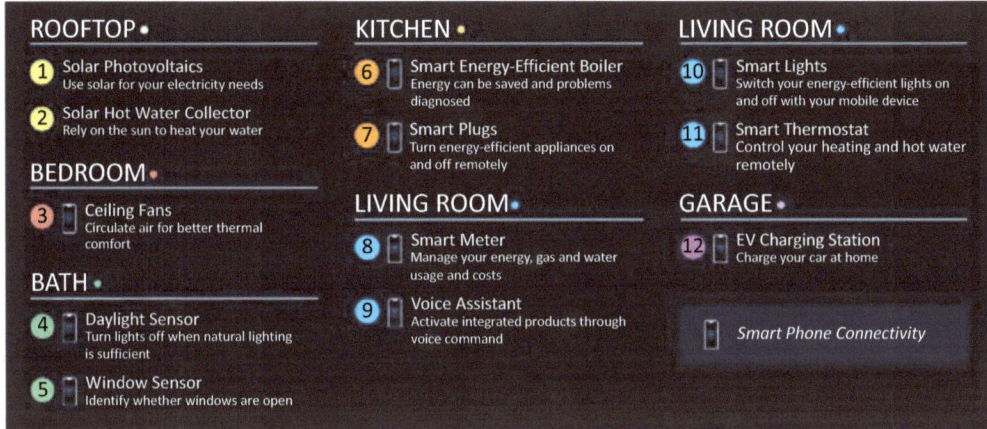

ROOFTOP •
1. **Solar Photovoltaics** Use solar for your electricity needs
2. **Solar Hot Water Collector** Rely on the sun to heat your water

BEDROOM •
3. **Ceiling Fans** Circulate air for better thermal comfort

BATH •
4. **Daylight Sensor** Turn lights off when natural lighting is sufficient
5. **Window Sensor** Identify whether windows are open

KITCHEN •
6. **Smart Energy-Efficient Boiler** Energy can be saved and problems diagnosed
7. **Smart Plugs** Turn energy-efficient appliances on and off remotely

LIVING ROOM •
8. **Smart Meter** Manage your energy, gas and water usage and costs
9. **Voice Assistant** Activate integrated products through voice command

LIVING ROOM •
10. **Smart Lights** Switch your energy-efficient lights on and off with your mobile device
11. **Smart Thermostat** Control your heating and hot water remotely

GARAGE •
12. **EV Charging Station** Charge your car at home

Smart Phone Connectivity

Fig. (1). Twelve Ways to Save With Smart Home.

Source: IFC, EDGE [7]

Data collected from IoT devices are used to build machine learning and deep learning models to perform different types of intelligent automation and smart monitoring in the smart home. The following section discusses some of the related works on the applications of AI and IoT in smart home environments.

Smart Management of Equipment

Smart meters can alert users about the usage of energy, peak load, time-of-day tariff, voltage fluctuations, billing, and payment due. Smart management of electrical equipment can be done to control lights, fans, blinds, heating, cooling, noise control, *etc.* Data collected from smart homes in a smart city can be analysed to find interesting patterns and intelligent predictions. Machine learning models and deep learning models will have much better learning capabilities through the massive data collected from smart homes.

Human Activity Recognition

A major concern in today's environment is the aging of the population. This mandates a need for monitoring the aged residents at home, for their functional health and monitoring. Daily activities like eating, cooking, drinking, reading, and taking medicines can be monitored through the accelerometer sensors present in modern smartphones. Rishab *et al* [7] have designed a deep learning-based smart home system that recognizes human activities. The model is implemented through a Long Short-Term Memory (LSTM) algorithm that was able to predict the activities, based on which necessary actions could be taken to prevent any unpleasant situation.

Activity recognition not only helps in senior citizens' care in terms of assisted living and fall detection, but it can be helpful in identifying potential persons involved in the events of a theft, and other violent activities. Various deep learning algorithms like Restricted Boltzmann Machine (RBM), naïve Bayes classification, and hidden Markov models are used by different researchers to implement human activity recognition in different setups and environments. These algorithms integrate video analytics, interaction modeling, sensing the emotion of the crowd, cognitive computing, *etc.* Predicting the activity can help in the development of early alert systems in the home security system. Abnormal activity detection can be extended to crowded areas also.

Smart Healthcare

Implementing smart healthcare in smart cities requires IoT and AI technologies [8]. It includes information sharing between patients, hospitals, and healthcare providers, services of telemedicine, potable monitoring devices, robotic surgery, prognosis, *etc.* Fig. (**2**) represents the various components of smart healthcare [9]. Various sensor devices collect the data from the patients, and doctors and input the data. AI-driven algorithms such as machine learning algorithms, neural network algorithms, NLP, and deep learning algorithms, analyse the collected data and based on the analysis, the devices decide whether to send the data to the cloud environment or to act accordingly.

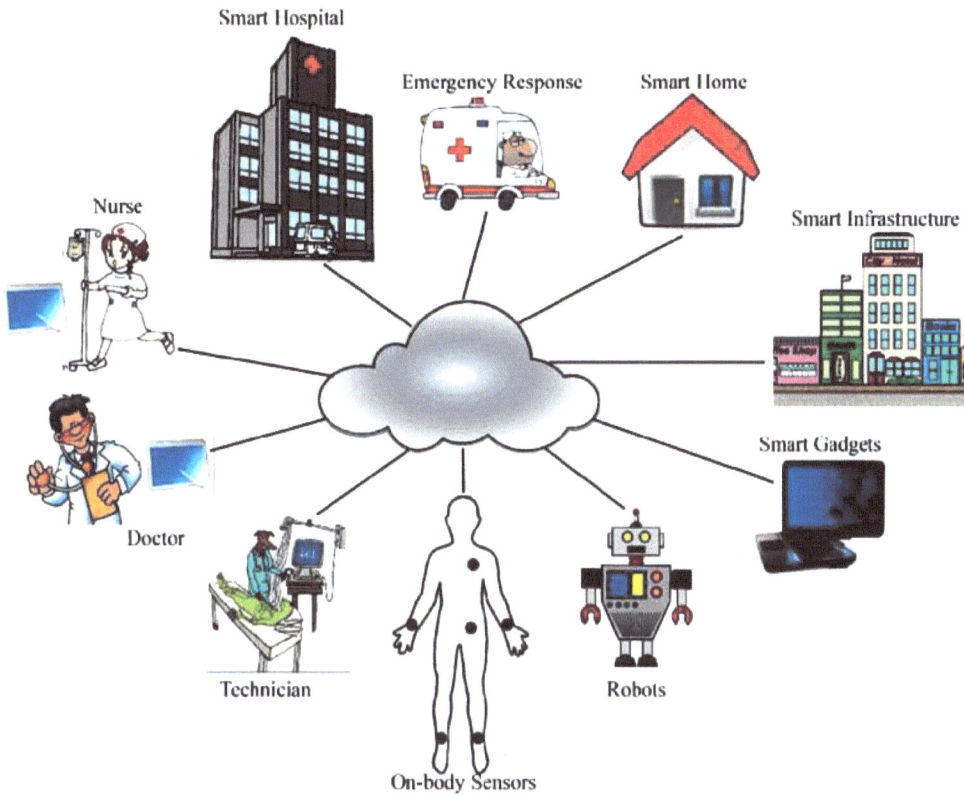

Fig. (2). Components of Smart Healthcare [20].

Role of AI Algorithms in Smart Healthcare

The most important AI algorithms that deliver the analytics and forecast future events in smart healthcare are discussed below [10]:

- K-means – It is the most popular clustering algorithm. It partitions the dataset into k pre-defined non-overlapping clusters. One simple application of K-means in smart healthcare is the suggestion for a hospital network to open Emergency-Care units within a particular region.
- Support Vector Machines (SVM) – It is a supervised machine learning algorithm used for both classification and regression-related problems. The various applications of SVM in healthcare are lifestyle pattern recognition, health pattern recognition, sensing of blood sugar levels, *etc* [11].
- Anomaly detection algorithm – It is an unsupervised machine learning algorithm that can be applied to unlabelled data to analyze the probability distribution using historical data. Specific applications in healthcare are blood pressure

monitoring, ECG monitoring, detecting abnormalities in patients, *etc* [12].

- Neural Networks - These algorithms work in a way similar to that of a human brain. The learning model provided by neural networks in healthcare improves the functionality of healthcare tools, devices and applications.
- Dbscan – It is a density-based clustering algorithm. One of the most important applications of Dbscan in healthcare is the feedback on body temperature through an IOT-based network.
- Decision Tree – It is a supervised learning algorithm. It identifies the rules of decision-making on the available data. One of the most important applications of a decision tree in healthcare is the management of Parkinson's disease patients.
- LSTM - Long Short-Term Memory is a kind of recurrent neural network which is dependent on the gradient-based learning algorithm. Cardiovascular risk prediction is an example of its application in healthcare.
- Genetic algorithms - It is a search-based algorithm that belongs to the category of evolutionary algorithms. One of the most notable applications of genetic algorithms in healthcare is categorizing the brain's signals.

Fitness-Tracking System

It measures the physical activities of athletes using smart wearable devices, analyzes and predicts the performance, and as a result, provides suggestions that increase the chance of winning using a Random Forest algorithm. Physical activity tracking wearables make a continuous analysis of the physical activities such as the number of walking steps, the duration of the activity performed, the quality of the activity such as moderate or vigorous and help them follow well-informed balanced decisions. The data would also be available as an activity report to the doctor. Tracking patients with cardiovascular diseases, tracking of cancer patients who receive chemotherapy to predict the complications, and tracking patients with rheumatic diseases are some of the use cases of activity tracking.

Glucose-Level Monitoring System

A glucose sensor measures the patient's glucose level. The Node MCU stores the data in the cloud, and classifies the patient as normal or diabetic using Naïve Bayes, Random Forest, oneR and J48 classification algorithms, and finally the notification is sent to the patient [13]. Finally, the data allows the doctors to plan the treatment for the patients. Some of the use cases are monitoring the blood glucose level of patients with type 1 and type 2 diabetes, identification of pre-diabetes patients, and diagnosing cardiac conditions of diabetic patients.

Body-Temperature Monitoring System

It measures the temperature in real-time and transmits the data [14]. The IoT-CBTM device automatically tracks the body temperature of patients using a wireless infrared sensor that is embedded in an IoT-Microcontroller module with AI-based software components. The device reduces the contact and proximity between patients and doctors. Furthermore, the information data that is collected is organized, sent, and recorded in the cloud database system, which makes the relevant expert to analyze and evaluate it easily [15]. Some of the use cases of body temperature monitoring systems are COVID – 19 disease detection at the earlier stage, helping the parents of babies and infants to save their energy and time, and protecting the visitors, staff, and suppliers in the business.

Stress Detection System

An AI-based fuzzy assisted petri net (AI-FAS) is proposed for stress assessment by monitoring heart rate and blood pressure [16]. Various stress-monitoring wearables are Spire, Muse, Flowtime, Fitbit charge 4, Apple Watch, Bellabeat leaf chakra, Fitbit Versa3, Fitbit Sense, Pip. Some of the use cases are providing feedback based on the current state of emotions, abnormal skeletal-muscle behavior detection based on the current emotional state, and detection of abnormal breathing rate which is most useful during the COVID-19 situation.

Oxygen-Saturation Monitoring System

The smart wearables help in monitoring the oxygen saturation level and indicate health experts about body changes in real-time [17]. Some of the wearables that monitor oxygen saturation are Fitbit Versa 2, Amazfit Bip U Smartwatch, Oneplus Smart Band, Apple Watch Series 6. The main functions of these wearables are always-on retina display, and tracking the activities such as swimming, walking, yoga, *etc.* One of the most important use cases is the detection of COVID-19 infection at home.

Other Healthcare Applications

Other applications of AI and IoT in Smart Healthcare are as follows [18]:

- Wheel Chair Management System – Creates a smart wheelchair based on the patient's health.
- Rehabilitation System – Shortens the duration of the rehabilitation process by assessing the mental state of patients undergoing rehabilitation.
- Electrocardiogram Monitoring - Monitors ECG using a device that detects electromagnetic signals.

- Medication Management – Verifies the authenticity of prescribed drugs.
- Wearables such as ECG Monitors, Biosensors, Patient therapy delivery, DIY health Trackers, Heart-Monitory Jewelry, *etc.*

Smart Transport

The main objectives of smart transport are to reduce pollution, increase the safety of passengers, reduce traffic congestion, reduce travel cost, and improve transfer speed [19]. Some of the AI algorithms that help to make transportation smarter are Genetic Algorithms (GA), Artificial Immune Systems (AIS), Artificial Neural Networks (ANN), Simulation Annealing (SA), Convolutional Neural Networks (CNN), Recurrent Neural Networks(RNN) and optimization algorithms such as Ant colony optimization, and Bee Colony optimization. Self-driving cars, Smart traffic lights, Smart and connected buses, Smart and connected streets, Smart delivery, and Smart trains are the various components of Smart Transport. The following section discusses some of the related works on the applications of AI and IoT in Smart Transport.

Connected-Vehicle Infrastructure Pedestrian (VIP)

In a connected environment, the exchange of information between vehicles, pedestrians, and infrastructure can be done either through a peer-to-peer connectivity protocol or through a centralized system such as 4G or any advanced network. The exchange of information in this case can be vehicle-to-vehicle or vehicle-to-infrastructure or pedestrian-to-infrastructure or vehicle-to-pedestrian. Three main phases of VIP are data collection, analysis of collected data, and data information transmission. Data-collection components gather all observable information from the transportation system (*e.g.*, traffic flow at a particular point of the road network, average travel time for a particular road section, number of passengers boarding a transit line, *etc.*) for further analysis of the current traffic conditions [20, 21]. Due to advances in technology, scanners are used to collect traffic data, and due to the extensive usage of smartphones and technologies such as GPS and WiFi, components analysis of traffic conditions becomes easier. The data transmission component communicates the collected and analysed data to operation centers for evaluation, to undergo control measures for travelers and infrastructures.

Smart Parking System (SPS)

Initially, the AI-based smart parking system counts the number of parked vehicles and balances parking spaces using IoT tools. It passes the information to the management after detecting the presence of a car in the parking space. At any time, the parking manager or decision-maker or parking analyst can optimize the parking strategy. Due to the availability of real-time data about the availability and occupancy of parking, users can find the slot to park their vehicles. Various approaches to smart parking systems are WSN-based SPS, Multi-agent system based SPS, Computer Vision based SPS, VANET-based SPS, Machine learning based SPS, Deep Learning based SPS, Neural Network based SPS, Fuzzy logic based SPS, GPS-based SPS, GSM-based SPS [22].

Automated Incident Detection System (AID)

The data from the traffic detectors are collected and analyzed by AID systems to identify the presence of vehicles and their characteristics. During the analysis phase, when it identifies incidents such as fire in vehicles, crashes, or wrong siders then it sends an alert in the Traffic Management System. Then the TMC team verifies it by checking the IOT-enabled sensor results and AI algorithms classify the action to be taken. In the near future, Qatar AID systems will use fixed-point traffic detectors [23].

Various other applications of AI and IoT in Smart Transport are:

- Lane Control System - LCS provides lane-specific information such as speed, and lane usage to the road users.
- Weigh-In-Motion Systems - WIM detects overweight vehicles.
- Overweight Vehicle Detection Systems – OVDS detects overweight vehicles.
- Road Weather Information Systems – RWIS uses sensors to monitor roadway weather conditions.
- Dynamic Pricing of Parking lots - Parking Telecom's AI-based parking solutions solves every parking management problem.

Smart Infrastructure

Devices are the building blocks for IoT. Heterogeneous devices from various vendors are interconnected to perform different functions for different purposes. When these devices are compromised by exploiting their vulnerabilities, a lot of malicious activities can happen. It is very much mandatory to identify the compromised devices before any disaster occurs. Ivan Cvitic *et al.* [24] analysed the features of traffic flow data generated by IoT devices and classified them based on their behaviour. Additive logistic regression (logit boost) as a method of ensemble machine learning is used to build a multiclass classification of devices that classified the devices into four classes. Clustering and classification are also used by researchers to identify unauthorised activities, unauthorized devices, and malicious software in an IoT environment.

This model can be extended and implemented to monitor IoT environments like smart homes, industrial IoT, and other real-life applications. Machine learning models can be built to identify interesting patterns through the analysis of traffic data from which anomalies can be detected in the communication network.

Smart Grid and Energy

IoT and AI control traditional grids to be more capable in terms of energy generation, distribution, monitoring and self-healing. This in effect would have a significant impact on the energy cost and carbon emissions. Real-time collection of related data facilitates building prediction models for better planning and management of energy consumption. Intelligent building-specific dynamic adaptive controlling mechanisms can be built with advanced machine learning algorithms.

Energy Consumption Forecasting

Forecasting energy consumption facilitates a proper supply demand management. A forecasting model was built for energy consumption using regression [25]. It uses clustering to cluster the users having similar consumption patterns and the distance function is used for prediction. Techniques like K-Means clustering, SVM, and RNN, are used by different researchers for this purpose. Electric power, temperature, humidity, time and holiday are some of the attributes used for analysis.

Smart Grid Monitoring and Management

Abnormal patterns of power usage can be used to detect electricity theft using supervised machine-learning techniques [26]. Fault identification and differentiating them is a critical task in smart grid management, which can be implemented using deep convolutional neural networks and decision trees [27]. Vázquez-Canteli, J.R., *et al.* [27] have introduced a simulation environment for energy scenarios using CitySim and TensorFlow, on which machine learning algorithms can be applied for significant problems in the energy sector in smart cities. This tool can be used for implementing self-tuning controlling algorithms that work in an optimum manner in the distributed smart grid environment.

Structural Health Monitoring

Smart infrastructure is the backbone for a smart city. When applied to civil engineering, it is referred to as smart monitoring, implemented through smart wireless systems. Smart monitoring detects structural damage or degeneration and prevents the same through pre-planned maintenance and repair, thereby reducing the cost anddamages to the infrastructure. Data collected from structural components are analyzed using artificial intelligence, agent-based models, and big data to detect, classify and localize damage, and predict the lifetime of the structure of bridges, dams, subways, railway lines, railway-crossing, turbines, *etc* [28]. Smart sensing technology including smartphones, UAVs, cameras and robotic sensors are utilized for monitoring the structure's health.

Support Vector Machines (SVM), with lamb waves, Gaussian radial basis function (RBF), wavelet transform, Hilbert-Huang transform, Teager-Huang transform, and multidimensional orthogonal-modified Littlewood-Paley wavelets, logistic regression, Convolutional Neural Networks (CNN), Artificial Neural Network (ANN) and k-nearest neighbour algorithms (k-NN) are used by researchers for damage detection and classification. To localize the damage, ANN-based algorithm is implemented. Outlier detection through k-means classification can isolate and localize the damage as well. SVMs, ANNs, and Gaussian naïve Bayes techniques are used to assess the condition of the damage identified. Lifetime prediction objective is realized through principal component analysis (PCA), and partial least square regression. Most of the monitoring is implemented as a separate task or a combination of them, using the finite element model.

Smart Water

Water is a scarce natural resource. Countries across the globe are striving to save water as water scarcity is considered to be one of the most important threats to any nation and it is directly related to a calm and peaceful society. Conservation of water resources, efficient planning and distribution to people are the primary objectives of a smart city. The water supply network in a smart city should be able to schedule the distribution in an efficient way, detect the leakage, and locate and lock the leakage. Hidden leakages and aged pipelines that are prone to damage would cause a lot of waste of water. The quality of water has to be maintained properly to ensure a conducive health condition for people. The pressure of water in the pipes, operation of pumps, scheduling of water supply, maintenance of water quality, detection of leakage, and its location identification, all put together make the management of water a very complex and demanding task.

Leakage Detection and Isolation

IoT and AI help in alleviating these challenges and improve the quality of every phase of smart water management systems. Leakage in pipelines can be detected using vibration sensors. A sample application of artificial intelligence applied for the detection of the location identification of hidden leaks is described [29]. A multi-layer perceptron neural network algorithm is developed that integrates SCADA (Supervisory Control and Data Acquisition) monitoring system with the water supply network, and formulates a hydraulic model that calibrates the measurements from the monitoring system. Leaks were simulated and flow distributions were stored in the database. This data was fed to the neural classifier to detect the water leaks.

Efficient Distribution and Consumption

Descriptive analytics can be applied to analyse the trends and behavior of the use of water to improvise water distribution plans. Consumption of water can be improved by monitoring and alerting the consumer whenever needed. Predicting a city's future utilization trend based on historical data on water usage, water availability, current events like festivals, and weather predictions would help the planning authorities for efficient planning and tune the pumping zones accordingly. IoT can facilitate automated scheduling to ensure necessary supply based on demand and duration. Water quality meters can monitor the quality of water in real-time. Underground water resources can be monitored with appropriate IoT components. Water flow in the smart homes can be monitored and this data can be used for future planning and billing. Insufficient water levels can come to the notice and people can be alerted. These steps put together aid in the efficient distribution and consumption of water and energy conservation.

IoT and machine learning are integrated for monitoring and forecasting of water usage in a smart home [30]. Ultrasonic and water flow sensors are used to monitor the inflow and outflow, and users are alerted when water wastage is identified. Data collected from these sensors are analysed using Random Forest Classifier and Support Vector Machine to predict future monthly and yearly water requirements. This work can be applied to industrial usage and farming as well.

The limitations of AI and IoT in smart city applications are as follows:

- Since AI algorithms used past data to predict the future, the need for cleaned and trained data would offer a proper examination for decision-making. IoT devices depend on electrical resources as they need a high level of energy to transmit information. Energy adequacy and the protocols used for communication are the most important challenges in developing IoT devices.
- Incomplete and noisy data that reduces the probability of deriving a conclusion.
- Poor QoS reduces the reliability of the system.
- Collection of a vast amount of data both structured and unstructured. In maintaining the entire data, the data that may be truly needed may be removed.

Real Estate Investment

In a Smart city construction, real-estate business could have effective consequences with an aim to boost the trust of the consumer, manage the completion in the market and increase the property value. Factors such as location, the income of the person, self-satisfaction, property value, and ownership rules influence the real-estate development [32]. It helps the respective industry to get prepared to avoid cyclic fall apart from the rise of returns in the market of real estate. The various stakeholders of real estate investment are modular buildings, smart logistics, smart materials, smart retails, and digital twins. The expected impacts of real estate investment in smart cities are data-driven development of a real estate, competitive advantage of smart buildings, demand in data centre, and flexibility in asset purchase.

CONCLUSION

IoT and AI offer wonderful applications for the implementation of a smart city environment. At the same time, certain challenges need to be addressed in this context. Not all people in smart city are well versed with digital environment and all the stakeholders should be educated well, which is not an easy task. These people can become a target for attackers.

Interconnection of IoT devices and communication with them is a potential vulnerability due the presence of complex social and trust relationships [31]. Access control mechanisms should be implemented with utmost care to prevent security breach and insider threats. Data being the valuable asset, security and privacy of the same has to be maintained. A compromise on IoT devices could expose citizen's data and activities to malicious entities, which is a threat to national level security, and lives and properties would be at risk. Safeguarding the data and flow of data and control should be ensured in the event of failure of equipment. Security implementations in different equipment manufactured by different vendors should follow standard mechanisms in order to eliminate the vulnerabilities present in them. Cyber terrorism is a national level threat that is always present in the society, and smart city is one of the major weak-links for the attackers.

All sorts of network security issues are pre-dominantly present here. Security and privacy challenges are a norm in a smart city, rather than an exception. Security mechanisms namely encryption, hashing, biometrics, access control, and multi-factor authentication are used to achieve security in smart city. IoT devices and real-time data transmission require continuous power supply, bandwidth, high computing power, new technologies for storage and memory, development of relevant algorithms and techniques for handling data, and so on. Industry 5.0 is completely designed based on AI, IoT, Computer Vision, Cloud, Analytics, Cyber physical systems and Cyber Security. When potential challenges in smart city environment in today's scenario are addressed, the application of AI and IoT will leverage smart city implementation further for optimal benefits of society at large.

REFERENCES

[1]   S. Joshi, S. Saxena, T. Godbole, and Shreya, "Developing smart cities: An integrated framework", *Procedia Comput. Sci.,* vol. 93, pp. 902-909, 2016.
[http://dx.doi.org/10.1016/j.procs.2016.07.258]

[2]   P. Wang, "On defining artificial intelligence", *J. Artif. Gen. Intell.,* vol. 10, no. 2, pp. 1-37, 2019.
[http://dx.doi.org/10.2478/jagi-2019-0002]

[3]   X. Chen, "The development trend and practical innovation of smart cities under the integration of new technologies", In: *Front Eng Manage,* vol. 6. , 2019, pp. 485-502.
[http://dx.doi.org/10.1007/s42524-019-0057-9]

[4]   M. Kuzlu, F. orinne, and V. Ozgur Guler, "Role of artificial intelligence in the internet of things (IoT) cybersecurity", *Disc. Int. Thin.,* vol. 1, no. 7, 2021.

[5]   Gartner, "Gartner Survey Shows Connected Home Solutions Adoption Remains Limited to Early Adopters". https://www.gartner.com/en/newsroom/press-releases/2017-03-06-gartner-survey-shows-connected-home-solutions-adoption-remains-limited-to-early-adopters

[6]   Z.B. Celik, E. Fernandes, E. Pauley, G. Tan, and P. McDaniel, "Program analysis of commodity IoT applications for security and privacy", *ACM Comput. Surv.,* vol. 52, no. 4, pp. 1-30, 2020.
[http://dx.doi.org/10.1145/3333501]

[7]   R. D. Manu, S. Kumar, S. Snehashish, and K.S. Rekha, "Smart home automation using iot and deep learning", *Int. Res. J. Eng. Technol.,* vol. 6, no. 4, pp. 2395-0056, 2019.

[8]   T. Pawar, and N. Anantakrishnan, "Engineering, S. Chaudhary, Biomedical Impact of Ambulation in Wearable. ECG", *in Springer,* 2018.

[9]   P. Saraju, "Mohanty , " Everything you wanted to know about smart cities"", *IEEE Consumer Electronics Magazine,,* vol. 5, no. 3, pp. 60-70, 2016.
[http://dx.doi.org/10.1109/MCE.2016.2556879]

[10]   P. Sunhare, R.R. Chowdhary, and M.K. Chattopadhyay, "Internet of things and data mining: An application oriented survey", *in Comput.Inf. Sci.,* 2020.
[http://dx.doi.org/10.1016/j.jksuci.2020.07.002]

[11]   P. Deshmukh, "Design of cloud security in the EHR for Indian healthcare services", *J.King. Saud. Univ. Comp. Inform. Sci.,* vol. 29, no. 3, pp. 281-287, 2017.
[http://dx.doi.org/10.1016/j.jksuci.2016.01.002]

[12]   A Gupta, and R Jha, "Security architecture of 5g wireless communication network", *in Sensors. R.D.-I.J., ingentaconnect.com,,* 2018.

[13]   R. Amine, A. Naja, and J. Lloret, "An IoT based diabetic patient monitoring system using machine learning and node MCU", *J. Phys. Conf.,* no. 1, p. 012035, 1743.
[http://dx.doi.org/10.1088/1742-6596/1743/1/012035]

[14]   Z.L. In, "Patient body temperature monitoring system and device based on internet of things", *in Chinese Patent,,* vol. 103, pp. 577-688, 2012.

[15]   W. Boonsong, S. Narongrit, and P. Piya, "Wireless Personal Communications" in Contactless Body Temperature Monitoring of In-Patient Department (IPD) Using 2.4 GHz Microwave Frequency *via* the

Internet of Things (IoT) Network,", *Wireless Personal Communication..*

[16]   Q. Lin, Li. Tongtong, S. Mohamed, and R. Dinesh Jackson Samuel, "Advanced artifcial intelligence in heart rate and blood pressure monitoring for stress management", *in Springer-Verlag GmbH Germany, part of Springer Nature, 2020.*

[17]   JJ. Kang, and H. Larkin, "Intelligent personal health devices converged with internet of things networks", *J. Mob. Multim.,* 2017.

[18]   M. Alshamrani, "IoT and artificial intelligence implementations for remote healthcare monitoring systems: A survey", *J. King. Saud. Univ. Comp. Inform. Sci.,* 2021.

[19]   C. Benevolo, R.P. Dameri, and B. D'Auria, "Smart mobility in smart city action taxonomy, ICT intensity and public benefits", *Empowering Organizations: Enabling Platforms and Artefacts,* pp. 13-28, 2016.

[20]   X. Henry, Liu. Xiaozheng, and He. Will Recker, "Estimation of the time-dependency of values of travel time and its reliability from loop detector data", *Transp.Res. B,* vol. 41, no. 4, pp. 448-461, 2007.

[21]   F. Soriguera, and F. Robuste, "Estimation of traffic stream space mean speed from time aggregations of double loop detector data", *Transp.Res. B,* vol. 19, no. 1, pp. 115-129, 2011.

[22]   H. Mehedi, and A.C. Muhtasim, "Smart parking systems: Comprehensive review based on various aspects", *in Heliyon,* vol. 7, no. 5, 2021.

[23]   K. Shaaban, M. Elamin, and M. Alsoub, "Intelligent transportation systems in a developing country: benefits and challenges of implementation" in 14th International scientific conference on sustainable, modern and safe transport", *Transp. Res. Procedia,* vol. 55, pp. 1373-1380, 2021.
[http://dx.doi.org/10.1016/j.trpro.2021.07.122]

[24]   I. Cvitić, D. Peraković, M. Periša, and B. Gupta, "Ensemble machine learning approach for classification of IoT devices in smart home", *Int. J. Mach. Learn. Cybern.,* vol. 12, no. 11, pp. 3179-3202, 2021.
[http://dx.doi.org/10.1007/s13042-020-01241-0]

[25]   D. Nguyen, R. Barella, S.A. Wallace, X. Zhao, and X. Liang, "Smart grid line event classification using supervised learning over PMU data streams", *Proceedings of the 2015 6th International Green and Sustainable Computing Conference,* 2015.
[http://dx.doi.org/10.1109/IGCC.2015.7393695]

[26]   Z. Zheng, Y. Yang, X. Niu, H.N. Dai, and Y. Zhou, "Wide and deep convolutional neural networks for electricity-theft detection to secure smart grids", *IEEE Trans. Industr. Inform.,* vol. 14, no. 4, pp. 1606-1615, 2018.
[http://dx.doi.org/10.1109/TII.2017.2785963]

[27]   J.R. Vázquez-Canteli, S. Ulyanin, J. Kämpf, and Z. Nagy, "Fusing TensorFlow with building energy simulation for intelligent energy management in smart cities", *Sustain Cities Soc.,* vol. 45, pp. 243-257, 2019.
[http://dx.doi.org/10.1016/j.scs.2018.11.021]

[28]   E. Kabalci, and Y. Kabalci, *From smart grid to Internet of Energy* 1st. Academic Press: London, UK, 2019.

[29]   S. John Livingston, M. Raj Sandeep Simeon, P. Bommi Vikas, and C. Hari, "A hybrid approach for water utilization in smart cities using machine learning techniques", *Int. J. Innov. Technol. Expl. Eng. (IJITEE),* vol. 8, no. 6S, pp. 2278-3075, 2019.

[30]   A. Al-Wakeel, J. Wu, and N.K. Jenkins, "Means based load estimation of domestic smart meter measurements", *Appl.Energy,* vol. 194, pp. 333-342, 2017.

[31]   R. Petrolo, V. Loscrì, and N. Mitton, "Towards a smart city based on cloud of things, a survey on the smart city vision and paradigms", *Transactions on Emerging Telecommunications Technologies,,* vol.

28, no. 1, p. e2931, 2017.

[32]   W.   Yiyao,   Real   estate's   contribution   to   GDP   falling.   Chana   Daily. https://www.chinadaily.com.cn/business/2017-01/21/content_28017345.htm Accessed 22 November 2019.

CHAPTER 12

Analysis of RGB Depth Sensors on Fashion Dataset for Virtual Trial Room Implementation

Sonali Mahendra Kothari[1,*], **Vijayshri Nitin Khedkar**[1], **Rahul Jadhav**[1] and **Madhumita Bawiskar**[1]

[1] *Department of Computer Science and Engineering, Symbiosis Institute of Technology, Symbiosis International [Deemed University], Maharashtra, India*

Abstract: This paper presents a Virtual Trial Room software using Augmented Reality which allows the user to wear clothes virtually by superimposing 3d clothes over the user. These sensors are valued particularly for robotics or computer vision applications because of their low cost and their ability to measure distances at a high frame rate. In November 2010, the Kinect v1 (Microsoft) release encouraged the use of Red Green Blue (RGB)-D cameras, and in July 2014, a second version of the sensor was launched. Because high-frequency point nuclei can be obtained from an observed picture, users can imagine employing these sensors to fulfill 3D acquisition requirements. However, certain issues such as the adequacy and accuracy of RGB-D cameras in close-range 3D modeling have to be addressed owing to the technology involved. The quality of the data obtained therefore constitutes an important dimension. In this study, the usage of the current sensor Kinect v2 is explored in the three-dimensional reconstruction of tiny objects. The advantages and problems of Kinect v2 are addressed in the first section and then photogrammetry versions are presented after an accurate evaluation of the generated models.

Keywords: Augmented reality, Depth Sensor, Fashion Recommendation, IOT, Virtual reality, Virtual trial room.

INTRODUCTION

As Vivienne Westwood has said, "fashion is very essential. It is enhanced life and worth doing well, like everything that brings joy". In the 14th century, there were the first changes in fashion in European culture; subsequently, the number of fashion designers across the globe grew because of the industrial revolution [1]. In the 21st century, every year fashion trends change. Trends in fashion influence

* **Corresponding author Sonali Mahendra Kothari:** Department of Computer Science and Engineering, Symbiosis Institute of Technology, Symbiosis International [Deemed University], Maharashtra, India; E-mail: sonali.kothari@sitpune.edu.in

Sonali Mahendra Kothari, Vijayshri Nitin Khedkar, Ujwala Kshirsagar and Gitanjali Rahul Shinde (Eds.)

local culture and climate change; yet these trend communities tend to be the world's leading fashion industry [2]. Unattended future popularity in fashion pictures must be predicted by a training prediction model to represent their trends throughout time [3].

The number of shopping malls owing to fast urbanisation is rapidly increasing and apparels is one of the best-known categories in shopping malls. The experience of cloth buying in shopping centres is mostly based on the availability of clothing that fit trends and hassle-free cloth testing. At the present time, in shopping centres or clothes stores, the trial of clothes is time-consuming because clients need to be in long queues and wait for their turn while they wear all the selected clothing and if they're not satisfied with the testing of selected clothes, they need to wait again in a queue with new clothes. The virtual test room is an Android application, which enables clients to choose clothing from the catalogue and try out to chosen garments on the virtual 2D/3D model [4]. The goal of the virtual test room is to maximise the accurate depiction and adjustment of the look and the customer preferences on the screen by overlaying the modelled clothes with the figure of the customer [5]. Two factors are thus necessary: information on the client's body size ("height, neck, breast, waist, hips, and arm measurement"), and the size of the chosen item of clothing, which should be taken into consideration. However, varying on whether it deals with 2D or 3D modelling, the method for adapting the garment to customer's body figure is different [6].

Due to the development in digitization and online platforms, Retail has undergone seismic changes over recent years [7]. A study claimed that the pace of change made possible *via* new technologies is accelerating [8]. One such technology, which "provides the shopping experience with the potential to revolutionise". By overlaying virtual components directly in the real-time environment, Augmented Reality (AR) may improve sensory impressions for customers [9].

Internet of Things (IoT)

IoT is a system of internet-based linked gadgets. It includes a desktop, a mobile, a laptop, mechanical equipment, sensors, household appliances, and automobiles. These gadgets are intended to exchange data *via* the internet with other devices. Many of the things around us are on the network in one way or another under the Internet of Things (IoT) concept. The new problem in which information and communication systems are invisibly integrated into the environment around would be tackled through Radio Frequency Identification (RFID) and sensor network technology. This leads to huge quantities of data being kept in a seamless, efficient, and easy-to-understand manner, processed and displayed. This model consists of goods and services that are supplied in a way such as conventional goods. With monitoring, storage, analytical tools, visualisation platforms and customer delivery, cloud computing may offer a virtual infrastructure for such utilities. Cloud computing's cost-based approach allows end-to-end service delivery, enabling companies and consumers to access apps from anywhere. It is an essential component of smart connectivity and context-friendly computing using network resources. The increasing availability of wireless internet connectivity such as Wi-Fi and 4G-LTE already demonstrates a development toward ubiquitous communication and information networks [10].

Components of IoT

However, all complete IoT systems are the same in that they represent the integration of six distinct components: sensors/devices, gateway, connectivity, data processing, analytics, and a user interface. Some of the major elements are required. The components are shown in Fig. (**1**) [10].

Fig. (**1**). Components of IOT.

• Sensor

The sensor is linked to the Internet of Things device to the outside world or a person. As the name implies, it detects changes and transmits data to the cloud for processing, as the name implies. Pressure sensors, temperature sensors, and light intensity detectors are examples of sensors that constantly gather data from the environment and send it to the next layer.

• Gateway

The gateway makes it easier to control data flow and layer protocols to transmit data across devices. It interprets device network protocols and encodes data traveling across the network. It is like a cloud layer and gadgets that remove cyber assault and unauthorised data access.

• Connectivity

The data gathered by sensors must be sent to the cloud for analytics. As a means of transferring data from one device to another, the internet is required. All IoT devices must always be linked to the Internet. Networks such as wireless internet, Bluetooth, and Wide Area Networks (WAN) are easier to maintain. These networks can send data to the cloud.

• Cloud

IoT systems transmit large amounts of data from devices and this data should be effectively handled to produce meaningful results. The IoT cloud is used to store this vast quantity of data. It offers tools for data collection, processing, and storage. Data is available and accessible *via* the Internet from a distant location. It also offers an analytics platform. The IoT cloud is an advanced server network that processes a large quantity of data at a fast speed.

• Analytics

Analytics is the process through which raw data are converted into a user-friendly format. The real-time analysis, capturing and anomalies happen in IoT analytics. The data are transformed into an end-user-friendly format. Users or companies may analyse trends in reports, forecast the market and get prepared to execute their ideas successfully.

• User interface

A physically visible portion of IoT systems is the user interface. This component of the IoT interacts with the end user. The information would be accessed as reports or as measures such as an alert, a notice, and so on. Some activities may also be carried out by the user. It is essential to develop an easy-to-use interface that is easily and technically useable.

AUGMENTED REALITY (AR)

AR is a communicating skill in a real-world setting in which computerized perceptual information occasionally enhances the items in the actual world in many sensory forms, including visual, aural, and tactile [11]. AR could be described as a system that combines three important features: mixing real and virtual worlds, networking in real-time and recording virtual and real things with precision in 3-D. Enhanced reality is utilised to improve natural settings or circumstances and to provide experiences with a perceptual enrichment. The information about the users is interactively and digitally altered *via* the use of sophisticated AR technologies (such as combining computer vision, integration of AR cameras into smartphone apps, and object identification). Increased reality is any artificial experience that adds to the existing or actual reality, *e.g.,* viewing other real felt or measured data such as electromagnetic radio waves [12].

Augmented reality offers a great deal of potential to collect and share knowledge. Some enhanced methods are usually used in real-time with environmental components and in semantic settings. Immersive perceptual information is coupled with other information, such as scores for a live broadcast of a sports game. This combines the advantages of both the technology of augmented reality and display technology.

VIRTUAL REALITY

The use of computer technology in the production of a modeled world is virtual reality (VR). In distinction to conventional user ports, VR puts the customer inside some knowledge. The customers are capable of connecting with 3D ecosystems as an alternative to seeing a screen in front of them. The computer transforms into a gatekeeper in this artificial environment, mimicking as many senses as possible, such as vision, hearing, touch, and even smell. The accessibility of a substance and inexpensive computer power are the only limitations to almost genuine VR experiences. VR uses computer science for creating a simulated world. The Head-Mounted Display (HMD) is the immediate part of "virtual reality" [13]. Human beings are visual beings and display technology is frequently the biggest gap among immersive systems like "virtual reality and conventional user interfaces". "HTC Vive, Oculus Rift and PlayStation VR (PSVR)" are major participants in "virtual reality".

FASHION ANALYSIS AND RECOMMENDATION

Recommendation on product sizes and fitness forecasts are essential to enhance the shopping experiences of consumers and minimise product returns. The fit feedback of consumers is difficult because of its complex semantics, its subjective assessment of goods, and its unbalanced label distribution. The first step is to determine human body dimensions, such as shoulder width, bush circles, hips, and waist, and to suggest goods to the consumers based on the current trends, acquisition and feedback history, and customer feeling analysis.

Mishra *et al.* [14] developed a predictive frame to address the product adjustment problem, which captures the semantics underlying consumers' correct input.

V. Sembium *et al.* [15] suggested the latent factor model for recommending product size fit to consumers (small, fit, large). Latent variables in this model relate to their real physical size for consumers and goods, which are learned from the previous products and returns. Latent factor models that include people, and the use of return codes demonstrated a 17-21% increase in the Area Under the Curve (AUC) against basic principles in tests using Amazon shoe datasets.

T. Xiaohui *et al.* [16] suggested a new method for the calculation of human body size, such as shoulder width, breast gyros, and waist, First, a depth camera is utilised to obtain the 3D human body model as a 3D model acquisition. A random forest deterioration assessment study of geodetic spaces then utilised the automated extraction technique of characteristics of the human body by means of a 3D forestry extraction. Finally, the various sizes of the human body are established based on these distinguishing facts and features.

Ashmawi *et al.* [17] developed a model, which estimated human body measures using machine learning techniques such as Har Cascade classifiers and vector machine support.

RGB-DEPTH SENSOR

Through the "multi-point level sensing, object counting and navigation systems", depth sensors that are used regularly in developing human-machine interfaces (motion detection, motion monitoring, *etc.*) can be used to measure the size of the customer's bodies and track customer movement in virtual mirrors. Red, Green Blue (RGB)-D sensors are used for digitalization into per pixel RGB colour and depth data of real-world 3D items and surroundings. "PrimeSense-based sensors" use "Structured Light" (SL) sensing technologies. Some examples of consumer RGB-D sensors are the Microsoft Kinect v1 and Asus Xtion as shown in below in Table **1**. Based on the Kinect v2 concept, Microsoft launched the range sensing system by 2015 in Microsoft. Intel also developed its own stereo, portable RGB-D sensor series. The Active Stereo Vision (ASV) is based on the R200 (2015) Intel, D415 and D435. It employs an NIR texture projection unit coupled with 2 NIR depth sensing cameras [18]. Table **1** shows the comparison study of an RGB-D sensor and defines the various parameters such as software, image resolution, and field of view between Asus xtion, Microsoft kinectv2, and intel realsenseR200.

Table 1. Comparative Study of RGB-D Sensors.

Parameters	Asus xtion Pro live	Microsoft Kinect v2	Intel realsense R200
Sensing principle	Projects a continuous form of NIR light speckle onto the scene and associating the took shape against a reference pattern to obtain depth data.	Emits a modified NIR light from its infrared projector. It then determines the phase offset of the reflected NIR light caught by the sensor to acquire depth data.	Utilizes the principle of an ASV and dual NIR cameras and a NIR pattern projector for enhanced stereo correlation identical to achieve depth data of a scene.
Image resolution	480p depth image and a 720p color image.	512x424 depth image and 1080p color image.	480p depth image and a 1080p color image.
Operational Distance	0.8 to 3.5m	0.8 to 4.5m	0.6 to 3.5m
Field of view	58H, 45V, 70D	57.5H,43.5V	59H, 46V
Software	OpenNI SDKBundle	Kinect for Windows SDK	Intel Real sense SDK
Programming Languages	C++, C#, JAVA	C++, C#, JAVA	C++, C#, JAVA

In collecting depth data, each sensor uses various techniques of depth sensing. All three sensors at home can record the surfaces of the subjects examined considering the distance, surface angle and material restrictions of each sensor. "Kinect v2" and the Asu's sensor surpass R200 to collect accurate and exact depth data from an object area. The Asus sensor cannot collect any depth data at any distance with substantial sunshine interference in the open air [19]. These sensors may serve for low-tolerance applications such as farm phenotyping, the mobilizing manufacturing, close-range 3D imaging, and face scanning in a wider variety of illuminated situations [20]. Microsoft Kinect may also be helpful for robotics and computer applications for Windows v2 (Kinect v2), since accurate, high-rate pictures can be obtained [21]. The R200 has been also incorporated into many commercial hardware platforms, which occlude the multi-rotor "Yuneec Typhoon H, the home robot ASUS Zenbo, the HP Spectre X2, and the robotics platform TurtleBot3" [22].

VIRTUAL TRIAL ROOM TECHNIQUES AND FASHION DATASETS

Recently, the virtual test room gained considerable attention owing to its business possibilities. The choices can be reduced by many styles and sizes, for online buying or smart suggestions. For the virtual test room, several techniques are provided below [23].

12.6.1. Virtual Trial Room Techniques

A virtual test room would be used for the test in the case of size, fit, style or colour. Depending on whether it works with 2D or 3D modelling [6], the method for customization would be different. Ramesh *et al.* [21], who used OpenCV and a camera to record video, presented a virtual test room application utilizing AR to enable an operator to try on various colours of dresses. When the video was caught, it detected the human backdrop and object, modified the T-shirt colour and inserted the chosen logo, depending upon the decision of the user. OpenCV is used to recognise the user and alter the colour and logo as the user wants.

Kamani *et al.* [24] developed a Virtual Trial Room application that enables a user, using the Microsoft Kinect sensor, to attempt on virtual clothing and to monitor depth using virtual clothes. The clothes are moved and folded in a realistic manner and the fabric luminance is adjusted for environmental illumination. In 2019, Masri *et al.* introduced an application of the virtual dressing room using a sensor based on Microsoft Kinect, using models and colours detection for the positioning, scaling, and rotation of joints to align the user's 2D cloth model and the model was then superimposed on the user in real-time. In 2020, an "android-based mobile application, along with OpenCV and TensorFlow lite technologies" was designed to enable consumers to practise their clothing digitally without waiting for long in line. OpenCV is used for mapping clothing to the body of the client [25].

Fernandes *et al.* [26] suggested a 3D virtual clothing mixed reality system. It automatically adapts an unseen (or partly visible) avatar based on the size of the "body and skin colour" of the individual and utilises it for correct clothing fit, configuration, and garments model. The technology allows consumers to undergo a private virtual trial at home and Fig. (**2**) presents three scenarios:

- Avatar virtual clothing,
- Users' picture virtual clothes and
- Avatar virtual clothes combined with the customer's face picture.

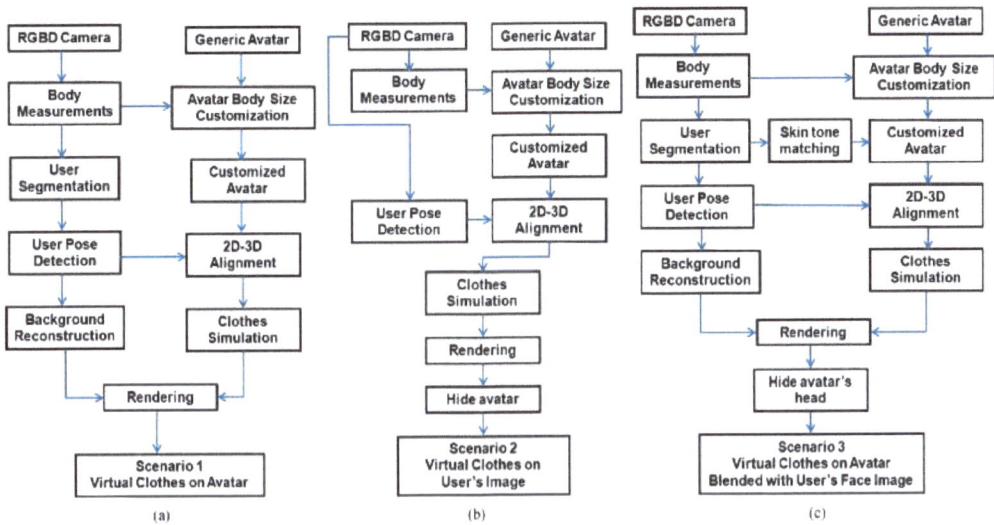

Fig. (2). Three scenarios for virtual clothes try-on system.

The user automatically adapts a standard 3D avatar first created on the body size and their skin tone is paired with the skin colour of the user's face. Then, it applies a new technique to match the 3D-custom avatar in real-time with the picture of the user. Due to its speed and precision for the physical garment model, it utilises the simulation technique [27] for the animation of virtual clothing. It removes the picture of the user in the first scenario from your screen and substitutes it with the clothed avatar. 3D virtual clothing would be added to the customer's picture in the second version, without the avatar display. It first removes the picture of the user behind the neck from the third version, replacing it with a rebuilt context using the backdrop picture pre-captured. Then on the screen, a bespoke headless avatar is produced with virtual clothing. Therefore, the viewer sees her appearance-like avatar with simulated clothing on the screen. The virtual clothing follows the motions of the user in all three situations, providing an idea of the usage of virtual dress in front of a mirror. Customization by Avatar must be a powerful tool for applications of modelling and simulation. Instead of having to produce models for a particular application with various body forms and sizes, it is set up if a standard can be accurately changed depending on certain criteria. This suggests a new way to alter a generically based avatar for a virtual system based on conventional human body measurement [28]. The process is quicker than current techniques and may yield outcomes that appear natural.

Since, an accurate user-like avatar would be produced on the basis of twelve main measures of the body of humans, *i.e.*, height, width of the shoulder, breast circle, hip circles, thigh circles, hook, "height, knee height, upper arm long" and forearms longitude. Some of these dimensions can be acquired by the RGB-D sensor directly (such as height, shoulder breadth, hair, "height and arm length") and can be used to personalise a virtual trial avatar. It provides the ability to manually hold all the essential measures for each registered user for more precise customisation. The new Kinect-based human models may also be used in these crucial measures [29, 30, 31].

Fashion Datasets

Most datasets concentrate on the issue of the clothing category or the categorization of attributes. Some of them are discussed below.

Chen *et al.* [32] introduced an attribute clothing dataset intended for the categorization of the attributes. This data collection only includes 1856 pictures and a total of 26 characteristics. Most clothing has an image size of 260×400 to 500×750 pixels, with a slightly inadequate resolution to analyse details.

"Colorful Fashion dataset" [33] is a useful basis for a study of "fashion data". It contains a total of 2,682 pixels, with colours and category labelling in all pixels, involving 13 colors and 23 categories. This dataset has a picture resolution of 400×600 pixels.

Apparel Style Dataset [34] is another publicly accessible data set utilised in two jobs: the categorization of clothing type and the identification of attributes. The authors gathered a data set specifying 15 clothing kinds with over 80,000 pictures of the type of categorization. Another dataset with 25,002 pictures has been built with 78 characteristics for attribute detection. The picture resolution is less than 200 pixels in most outfits. Although the dataset is considerably larger than the two previous datasets, it has the lowest resolution.

Multi-vision clothing dataset (MVC) [35] contains "37,499 items and 161,638 clothing photos", most of which contain at least four video views. Most of the picture resolution is "1920×2240 pixels", which thus provides enough information for several research relating to clothes, including the localisation of clothing attributes and type rating.

Fashion-MNIST [36] is a dataset of Zalando's pictures of articles—which comprise 60,000 training sessions and 10,000 instances. Each case is a picture of 28 x 28, with a label of 10 classes in association. For testing machine learning techniques, the Fashion-MNIST is designed to act as a direct reverse for the original MNIST data set.

Table **2** compares a few such available fashion datasets to provide glimpses of various datasets which can be referred by researchers.

Table 2. Comparison of fashion datasets.

Dataset	Number of Images	Attributes	Image Resolution	Source Link
Clothing Attribute	1,856	26	$\leq 500 \times 750$	https://exhibits.stanford.edu/data/catalog/tb980qz1002
Apparel Style	25,002	78	$\leq 200 \times 300$	https://data.vision.ee.ethz.ch/cvl/lbossard/accv12/
Colorful Fashion	2,682	36	400×600	https://github.com/hrsma2i/dataset-CFPD
MVC	161,638	264	1920×2240	https://github.com/MVC-Datasets/MVC
Fashion-MNIST	60,000	10	28x28	https://github.com/zalandoresearch/fashion-mnist

DISCUSSION AND FUTURE DIRECTIONS

This work is new and can be implemented in the near future so that many procedures can be performed automatically to enhance the program. The interface offered by the modified colorimeter in this program has not been fully used. The RGB data directly from the modified colorimeter can be turned into the new software. All work was carried out using just the usual bilirubin solutions.

Even though it works with RGB, depth, and RGB-D data, it's essential to look at the wider function of synthetic RGB data in human action detection. In contrast to depth films, deep action models use a variety of large-scale RGB video action datasets. This may reduce the requirement for synthetic data in this area. These may readily guarantee a broad range of action-independent data changes, such as camera views, textures, and illuminations. Even with huge datasets, such diversity, and magnitude of changes cannot be readily ensured.

SUMMARY

This paper compares the capabilities of three-degree sensors for consumers, "MS Kinect v2, Intel R200 and Asus Xtion Pro Live", in collecting outside depth data. In collecting depth data, each sensor uses various techniques of depth sensing. All three sensors at home can record the surfaces of the subjects examined considering the distance, surface angle and material restrictions of each sensor. In general, the sensor characteristics both of Kinect v2 and Asus exceed the R200 in the collection of valid and accurate object-surface depth data. This article also addressed the RGB depth sensors in the virtual trial room method that utilises their software to follow the user position and the Skeleton Application Programming Interface (API) used to detect depth. OpenCV is an open-source cross-platform package that includes a large variety of software design features that enable the customer to cooperate with computer images and perform tasks such as facial recognition, object identification, video detection, and many more. It has also compared various fashion datasets in this study. To depict broad patterns of what people are purchasing months or years from now, computer models able to generate such projections would be very useful to the fashion sector.

But even those of us who are not attracted by high couture, money and glamour are interested in fashion predictions. Intel has produced many stereoscopic depth cameras. However, many share images, projectors, and picture processors, which are similar or identical. All of these items are referred to as Intel R200, even though this analysis is equally valid for LR200 and ZR300. These modules are linked and operated *via* an individual USB interface, are around "100 x 10 x 4mm" in volume, and help in a variety of frame rates. For all three lenses on the board, each device is calibrated separately in a factory to an exact subpixel camera model. Distortion and rectification of the left-right pair of images in hardware are done and the colour camera is used in the host.

CHALLENGES IN SENSOR SELECTION AND TRIAL ROOM SETUP

Sensor performance can vary under different conditions so the overall performance of sensors under various conditions is investigated such as Light Intensity and Object Distance, Sensor-Angel Effect, and Light Incidence angle Effect in the test room Setup. Sensor performance may vary under different conditions. Trial rooms are extremely scarce and thus widely occupied in most textile and retail malls. And individuals also must wait a long time for this test room and waiting for such a test room is a waste of time. Test rooms are not as secure as we cannot make sure that there are no concealed cameras in the changing room. As a result, ladies changing their clothes in the trial room face a significant safety risk. These are some of the safety problems that occur in the conventional method of testing. The user may virtually alter his outfit utilising virtual clothing in a virtual test room programme. The user faces the Kinect sensor. With the skeletal tracking method, the Kinect scans the human body. The monitor linked to the Kinect sensor and CPU show the user and the clothing list that can be virtually made. The Kinect scans live video streaming of the surroundings and displays it on the monitor. The monitor also lists outfits that the user can wear, while selecting the garment. The garment is extremely imposed on the worn clothes by scanning a person's skeletal joints. The fitting garment moves by the user's movements in front of the Kinect sensor [37].

"Virtual Mirror with Virtual Human Use Kinect Sensor" offers virtual image managing software and an app to let users test virtual clothes from a virtual mirror. In a virtual changing room, a virtual version of the dress is shown. The hand movements of the user pick clothing from the screen list. The chosen virtual clothing then appears in the virtual mirror of a humanoid figure. The Kinect sensor helps scan the dimensions of the customer's image. 3D joints are utilised for positioning, resizing and rotating to align the 3D clothing with the models. Computer graphics offers us the ability to model virtual people and animate them. To mimic human beings, it is necessary to see and animate in real time, taking into consideration the limitations of the data utilised by these people. Here the user scans the Kinect to produce a 3D representation of a human. The user is scanned using AGPL3.0 software for the creation of the 3D user model, *i.e.*, a humanoid model and a unit for 3D models. Keyboards and mouse carry out the customer's interface with the system. Since the application is about the user's 3D model, the customer requirements are not met. The client cannot experience the idea of live dressing. These suggestions are inapplicable to online purchasing while unitary clothing may only be used in the application. The GUI (Graphical User Interface), allows users to utilise clothing in humanoid mode, and receive and interpret data arriving in the form of the input keyboard, mouse, camera or Kinect [37].

In a study [38], authors have proposed a system to use AR with the physics motion for a more realistic approach and for greater satisfaction. It suggests the use of 3D models for cloth designs which will help in improving scalability. The developed system uses a Kinect V2 sensor with an IR sensor, a camera sensor for color identification, and audio capturing using an inbuilt microphone array. Windows Presentation Foundation is used for capturing body measurements, Kinect skeleton joints are used for accessing necessary body parameters, while the Unity3D model overlays cloths on the user for trial.

Human action recognition is widely used by many researchers for a long time but recently this topic has gained huge attention from researchers looking into its various uses. Some authors [39] have discussed RGB-D modality and data acquisition. It gives a review of the classical machine learning-based methods and deep learning-based methods. The review also highlights the use of different data fusion techniques used in HAR and summarizes applications of state-of-the-art RGB-D methods in different scenarios. The authors have highlighted different challenges in data fusion and action recognition techniques.

FUTURE DIRECTION

"Fashion is time-dependent". It continually evolves owing to the impact of global actions, social and sub-cultural actions, financial circumstances, technological progress, social figures and fashion managers such as graphic designers and famous icons.

Fashion analysis and prediction comprise three important components, namely the environment, market, and product. Each aspect is based on five phases of study: awareness and observation, information investigation and collection, analyses, interpretations, and syntheses. The interface between all the components is the multidirectional arrows. Analysis of content, observation, drafting of scenarios, and interviews are some of the techniques utilised for prediction. Considering that content analysis is the most frequent method that forecasters choose and is more advantageous in long-term prediction, the most common sources of social content data in today's world are social media websites like Facebook, Twitter, Flickr, *etc.* Social contents are accessible in a variety of forms, such as numerical (for instance number of tags or likes), text (for instance, references), pictures (for example the profile/timeline image, posts), audio (for example songs), video (for example, humorous videos, clips), *etc.* "Image data is one of the most compelling data types". It contains both useful and amusing information. Image data is useful for studying content data.

Trend analysis of the fashion industry plays an essential function as it provides information about future and outgoing trends. It is essential in the end when it comes to making business choices. Along with intuitive information about characteristics that influence fashion trends, excellent judgment, inventiveness, and analysis of data from social material are useful. Due to its vast, unlabeled and diverse character, the job of analysis is very difficult. For data analysis, many data mining tasks such as categorization, cluster, deterioration, involvement, and external exposure are helpful. The appropriate data mining tasks are accomplished in the suggested system based on the features of social image data.

The programme is currently solely designed for clients to test virtual clothing. It intends to implement a further application, particularly for shopkeepers or owners. This software gives the owner daily data on how many people tried clothes, how many people ended up purchasing the clothes, etc. It intends to additionally integrate a machine learning model to give the client guidance on what clothes to purchase, based on his past clothing selections and other factors.

CONCLUSION

This paper presents a summary of a series of tests using an RGB-D camera to evaluate its capacity for 3D modeling applications in close range. The Kinect v2 sensor gadget examined is a low-cost Microsoft motion-detecting device. The primary aim was to assess its accuracy and capability for measuring performance for a certain metrological job. To achieve this, experiments were performed for the improvement of raw data and the calibration method. An experimental 3-D reconstruction technique using Kinect and its associated problems have also been presented. Various experiments have led to the emphasis on environmental and captured scene faults as well as sensor-related mistakes. A pre-heat time must be addressed to achieve consistent readings, according to numerous contributions dealing with RGB-D cameras. In addition, measurements made by the camera seem to have a major effect on the hue and the reflection of the objects. Finally, there is an experimental 3-D reconstruction technique for an archaeological piece. However, the use of a Kinect sensor proved a significant difficulty in achieving that objective. However, for many additional applications, the technology of the RGB-D camera seems promising once significant performance constraints have been solved. A 3-D scanning solution established based on structured light projecting and exposure with a tablet is offered with a structure sensor comparable to the original version of Kinect. As the evaluation of data quality is an open problem in such initiatives, there is little doubt that future contributions would center on the achievements made using such novel methods.

REFERENCES

[1]   K. Abe, M. Minoguchi, T. Suzuki, T. Suzuki, N. Akimoto, Y. Qiu, R. Suzuki, K. Iwata, Y. Satoh, and H. Kataoka, "Fashion culture database: Construction of database for world-wide fashion analysis", *In 2018 15th International Conference on Control, Automation, Robotics and Vision (ICARCV),*, pp. 1721-1726, 2018.

[2]   K. Abe, Suzuki. Teppei, Ueta. Shunya, Satoh. Yutuka, Kataoka. Hirokatsu, and Nakamura. Akio, "Changing fashion cultures", *arXiv,* vol. 1, 2017.

[3]   Al-h. Ziad, S. Rainer, and G. Kristein, ""Fashion Forward: Forecasting Visual Style in Fashion," no. Iccv,",

[4]   S. Kshitij, P. Mridul, P. Sharvesh, and S. Radha, "A virtual trial room using pose estimation and homography", *Proc. Int. Conf. Intell. Comput. Control Syst. ICICCS 2020, no. Iciccs,*, pp. 685-691, 2020.
      [http://dx.doi.org/10.1109/ICICCS48265.2020.9120947]

[5]   E. Bazaki, and V. Wanick, "Unlocking the potential of the salesperson in the virtual fitting room", *Conference Proceedings of the Academy for Design Innovation Management,* vol. 2, no. 1, 2019.
      [http://dx.doi.org/10.33114/adim.2019.10.387]

[6]   M. Moroz, "Tendency to use the virtual fitting room in generation Y : Results of qualitative study", *Foundations of Management,* vol. 11, no. 1, pp. 239-254, 2019.
      [http://dx.doi.org/10.2478/fman-2019-0020]

[7]   P.C. Verhoef, T. Broekhuizen, Y. Bart, A. Bhattacharya, J. Qi Dong, N. Fabian, and M. Haenlein,

"Digital transformation: A multidisciplinary reflection and research agenda", *J. Bus. Res.,* vol. 122, pp. 889-901, 2021.
[http://dx.doi.org/10.1016/j.jbusres.2019.09.022]

[8]   D. Grewal, S. Motyka, and M. Levy, "The evolution and future of retailing and retailing education", *J. Mark. Educ.,* vol. 40, no. 1, pp. 85-93, 2018.
[http://dx.doi.org/10.1177/0273475318755838]

[9]   A. Watson, B. Alexander, and L. Salavati, "The impact of experiential augmented reality applications on fashion purchase intention", *Int. J. Retail Distrib. Manag.,* vol. 48, no. 5, pp. 433-451, 2018.
[http://dx.doi.org/10.1108/IJRDM-06-2017-0117]

[10]   https://www.educba.com/introduction-to-iot/?source=leftnav

[11]   H. Sharma, N. Jain, and A. Chauhan, Learnify: An Augmented Reality-Based Application for Learning. In Advances in Manufacturing and Industrial Engineering (pp. 349-359). Springer, Singapore 2021.

[12]   S. Mann, S. Feiner, S. Harner, M.A. Ali, R. Janzen, J. Hansen, and S. Baldassi, "Wearable computing, 3d aug* reality, photographic/videographic gesture sensing, and veillance", *Proceedings of the Ninth International Conference on Tangible, Embedded, and Embodied Interaction,* pp. 497-500, 2015, January.
[http://dx.doi.org/10.1145/2677199.2683590]

[13]   Grigore Burdea, and Philippe Coiffet, "Virtual reality technology", 2003: 663-664.

[14]   R. Misra, Wan. Mengting, and McAul. Julian, "Decomposing fit semantics for product size recommendation in metric spaces", *RecSys 2018 - 12th ACM Conf. Recomm. Syst.,,* pp. 422-426, 2018.
[http://dx.doi.org/10.1145/3240323.3240398]

[15]   S. Vivek, Wan. Mengting, R. Rajeev, S. Atul, and M. Srujana, "Recommending product sizes to customers", *RecSys 2017 : Proc. 11th ACM Conf. Recomm. Syst.,* pp. 243-250, 2017.
[http://dx.doi.org/10.1145/3109859.3109891]

[16]   X. Tan, X. Peng, L. Liwen, and Q. Xia, "Automatic human body feature extraction and personal size measurement", *J. Vis. Lang. Comput.,* vol. 47, no. December 2017,, pp. 9-18, 2018.
[http://dx.doi.org/10.1016/j.jvlc.2018.05.002]

[17]   S. Ashmawi, M. Alharbi, A. Almaghrabi, A. Alhothali, A. Maraham, A. Almaghrabi, and A. Alhothali, "FITME: Body measurement estimations using machine learning method", *Procedia Comput. Sci.,* vol. 163, pp. 209-217, 2019.
[http://dx.doi.org/10.1016/j.procs.2019.12.102]

[18]   Y.W. Kuan, N.O. Ee, L.S. Wei, Weng. Yau, Ee. Ng. Oon, and Wei. Lee. Sze, "Comparative study of intel R200, Kinect v2, and primesense RGB-D sensors performance outdoors", *IEEE Sens. J.,* vol. 19, no. 19, pp. 8741-8750, 2019.
[http://dx.doi.org/10.1109/JSEN.2019.2920976]

[19]   M.F. Hamid, and M.A. Alam, "Virtual wardrobe for physically impaired using microsoft kinect sensor", *Conf. Signal Image Process. ICSIP 2017,* pp. 331-335, 2017.
[http://dx.doi.org/10.1109/SIPROCESS.2017.8124559]

[20]   H. Kataoka, Y. Satoh, K. Abe, M. Minoguchi, and A. Nakamura, "Ten-million-order human database for world-wide fashion culture analysis", *Proceedings of the IEEE/CVF Conference on Computer Vision and Pattern Recognition Workshops,* 2019.
[http://dx.doi.org/10.1109/CVPRW.2019.00040]

[21]   A. Ramesh, R. Kushal Ankit, D. Brinda, S. Vaishnavi, and P. Shrinivasacharya, "3D virtual trial room", *Int. J. Eng. Res. Technol.,* 2018.

[22]   F. Peter, B. Michael, R. Diego, R. Kaestner, M. Hutter, and R. Siegwart, "Kinect v2 for mobile robot navigation: Evaluation and modeling", *Proc. 17th Int. Conf. Adv. Robot. ICAR 2015,,* pp. 388-394, 2015.

[http://dx.doi.org/10.1109/ICAR.2015.7251485]

[23]   P. Parmar, and B.T. Morris, "Learning to score olympic events", *Proceedings of the IEEE Conference on Computer Vision and Pattern Recognition Workshops,* pp. 20-28, 2017.

[24]   S. Kamani, Neel. Vasa, and K. Srivastava, "Virtual trial room using augmented reality", *Int. J. Adv. Comput. Technol.,* vol. 3/6, no. Dec, pp. 98-102, 2014.

[25]   S. Kshitij, P. Mridul, P. Sharvesh, and R. Shankarmani, "A virtual trial room using pose estimation and homography", *Proc. Int. Conf. Intell. Comput. Control Syst. ICICCS 2020, no. Iciccs,,* pp. 685-691, 2020.
       [http://dx.doi.org/10.1109/ICICCS48265.2020.9120947]

[26]   Clara E. Fernandes, and Ricardo Morais, "A review on potential technological advances for fashion retail: smart fitting rooms, augmented and virtual realities", *Science,* pp. 168-186, 2021.
       [http://dx.doi.org/10.26563/dobras.i32.1372]

[27]   K. Mustafa, H. David, V. Pascal, N. Magnenat-Thalmann, and F. Faure, "A simple approac to nonlinear tensile stiffness for accurate cloth simulation", *ACM Trans. Graph.,* vol. 28, no. 4, pp. 105-116, 2009.

[28]   K. Mustafa, H. David, and N. Magnenat-Thalmann, "Sizing avatar from skin weights", *in Proc. Virtual Reality Softw. and Techol,* pp. 123-126, 2009.

[29]   W. Alexandar, H. David, N. Tobias, and J.B. Michael, "Home 3D body scans from noisy image and range data", *in Proc. Int. Conf. Comput. Vis,,* pp. 1951-1958, 2011.

[30]   Cui. Yan, C. Will, N. Tobias, and S. Didier, "KinectAvatar. Full auto matic body capture using a single Kinect", *in Proc. ACCV Workshop Col Dep Fus Comput. Vis,* 2012.

[31]   T. Jing, Z. Jin, L. Ligang, P. Zhigeng, and Y. Hao, "Scanning 3D full human bodies using Kinects", *IEEE Trans. Vis. Comput. Graph.,* vol. 18, no. 4, pp. 643-650, 2012.
       [http://dx.doi.org/10.1109/TVCG.2012.56] [PMID: 22402692]

[32]   H. Chen, A. Gallagher, and B. Girod, "Describing clothing by semantic attributes", *ECCV 2012: Computer Vision : ECCV,* pp. 609-623, 2012.
       [http://dx.doi.org/10.1007/978-3-642-33712-3_44]

[33]   S. Liu, J. Feng, C. Domokos, H. Xu, J. Huang, Z. Hu, and S. Yan, "Fashion parsing with weak color-category labels", *IEEE Trans. Multimed.,* vol. 16, no. 1, pp. 253-265, 2014.
       [http://dx.doi.org/10.1109/TMM.2013.2285526]

[34]   L. Bossard, M. Dantone, C. Leistner, C. Wengert, T. Quack, and L. Van Gool, "Apparel classification with style", *ACCV'12: Proceedings of the 11th Asian conference on Computer Vision,* pp. 321-335, 2013.
       [http://dx.doi.org/10.1007/978-3-642-37447-0_25]

[35]   K.H. Liu, T.Y. Chen, and S.C. Chu, "MVC: A dataset for view-invariant clothing retrieval and attribute prediction", *ICMR '16: Proceedings of the 2016 ACM on International Conference on Multimedia,* pp. 313-316, 2016.
       [http://dx.doi.org/10.1145/2911996.2912058]

[36]   M. Kayed, A. Anter, and H. Mohamed, "Classification of garments from fashion MNIST dataset using CNN LeNet-5 architecture", *Proceedings of 2020 International Conference on Innovative Trends in Communication and Computer Engineering, ITCE 2020,* pp. 238-43, 2020.
       [http://dx.doi.org/10.1109/ITCE48509.2020.9047776]

[37]   M. Kotan, *Virtual Mirror with Virtual Human Using Kinect Sensor* Department of Information Systems Engineering, Sakarya University, 2015. Available from: http://www.isites.info/pastconferences/isites2014/isites2014/papers/C7-ISITES2014ID117.pdf

[38]   Sasadara B. Adikari, Naleen C. Ganegoda, Ravinda G. N. Meegama, and Indika L. Wanniarachchi, "Applicability of a single depth sensor in real-time 3D clothes simulation: Augmented reality virtual

dressing room using kinect sensor", *Advances in Human-Computer Interaction Volume,* 2020.
[http://dx.doi.org/10.1155/2020/1314598]

[39]   M.B. Shaikh, and D. Chai, "RGB-D data-based action recognition: A review", *Sensors,* vol. 21, no. 12, p. 4246, 2021.
[http://dx.doi.org/10.3390/s21124246] [PMID: 34205782]

SUBJECT INDEX

A

Active stereo vision (ASV) 208, 209
Activities, plant photosynthetic 10
Adaptive neuro-fuzzy inference system 21
Agricultural 1, 12, 18, 21, 54, 61, 116
    applications 1, 54
    machinery 12
    monitoring 116
    systems 18, 21, 61
Agriculture 13, 16, 18, 19, 21, 22, 27, 28, 54
    applications 27, 28
    automation 18, 19
    industry 13, 16, 21, 22, 54
    system 28
AI-based 39, 194, 195
    parking 195
    smart parking system 194
    systems 39
AI-based sentiment analysis 156
    systems 156
    technologies 156
AI-powered 13, 104, 113, 115
    autonomous vehicles 115
    cameras and drones 13
    IoT devices 113
    IoT systems 104
AI-trained devices 30, 74
AIoT 44, 47
    businesses 44
    in smart healthcare 47
AIoT applications 42, 46, 47
    innovative 42
    limitless 47
Air quality sensors 9
Algorithms 109, 150, 190, 191, 192, 194, 198
    artificial intelligence 109
    genetic 192, 194
    in smart healthcare 191
    machine-learning classification 150
    neural network 190, 198
Amazon shoe datasets 208

Amazon's Alexa 98, 114
Apollo program 125
Apple's SIRI 98
Application programming interface (API) 214
Artificial 18, 19, 21, 43, 194, 197
    immune systems (AIS) 194
    intelligence machines 43
    neural networks (ANN) 18, 19, 21, 194, 197
Aspect-based sentiment analysis (ABSA) 155
Atmospheric pressure sensors 9
Attacks, cyber security 96
Automated 14, 47
    machinery 14
    vehicles 47
Automatic 15, 18, 29, 64
    crop protection 29
    irrigation systems 15
    machine changes 18
    watering system 64
Automation 26, 27, 37, 38, 45, 167, 189
    for green houses 38
    greenhouse 27, 37
    industrial 45
    industry 26, 167
    intelligent 189
Autonomous driving 167, 168, 169, 170, 172, 183, 184
    systems 170
    vehicles 183
Autonomous harvesting systems 60

C

Cameras, sensing 208
Cardiovascular risk prediction 192
Cloud 45, 66, 193
    database system 193
    server 66
    storage system 45
Cognitive psychology 157
Communication 120, 124, 152, 159, 204

www.ingramcontent.com/pod-product-compliance
Lightning Source LLC
Chambersburg PA
CBHW050830220326
41598CB00006B/347